W9-AHH-693

For Debbie —

Christmas '96

Opinions of a

Tennessee Talker

A   Fireside   Book
Published by Simon & Schuster

Dixie Carter

Trying to Get to Heaven

FIRESIDE
Rockefeller Center
1230 Avenue of the Americas
New York, NY 10020

Copyright © 1996 by Dixie Carter
All rights reserved, including the right of reproduction
in whole or in part in any form.

First Fireside Edition 1996

FIRESIDE and colophon are registered trademarks
of Simon & Schuster Inc.

Designed by Bonni Leon-Berman

Manufactured in the United States of America

1   3   5   7   9   10   8   6   4   2

The Library of Congress has cataloged the
Simon & Schuster edition as follows:
Carter, Dixie.
Trying to get to heaven : opinions of a Tennessee talker / Dixie Carter.
p.   cm.
1. Carter, Dixie.   2. Actors—United States—Biography.
3. Singers—United States—Biography.   4. Conduct of life.
I. Title.
PN2287.C298A3   1996
791.45′028′092—dc20
[B]   95-32059
CIP
ISBN 0-684-80101-9
0-684-82699-2 (Pbk)

The author gratefully acknowledges permission to reprint the following
materials:

Poem by Edgar Guest: Reprinted by permission of the publisher, Amereon
Ltd., Mattituck, New York.

(continued on page 269)

A C K N O W L E D G M E N T S

I'*m forever grateful to the editor of this book, my young mentor, Marilyn Abraham, for agreeing with my business partner Steve Silas's notion that I could write a book. I'm grateful to him for coming up with the idea in the first place and to her for her gentle instruction and encouragement. Thank you, Marilyn. Thank you, Steve.*

I'm grateful to my daughters for being with me through this endeavor as they have always been through everything, and most especially grateful for their being, period. Thank you, Gigi. Thank you, Mary Dixie. Thank you for the light of your existence.

And finally, I wish to thank Hal Holbrook, who was kind enough to marry me ten years ago. In case I don't ever get to write another book, I want publicly to thank him for that action now, as well as for his genuine interest and delight in watching the number of pages grow, for taking the time to read it and urge me on, for putting up with the falloff in my appearance and with my shut-away hours on end, and for reminding me just twice that Mark Twain said, "The difference between the right word and the almost right word is the difference between lightning and the lightning bug."

*This book is dedicated
to my father, Halbert Leroy Carter,
to my mother, Esther Virginia Hillsman Carter,
and to my aunt Helen Hillsman.
It is intended as an expression of gratitude to them
and to my whole family.*

CONTENTS

They might not need me—yet they might
I'll let my heart be just in sight—
A smile so small as mine might be
Precisely their necessity—

—EMILY DICKINSON

*M*y first-grade teacher, Miss Ethelyn Taylor, often urged on her seven charges (well, eighteen to twenty, if you included the second and third grades who were in the same schoolroom with us) with that time-tested exhortation "Carpe diem," and mindful that we were none of us Latin whizzes quite yet, she completed the phrase with the English translation, so I always thought it was "Carpe diem seize the day," the whole thing. I thought it was a very high-sounding proposition and called upon it many a time to rally my little sister and big brother and whatever playmates were available for some game of flinging statues or kick the can. By the time Miss Audrey Mitchell got hold of me in high school Latin class and explained that I was saying the same thing twice, I was embarrassed and just had to stop using it at all, because it was too late to change. But I never gave up saying it in my mind, so when it was suggested that I write this book, I considered the invitation for one-half a minute and said to myself, *Carpe diem seize the day!* Thank you, Miss Ethelyn.

I love to read and feel indebted to the writers, great and less great, who have given me literally years of pleasure, and sometimes knowledge, and sometimes even understanding. I am grateful for the hours and hours I was read to as a child. I am grateful for the long rainy Sunday afternoons that we all spent reading in the living room, Daddy in his chair by the fire, and the weeks between Christmas and New Year's when we were allowed to do no chores, read all week long, and eat as much candy as we wanted. I am grateful for the friendly comfort offered by a book when I have needed to quit thinking about what was going on in my "real" life. (Many a dope fiend might have been saved by getting hooked on books before resorting to other forms of relaxation.) I am grateful for the books that have taken me, with no plane ticket, into that remarkable world where anything can happen, where dreams are real, and where the people we get to know are with us always. I am in deep respect of the writers of books. Hence it is not without trepidation that I presume to put pen to paper.

I am going to do it, however, in my roundabout, tangential way, because first of all I am pleased to be asked, but mostly because it has come home to me in speaking with the numbers of men, women, and youngsters who feel friendly toward the television character Julia Sugarbaker, with whom I perforce share many particularities, that she represented something people liked and admired and wanted in their lives and that, further, the conclusions I've drawn from my own experience might be interesting, even useful, to somebody else.

Just between us, living in Hollywood doesn't make it exactly easy to hold to my purpose. For example, the memories I hold dear, from which come the values I hold dear, often seem out of sync with most of what I read and hear around me. Much that gets ballyhooed fits Shakespeare's phrase, "full of sound and fury, signifying nothing." Often I don't get the reason for the hype.

All the same, I don't imagine that I'm a singular specimen; I believe that I must be one of many pilgrims who aspire to an existence of merit and who are willing to make an effort toward that end. I am writing this book for those of my kindred spirits who would like a little comradely encouragement in their own personal mission. And although it seems crazy to say it, that mission doesn't necessarily have to do with money. It has to do with how we use the life God has given us and the body He's put us in.

I was charging through the flower shop not long ago, late getting flowers for my dinner company, when in answering a question I don't now remember I said, "I'm just trying to get to Heaven." The young man responded pertly, "Yes, well, I'm sure we all are." I left the shop privately ashamed of myself that I had provoked that glib response with an expression that does in fact mean a great deal to me. Too easily said, I guess.

A few days ago I told our friend Oddvar Abrahamsen that I was writing a book I was going to call *Trying to Get to Heaven*, and he smiled at me and said in his gentle way, "But Dixie, you know we don't get there by trying. We get there by faith."

"I don't mean it to be taken that literally," I protested, realizing that I didn't want to get caught putting my intention into words. Oddvar didn't press his point, but he left me hoping that the content would explain the title.

Even though this book intends to discuss what we're doing in the here and now, I do believe that there is a Heaven, and I very much want to go there when I die. I want to see my mother again and all the people I miss who are gone, and I want to hear the music of Heaven, which I know will be heavenly. And notwithstanding Oddvar's reminder that working at it isn't what gets you there, still I don't see how it could hurt my chances toward that end to be doing the best I know how here on earth.

There is the story about the three questions put to Buddha at the end of his life. To the first, "O great Buddha, are you God?" he answered no. To the second, "O great Buddha, are you a prophet?" he answered no. The third question then came, "O great Buddha, won't you tell us what you are?" and Buddha answered, "I am awake." Well, I may not be completely awake yet, but I'm opening my eyes.

In the pages that follow I am hoping to elicit a response of "Yes, Dixie, that's just the way I feel" and as the case may be, "Do you really think I could do that too?" As I write I am picturing some very dear and familiar faces, faces that are beautiful far beyond their possessors' own ideas of themselves, and at the same time I am speaking to every kind person who is willing to spend a few hours with me, to you, Dear Reader, whom I am meeting for the first time. My mother used to say that we should "get to the heart of the matter," and the heart is indeed what I hope to get to; I hope that somewhere in the following chapters we may become friends. If I am able to communicate to you some of the joy and beauty life holds for me, and why I think it does, and how therefore it might hold the same for you if it doesn't already, then I will have achieved my purpose in attempting this manual. I like to imagine that those with whom I am closest as well as those whom I am meeting now will receive through these pages a reminder of their wondrous worth.

Tennessee Williams said, "The only somebody worth being is the solitary and unseen you that existed from your first breath and which is the sum of your actions and so is constantly in a state of becoming under your own volition." Now there's a writer.

PART ONE

There's Nothing Wrong with
Wanting to Be Beautiful

❧ Chapter One ❧
THE CULTIVATION OF NATURAL BEAUTY

How many Flowers fail in Wood
Or perish from the Hill—
Without the privilege to know
That they are Beautiful—

—EMILY DICKINSON

*T*HERE WEREN'T MANY ORTHODONTISTS practicing in West Tennessee when I was twelve years old, but when my father told my mother she'd better find one, she did. He had realized one day that Little Didi's overbite had become very pronounced, and he recommended immediate action, immediate being his only type of action. My mother was in complete accord; four years, two orthodontists, many dollars, and much pain later I had a satisfactory mouth. The process was particularly troublesome as I spent several hours each week playing the trumpet in the school band, and if my embouchure got tired, the pressure of the mouthpiece against my lips would cause the little steel wires around my teeth to cut into the inside of my mouth. So what with the letdown of having to change doctors after two whole years of continuous misery with no results, the trauma of having four great big healthy teeth yanked out (everyone crying including our family dentist), another two years of aching, exacerbated by the trumpet playing and the friendly observations offered here and there by local thinkers (as when Hazel Wyatt's funeral-loving mother stopped me in our store the day the braces finally came off to tell me in all honesty that that doctor over in Jackson had made me dish-faced), it took a strong resolve on my part not to lose heart. But strong resolve I had. I had not enjoyed being called Horsetooth at school. I endured four years of looking like a geek and hurting until I cried because I wanted to be beautiful.

My mother and father called all three of their children, including my big brother, "beautiful," and so we all thought we were. Or we thought they thought we were. We knew they were, that's for sure. My mother and father were so beautiful they were shiny.

For my part I thought I had potential, but I couldn't see it actually taking shape the way it had, say, in my mother. From the time I was six or seven, I would study myself in the mirror from all different angles, employing all possible expressions. The funny faces were easy and very enjoyable, the plain faces not as rewarding. I noted with deep interest the effect my permanent teeth were having, tipping my head way back so as to minimize their appearance, and expecting that surely they would look different, smaller, prettier one day. When school pictures were taken in the early fall, I always had an eager hope that I would look better this time. The pictures would come back and I would see that this wasn't the year I was going to look like I wanted to. But I just knew that one day things would take a turn, and I never told anyone—not my sister, not my mother—that I was disappointed in myself, or about my dream of loveliness.

> *Estranged from Beauty—none can be—*
> *For Beauty is Infinity—*
> *And power to be finite ceased*
> *Before Identity was leased.*

So Emily Dickinson wrote.

There's nothing wrong with wanting to be beautiful. It's as natural as can be, and we'd want to even if we'd never seen a movie or a glossy magazine. The desire to be attractive to others as well as to be pleased with what we see in the looking glass is as old as history. When mirrors weren't around, people peered at themselves in still water. Although we're all naturally interested in what we look like, most of us watch ourselves privately; we don't want to seem to care about our looks. We don't want to get caught trying. Why would a perfectly normal inclination be companioned by a disinclination to admit it? This shyness derives from an innate understanding that one of the desired results of any accomplishment is that it appear effortless, whether it's the dancer's grace, the singer's high note, the orator's command of language, or the French woman's elegant accoutrements. If we can see the work in it, the effect is less delightful.

But let's face it, work we must. As my grandmother Hillsman would always say, "There is no excellence without great labor." Not the happiest words to intrude upon a teenager's consciousness, but sadly true, sadly true. Certainly if we hope to enhance and extend whatever natural assets we were given, we must expect to make an effort, if not actually *great* labor. Natural beauty is the best kind, that we know; however, we know also that just like the roses in the garden, it won't bloom long if left untended.

The good news is that natural beauty can be cultivated and still be natural. And don't say, What good is it if you have to work for it? Say, What good is it if you *haven't* worked for it?

Notions of beauty are wide-ranging. We don't all agree upon what it is or even if it should be held up as desirable, since not everybody starts life with the same goods in the physical equipment department. We do agree that it's in the eye of the beholder, and we've all at some time or other been amazed to encounter a person who doesn't match our preconceived ideas and yet does strike us as beautiful. On one hand we recognize the felicity in being around somebody beautiful, and on the other hand many of us back off from the idea that we ourselves could and should be one of those pleasure givers. The Oxford dictionary's first definition of beauty is a "combination of qualities . . . in human face or form, or in other objects, that delights the sight." Nothing wrong with that, is there? The second definition is "combined qualities delighting the other senses, the moral sense, or the intellectual." Good, good, all to the good. The third definition of beauty is "exceptionally good specimen," and I for one would like to qualify. I think everybody would—man, woman, and child.

I repeat: there is nothing wrong with wanting to be beautiful —certainly not by the Oxford's standards. But maybe we should pay attention to where we're getting our definition. Who are we allowing to set the criteria for whether or not we're an "exceptionally good specimen"? *People* magazine? Is it our ambition to delight the senses of somebody who actually matters to us, or are we nagged by some half-conscious obligation to resemble the latest emaciated victim of media hype, for the silent approval of people looking out at us from our TV set?

I think we've gotten confused somewhere along the way, and who can blame us; it's certainly easy to do. Here's an idea. Why don't we see Tyne Daly on a magazine cover as one of the beautiful people? I just worked with her and spent a little time up close to her, and she is beautiful. Life pours from her; she is intelligent, she is funny, and let me tell you, she is not hard on the eyes. She exudes sensuality. The magazines seem interested in the ups and downs of her weight, in her marital difficulties, and in what she wore to some party. Why doesn't somebody say, "Hey, folks, here's a real beauty!" and put her on the cover of something and give us somebody we'd enjoy emulating. Europe does not have a corner on luscious women like Simone Signoret; we just for some reason keep quiet about ours. Wouldn't it be good for us to see women and men put forward as special who really *are* special, whom we can actually like? Wouldn't it be good for us to see icons of the kind of beauty that we all realistically could have a shot at?

Some days I have to take a deep breath not to respond to the newest displays in the airport newsstand with a little sinking feeling, even though I know it doesn't make sense. *We shouldn't want to look like anybody but ourselves, because we are the people we were intended to be.* I do firmly believe, however, that we were intended to take what we started with and work on it, bearing in mind if possible the distinction between working on it and working it.

With due respect for my southern sisters, and I surely have it, I might mention in passing that albeit the arts of pulchritude and charm have been well nurtured in the South, sometimes we go a little far. That certain amount of basic deception we have been used to employ in making our way through the early years of female power, and occasionally beyond, may have been necessary, considering that the theoretical objective was holy wedlock, until recent years a worthy and prudent aim, but I'm afraid some of us were liable to forget the goal and get sidetracked by the fascinating exercise of practicing up on just anybody around. Probably no one does this kind of thing anymore since women's liberation has made us pure and real, and some never, even way back, took it as far as some others. I was a member of the "some others" category. I have never understood, and I have wondered about it, how my mother, who was the epitome of dignity and grace, could have raised such a flighty girl, and I am not talking about my sister. My sister, Midge, and my brother, Hal, always understood that effect without substance was nothing. Not me. I thought a nice hollow effect was just fine. My mother heard me at about fourteen years of age chirp into the mirror as I was brushing my hair, "Vanity! Vanity! All is vanity!" then Midge's amused commentary, "Well, my dear, you ought to know."

At that time my idea of natural beauty was often quite self-conscious and so not natural at all. We southern girls just took everything too far in every direction. I'm speaking now of my friends at the University of Tennessee, Carole Jane Hassell, Joy Belle Travis, Judy Murray, Ansley Parker, Margaret Moore, Chici Fulton, Mary Parrot, Sissy and Melinda Midkiff, and Diane Meeks (not my closest friend all through high school, Barbara Clifton, who was perfect in all ways). We were wildly agreeable, riotously fun-loving, and overwhelmingly sweet. Not cloyingly, mind you, overwhelmingly. Heaven forbid anybody might have an ordinary or boring moment with a one of us. Whatever girls were supposed to be, we were and then some. Extreme was the name of our game. We were egged on by our young men. My young man was William Preston Moss, Jr. Billy Moss, as I called him, in the way southern girls have of using a boy's whole name (now the father of four with his Miss Tennessee bride Marcia), was the fine and good-looking oldest brother of three good-looking boys and a beautiful little sister. When we'd go by his home in Jackson to speak to his parents on our way somewhere, the staircase railing would most of the time be half torn out, and Miss Lou

Moss would shake her head and tell me she didn't know what
she was going to do with them, that they started roughhousing
upstairs and kept it up all the way downstairs and out into the
yard. Billy liked to call me Goon. Every time he said it, it
tickled me worse than before. I tried to live up to it. Our
carefree youth.

Although my girlfriends and I were close and loyal, and are
to the present time, we did not share pointers on enchantment
skills. Those tuitions we got from the water we drank and the
air we breathed. Yet we all understood that certain immutable
rules of beauty and desirability held true.

One of the biggest was the Rule of Natural Beauty. We
knew that it had to be unconscious and effortless. An extremely accomplished natural beauty would likely receive a
compliment with surprise, conveying the impression that
whatever about her had found favor was a happy accident,
artless and unsought after. We went on past effortlessness, as
in "Yes, I've looked just like this from the day I was born,"
through gauzy unawareness, to a reaction of mild revelation at
the moment of praise, if possible. At all costs one had to
get away from effects that seemed calculated or planned. For
example, matching elements in an ensemble were dangerous
no matter how lovely and tempting to wear; any unwanted
notice of them could test the accidental beauty's naturalness
and surprise to the limit, but the gifted ones could pull it off.
Trust me when I tell you I have witnessed a bold insinuation
that certain mauve silk shoes, blouse, and hat ribbons of exactly the same shade had been dyed to match, and have seen
that accusation blithely rebuffed with aplomb. (And sometimes a peach or a pear.)

Please forgive me. I have to say that after I say *aplomb*; it's a
compulsion. If my children can stand it, maybe you can too.
There are a number of such crosses my girls have had to bear;
most of them they have tolerated with something between
amusement and indulgence, but about ten years ago they put
their collective little feet down over my testing dinner guests

by saying "casting asparagus" when "casting aspersions" was the intended meaning, my goal being to take my own private sense-of-humor reading around the table. After one evening when we had guests none of whom knew each other or quite what they were doing at our house, which does happen sometimes, and Hal (that's my husband Hal, but I also have a brother Hal and a father Hal, which is no more confusing than having been born a Carter and marrying one) wasn't there, and the dinner was inedible, which also happens sometimes, and I had tried to jolly everything up with "casting asparagus" many more times than once, unfortunately, and failing the success of that conversational trump card, had started to proclaim everything everybody else said "fabulooloos" in an effort to raise the general level of merriment, and had finally had to accept defeat and allow the poor benighted souls to escape our portals, Ginna and Mary Dixie were ready for me when I came in to kiss them good night. They said I mustn't ever say "casting asparagus" again to people who clearly were not going to get it or enjoy it if they did, and that I must try to strike "fabulooloos" from my vocabulary, period, that I had said it enough that night to last forever. They are excellent reformers when they mean business, my little cherries jubilee.

I enjoy having a little fun about females, particularly southern females. My friends and I laugh about our foibles and our eccentricities because we have fun being women and being different from men and making sure that things stay interesting, from our first Easter Egg Hunt right on through. Contrary to the stereotypical view of southern females which I encountered to my consternation when I ventured north to New York City, we all always knew that intelligence was desirable, highly desirable. More than desirable, it was that without which all the rest had little value. We knew also that intelligence was especially effective if it were more or less kept under wraps. Flaunting intelligence was dumb—unintelligent, really. I don't cling to all the ideas I grew up with, but that one seems more valid all the time.

And without a doubt the most attractive, most winning, most beautiful person in captivity was the one who could close her mouth, gaze into the eyes of the speaker, and listen. Learning to sit enrapt in intense and sincere appreciation, to be caught up in eager and mute concentration, was perhaps not the easiest thing for self-centered young geese, but since it was pretty much the biggest Rule of Beauty, we had to do it, and a few of us may actually have learned something as a side effect along the way. At this time in our history we had not become acquainted with that superior slogan, "It takes a mighty good man to be better than no man at all." And it didn't seem excessively awful, since we didn't have to keep it up too long at one time, and we figured we could start talking again as soon as we were married. When my first husband, Arthur, left me, I wondered if maybe I had started talking again too soon.

I have mentioned Arthur now and will again during these rambles. I usually tease about my first husband, especially if what I'm talking about has anything to do with the breakup of our marriage. I joke because what else is there to do?

When I met Arthur I had just returned to New York from touring with *Carousel* out of the now defunct Music Theatre of Lincoln Center. My Memphis friends Toby and Dottie Sides and Toby's law partner Dunlap Cannon were sporting me to dinner at the Salum Sanctorum, a tiny and fancy restaurant over the Sign of the Dove. There was a piano player, so naturally I was singing song after song. Arthur had dropped in with Richard and Phyllis Graham to have a nightcap. When I went to the ladies' room he followed and introduced himself as I came out. The next day he called Richard Rodgers's office and got my address. That afternoon a dozen dozen (144) roses arrived and our romance had begun. At the time I thought that I was very pretty, and he had said that he loved the way I sang, so I put down his interest to a combination of those two things. Later, I think years later, Arthur told me that he had fallen in love because I was the happiest person he'd ever seen.

By the time I received this vital information, I wasn't happy anymore.

If only we could get it into our beans that happiness is the most beautiful thing about us, maybe we could hang on to it better. Arthur wasn't wrong.

ᴀ Chapter Two ᴪ
My Childhood as a Health Nut

ALTHOUGH IT HAS NEVER BEEN SUG-
gested that my mother, Esther Virginia Hillsman, was frivo-
lous, I know that she was a laughing girl, gay and maybe a
little reckless. She was five feet six inches tall, with a slender,
long-legged, almost boyish figure; straight hair, "black as a
raven's wing"; a straight-nosed, angular face; and a jaunty,
almost military carriage. The rarest beauty came from her
eyes, which were a most unusual shape and color, long trian-
gles of grey with flecks of green in them, and her flawless skin,
which looked like tan-colored satin, as if she'd been polished
and rubbed all over with a light wood stain, and which had
that translucent quality one reads about in poems. She had
the kind of roses in her cheeks usually seen only in very fair
complexions, and the effect was utterly captivating, as my father has testified time upon time.

She was high-spirited all her life, but by the time I came
along, whatever might have been capricious in her nature had
been tempered by the daunting task of making it through the
Depression and by the fact that she had lost her health. One of
her remarkable achievements was the gorgeous and vivacious
person she managed to be in spite of perilous physical handi-
caps. My mother was definitely interested in physical beauty,
her own and ours. She placed a great emphasis on our appearance and on the real determinants, glowing good health being
one of the majors.

As a nineteen-year-old college student in Baton Rouge,
Louisiana, living with her aunt, Gina became deathly ill with
ptomaine poisoning. (Let me explain about my mother's
name. My brother, as a baby striking at Virginia, began calling
her Ingie, and it sounded so sweet she let it go, then he got it
around to Gin-Gin, and finally Ginna, which stuck but got
spelled *Gina*, which is misleading because it looks like the
Italian pronunciation and it's not. We all three called our

mother Gina [pronounced *Ginna*] instead of Mother or Mama, and everybody liked it except Gina's mother, Grandmother Hillsman, who would often say, apropos of nothing in particular, "*Mothah* is one of the Most Beautiful Words in the English language!")

Before I get back to my story, I'll just say a little more about names. Gina was staying in Baton Rouge with Aunt Faustina. That's correct, Faustina. Her full name was Faustina Imogene Wingo McMakin. (Uncle Laurence McMakin had horrified his parents by becoming a riverboat captain on the Mighty Mississippi. Auntie, however, loved his occupation. He was splendid, and so was she.) Her brothers' names were Herschel, Spurgeon, and Clarence, and her sister, my grandmother, was named Esther, which Grandmother insisted be pronounced sounding the *h*. While I've gotten off on this, let me go on to note that my father's family boasted their fair share of redoubtable names: Daddy's name is Halbert Leroy, his brother was Leon, and his sister is Melba. Daddy thought it was a good idea to name me something short and cute and not a joke. Who could have foreseen that I might wind up someplace where my short cute name would be a joke after all? The best-laid schemes o' mice an' men gang aft agley. But I digress; forgive the lapse into my native tongue.

Auntie's cooking was very fine but her refrigerator wasn't; my mother got food poisoning from her delicious chicken salad, almost died but somehow didn't, was critically ill for months, and never for the rest of her life completely recovered from the damage done, principally to her heart. Gina told me during the last years of her life about the near-death experience she had had, about how she had seen angels and the pearly gates, and she was not speaking metaphorically; she meant that's what she had seen. My mother having been the farthest thing from a hysteric, I know that her vision was as she said. I have wished that she had told me more, but my asking her would have seemed rough, I thought, or intrusive.

Although she was never really well again, Gina's irrepressible spirit and her sparkling intellect were still intact, and she became the first "health nut" in our part of the country, no doubt the only one for a very long time. She must have known or suspected that the new ways of eating that people were adopting in the 1950s were bad for the human system, particularly hers. And she was ardently interested in feeding her family what was best for them. Cream of mushroom soup and Velveeta cheese were the enemy. She read everything Gayelord Hauser wrote (she pronounced it *Gaylaud*), and put a great deal of it into practice. She purchased one of the first juice extractors made and poured all kinds of fresh juices down us.

In the summer we ate out of the garden. Daddy and Gina made a game out of gardening with us. Daddy would come home from the store (H. L. Carter and Son, "A Good Place to Trade") just as early as he could so that there would still be daylight for us to go out and work together. Midge was a year and a half when she became interested in gardening. She judiciously studied the crop, picked out the largest and most inviting tomato plant, and sat down on it, seriously injuring both her dignity and the plant. Daddy tied it up again and it survived, but Midge's advanced little baby brain recorded her predation with deep chagrin. She still remembers her embarrassment. (My little sister, Melba Helen, nicknamed Midge by her aunt Melba, is eighteen months younger than me. She was round and dimpled, with blond hair, dark eyes, and a melting smile—the cutest little thing you could dream of. You'd have thought so, too, if you'd been around for her rendition of "My Country 'Tis of Thee," keeping perfect time astride the rocking horse with brother Hal's cowboy hat on, the only way she ever sang it. I adored her from the start and rode her around in my doll carriage until it broke down. Very early on she began to take up for me against mean girls and boys; I was a scaredy-cat and she was fearless. She was also stubborn. When her chin went out, even Gina and Daddy avoided debate. She turned "Dixie" into "Didi," which is what she calls me still. Our relationship is very like that of my daughters.)

Another summer each of us children was allowed to choose

our own small area to plant whatever we wanted. I planted corn. It came up. Every day I watched it stretch up out of the ground a little higher. It developed little ears with silk in them. It was very beautiful. I could picture my pride when we all sat down to enjoy it with fresh sliced tomatoes and hot buttered cornbread, and maybe some black-eyed peas, or maybe green beans, and even a little pickle relish, and everyone would ask for another ear and say they believed it might be the best corn they'd ever tasted. Then came the morning I went out to look at my corn and it was gone. Right down to the ground. And the fence close to where it was planted was bent way down where the cow had leaned over to plunder my crop. Daddy said he should've known better than to let me plant it so close to the fence. Everyone was very sympathetic, very. But the corn was gone, and the cow, whom I had thought I liked, had taken it. I guess I was too young to see this as a lesson in life.

Hardly any of our gardening experiences were other than happy ones. One more comes to mind as a bit chancy, but it ended safely, and it's fun to remember:

One evening after supper Mama Carter, my paternal grandmother, was hanging out the cheesecloth she had used to strain that day's milk (from the aforementioned cow) when she saw through the window that the garage was on fire. She called to Gina, who called to Daddy, who was at that moment soaking in a hot bath to relieve the soreness from several hours of plowing. Daddy leapt from the tub into his trousers and raced out to the garage barefoot. There he saw to his dismay that his pride and joy, our new Gravely walking tractor, was in flames, or more precisely, that the blanket which he had inexplicably thrown over the tractor was in flames. (Neither he nor anyone else has ever been able to figure out why he had done such a thing, unless out of absent-minded affection; the tractor was new and I surmise that he still unconsciously thought of it as a horse.) Instead of just yanking off the blanket, he grabbed the tractor and frantically retreated backwards with it, out of the garage, up the driveway, and into the coal pile, where he fell out flat over the coal and let the Gravely coast merrily back down the driveway into its original place in the garage, flames leaping higher and higher. Nothing would do then, of course, but that my father lunge to his feet and hotfoot barefoot over the gravel after it, waving us away and ordering us back into the house, with all of us imploring him to get away from the tractor before the gas tank exploded. He avoided the coal pile the second time, got the machine up the driveway, away from the garage and the house, and then and only then pulled the blanket off and let it burn itself out harmlessly. Since it hadn't exploded and killed him, and since he always laughed the most at the joke that was on himself, he thought the whole thing was hilarious and we eventually agreed. (The Gravely is still out in the toolshed, long since retired. Gina and Daddy couldn't stand to get rid of it.)

So in the summer we had very healthy fare. If we had fish, they had just come out of the Tennessee River, which wasn't polluted then. Our vegetables grew in lovely soil, and we didn't eat much meat until winter. (When she did fry fish or chicken, by the way, it was simply the crispiest, lightest, tenderest, and most delicious delectable anyone ever tasted.) And we never ate in restaurants unless we were making a trip. Gina had no time for restaurant dining. She thought it was common. By the time I got to junior high, most of my friends' families went out to eat after church on Sunday. Not us. Gina was ahead of her time in many ways and that was one. (You couldn't fool her with what was in style. She knew that the ladies' clubs were a waste of time. She knew that restaurant food wasn't as good as her cooking. She also knew that television was brainless. She held out against getting a set until our whining finally became too pitiful for her to stand. She kept her elegant aquiline nose turned up at the tube pretty consistently through the years, although she admired Dinah Shore, her wardrobe and her style, and enjoyed the family programs we could all watch together, especially mysteries. By the time I started appearing on TV, her utter delight in whatever I was up to removed most of her reservations about it. Naturally she was glued every moment I was on.)

In the winter we ate out of the freezer what had been harvested from the garden. Gina developed her own technique for blanching fruits and vegetables, then very quickly sealing them and getting them into the deep freeze. In the dead of winter when she'd thaw something, the flavor would pop out miraculously. We always marveled at her legerdemain; nobody else's frozen food tasted so fresh then or now; even gourmet frozen foods don't come close. In the fall our cousins John David and Mary Carter would give us half a cow, not all in one piece, thank goodness, but cut up and ready to freeze. Even though one of our stores sold groceries, we didn't eat out of it very much, not canned foods anyway. And when we sold our cow and started getting milk from the store, it was a bad day at Black Rock indeed. Pasteurized meant ptooey to me. Horrible-tasting stuff. How I longed for that cool jar with the thick layer of heavy cream at the top, or for fresh buttermilk right after Mama had churned it, or for the butter that Mama made with her own signature of pretty little designs she pressed into it with a knife while it was still soft. Uh-oh, now I have to veer off a moment and tell a story on my brother.

Our elders decided to have mercy on the children's names just a little late for my brother, who came first. He was named Halbert Leroy Carter, Jr., and became at the same time H. L. Carter III. (Daddy's father was Horace Leroy.) However, he turned out to be the most gorgeous child anyone had ever seen, so he could stand it. When he was two years old and still reigning alone and supreme, he was, as usual, settled in place beside his grandmama Carter's knee, watching her churn while she told him nursery stories. The butter came up, she took it out as usual, put the buttermilk in the refrigerator, made the butter cakes as usual, and put them on the dining room table to set, saying as usual,

"Hal, don't bother my butter."

Then she proceeded to go about her business in the kitchen. But on this particular day Hal lingered behind for just a minute before he appeared again in the kitchen, where he took a position against the kitchen table with one brown leg crossed importantly over the other, stomach prominent, eyes black as muscadines fixing her with his steady gaze, and announced,

"Ethel, I bothered your butter."

How Mama, as we called our grandmama Carter, enjoyed telling that story and imitating his unusually deep voice and the gravity of his manner. When she looked to see what he'd done, there was a barely discernible dent in one of the butter cakes where he'd pressed his sturdy little finger against it. If he was testing the waters, Mama's reaction should have sent him off to a life of crime, because she did not exact any penalty. She rarely got mad; she got tickled. And after his two-year-old uprising Hal never felt the need to address her by her given name again. She did spank him once for eating green grapes after she'd told him they'd give him a stomachache. He remembers it as the only time. That was Mama Carter for you, soft on children.

It doesn't take a therapist to figure out that the wonderful healthy food I remember having as a child was extra delicious because it was love given us in tangible form. The food itself was indeed pure and not like what we have to settle for today, but it's a fairly good bet that the feeling with which it was put before us was every bit as nourishing as any of its other essentials.

That was when somebody else was taking care of me.

Then came My Adulthood as a Child, or Twenty Years to Lose Ten Pounds, or Growing Up Is Hard to Do.

When I went away to college and left the structure and guidance I'd had at home, I was far less focused and less successful. As a youngster I was motivated and disciplined; I finished high school as valedictorian and winner of the mathematics award with a four-year average in math of 99 and an overall average of 96. I had become a good pianist and trumpet player. (My sister and I gave a piano recital together my senior year and played first chair first and second trumpet in the Tennessee state band.) I sang all over the place, popular, sacred, and classical music. I entered contests of all different kinds and won them, from oratory to beauty to 4-H Club. I was a good girl, and I was just naturally ambitious also. And except for not getting to be a cheerleader, and not getting to try out for majorette because of the trumpet, I was exceedingly happy.

I went away to college at UT Knoxville and in a year's time lost my focus. Here's another way to put it: I turned into a smart aleck and a fool. Perhaps those tendencies had been lurking around in me just waiting until I got far enough away from my parents' eyes to let them loose. I am not proud of much of my behavior during those years. I joke about it now, but the truth is I wasted so much of my talent and intelligence and energy in my late teens and early twenties that it has always been a sadness to me. I studied and worked assiduously at my music, which I loved doing, but I didn't do the organizing and putting myself forward that was hard for me. What I was doing was what I enjoyed doing, so I wasn't really working. I had lost discipline. I didn't realize then that those days and months and years of youth could never be exactly duplicated, and I more or less squandered them, and in doing so I was laughing away the career I might have had.

I've done well, I think, for someone who finally regained focus at around forty years of age. If I were perfectly honest, I would call this book *Sleeping Until Forty*. Much of what went on in my young adulthood is a blur now, probably because I am not proud of how I was conducting myself. I remember once when my mother, visiting me in New York, mildly admonished me about going to the beauty shop twice a week, mentioning that even though Arthur was making a terrific success in business, as a good wife I should be trying to save money, not letting it run through my fingers so fast. With some queasiness I have to tell you what I said to her. I was a little indignant. I told Gina in a pitiful voice that my hair was so long and thick that it made my arms too tired when I washed my hair myself. I don't know how she kept from knocking me down. I do know she looked at me in a quizzical way, which I can interpret now as, "Are you really my same little daughter whom I thought I knew so well? And if you are, where on earth did I go so far wrong raising you?" No wonder I don't recall those years perfectly. Who would want to?

I first met Arthur's three children, Jon, Wendy (now Whendy), and Ellen, at nine, seven, and four years of age, respectively, and became their stepmother when they were ten, eight, and five. Now when it comes back to me how Jonny would rush to get in the car seat beside his father before I did, it breaks my heart. When I think of Ellen's and Whendy's trusting little faces, it breaks my heart. They were all so sweet and so scared, at the mercy of circumstances out of their control, the agendas of adults. Understanding almost nothing about what I could have done to make their lives a little more stable, I opted for buying them clothes and taking them to Twenty One for lunch. I am thankful that it came out well between us over the long haul. Since I seem to have been forgiven both somnambulism and self-centeredness by those I love, and since the years between twenty and forty were not without what we call life experience—some of it in the most exalted reaches of joy, including the crowning moments of my existence, the birth of my two daughters—and since woulda-coulda-shoulda is so pointless anyway, I'm just happy with the way things are now.

The disciplines we are able to impose upon ourselves bring the greatest rewards and are of course the hardest. That's why they bring the greatest rewards.

You don't have to be in show business to benefit professionally and personally from staying in good physical condition or getting there if you're not already. Now more than ever an attractive physique is essential to high self-esteem, and self-esteem is that without which we all have a hard time getting up in the morning and that which we acquire only through our own actions. Clean hair, clean skin, no matter what your job is. And I'm not kidding: go to the dentist and get your teeth capped or whitened or whatever it takes to have a relaxed and bright smile. With all the products available, everyone can have a sparkling smile these days, and it does make a difference to the people who have to look at you all the time, not to mention those who might be deciding to give you a job.

Television is running our country now and what is left of our culture, and television has put it into our national consciousness that how we look is really, really, really important. I agree that looking the way we want to is important to our psyches, even though I don't usually agree with the way television puts that message across. I say this with full awareness and gratitude for how kind television has been to me. I just think too much is too much, although I'm not quite as mad about it as Naomi Wolf.

Well, all right, what about our looks? What's the first thing that comes to mind? Weight. Statistics indicate that America has weight on the mind in a big way, and with good cause, since it has turned into a national problem. But it's a fairly recent problem, only a couple of decades old. Going through a bunch of old family tintypes with my cousins Sam and Louise this summer, I noticed that almost all the people in those pictures were slender. What happened since then? Fast foods and preservatives, sitting down a lot, and having what used to be holiday fare available to us all the time. Daddy often mentions how oranges smell like Christmas to him. (I guess he's referring to the occasional few that actually have an aroma.)

Since I grew up before the fast-food establishments set about to make America fat and pimply, I didn't have to resolve and reresolve not to eat that stuff. Lucky for me, because a lot of it tastes good. Well, grease does taste good, face it. Stroke food, as I call it, has its own undeniable allure, especially if you've gotten real used to it. We have to wean ourselves away from it somehow. For me, for most of us, I imagine, realizing that it's bad for our health isn't enough, at least not while we're still young and reasonably healthy. Too often it takes some dire physical alarm to force us to change our eating habits. If we could connect how we feel with what we eat from the time we are forming habits, we'd save a lot of struggling.

The connection with our looks is more obvious and therefore probably a clearer motivator. People who can accept as actual fact that what is hanging over their belt is literally pizza can possibly quit on the pizza. Accepting that fact—aye, there's the rub.

One of the words I'd love not to hear again for a while is *denial*. It's one of those words that had been yanked around until it's silly. Anybody who doesn't see his or her behavior in the way we see it is "in denial," which phrase, by the way, is grammatically incorrect. (A denial is a refusal, a contradiction, or a disavowal. It is not a state.) He thinks he's right and I'm wrong, so he's in denial. Why not just say that he won't admit he's wrong? I wish the fact that it isn't correct use of the language bothered somebody besides me.

Anyway, I'm misusing that poor misused phrase now to suggest why it's hard to eat so as to maintain whatever weight we want, presumably one that pleases us aesthetically or at least does not tax our heart. We find it hard to do because we are in denial. We're all inclined to deny the connection between putting something into our mouth and swallowing it, the connection between swallowing it and finding it on our body—not inside our body, outside, sticking out where we can see it and not like it. (We look at it and blame our poor body; separating ourselves from our bodies doesn't make us happy or healthy.) We simply refuse to let our minds take in the journey of that happy morsel as it makes its way calmly but certainly to a comfortable resting place around the pocket line of our slacks. We refuse to acknowledge how much we really do eat. Unconsciously we think that we get away with what we pop into our mouth when nobody's around. We shut down our memory when we're snacking so that we can light-heartedly pull up to the dinner table with no thought of the meal we were eating all afternoon. Not only do we refuse to acknowledge or remember what we ate, much of the time we do not even realize what we're eating when we're eating it. We dare not realize it.

If we really took in what we're doing to ourselves, we wouldn't enjoy doing it. We'd eat what would make us feel good.

We can't stand to face the fact that the way our bodies look is mostly a result of what we eat, and *what we eat is entirely up to us.* "You are what you eat" has been jingling around for years. Interestingly, I happened across a copy of that very book, *You Are What You Eat*, the last time I was home. It was first published in 1940, and five printings are recorded on the flyleaf, the last in 1942. It's a wonderful book written by Victor H. Lindlahr, based upon findings of his father, Dr. Henry Lindlahr. At his clinic, the Lindlahr Sanitarium, Dr. Henry prescribed fresh fruit, vegetable juices, and pot liquors. He proved that "many illnesses could be prevented, relieved, and even remedied by nothing more complicated than correct eating." The information has been around for a while; by now there's such a glut of information that it's gotten confusing. Why hasn't all that knowledge come to the aid of me or you? Because, I believe, we affect a disassociation between our "bodies" and our "selves."

People who weigh more than they want to often refer to their extra poundage as "the weight," as if it had descended upon their poor body of its own will and without their participation. Victims of "the weight" prefer to avoid the actual history of how that pizza got out of the pizza parlor or grocery store, into their car, into their house, onto their plate, and down their little red lane. The moment we make that connection, we're more than half way there.

Nobody, but nobody, has to be ignorant of the basic facts of nutrition. Pick up one of Susan Powter's books, and if you're still pretending that a salad with fat salad dressing on it is light eating, your nose will start growing like Pinocchio's. If we can get honest with ourselves, we can deal with "the weight." This I believe because I have lived it myself. Very few people have a condition that causes them to be fat. Food intake causes fat, and the person has to do the intaking. Seems obvious, but it's not. Talk to people who are overweight; most avoid the subject as if it were shameful. If overweight is discussed, the discussion is very roundabout and never with the stated understanding that the person can control the condition. I so strongly believe that when average people get it into their understanding that they do have the power to determine how they look and feel, they will find it possible to do something about it. To get to that point we have to quit making excuses to ourselves, demystify the whole process of eating, and decide to start eating for real pleasure, not for the pleasure of killing ourselves by degrees. It's not an instant or easy mental reframe, but the results are surefire, and one of the biggest results is self-respect. (*Self-respect* is another overworked word, along with *self-esteem*, both of which are hard to come by. Neither one can be acquired in a therapist's office; they have to be earned all by oneself.)

Changing the way we think about our weight and how it gets on us is the only place to start. All the greatest eating plans going will amount to just another set of constrictive rules if we don't feel in charge. Once we take charge, we can decide which kind of gasoline to put in our tank. We will decide not to buy food that we don't want to wind up eating, with the excuse that someone else in the family likes it; nobody we love needs to eat the wrong kind of food. We won't rationalize that we went ahead and ate the fancy dessert so that our dinner guests would feel like they could too. When we eat bad stuff or just plain too much, we will own up to it. We will stop cheating on ourselves and shortchanging ourselves and fooling ourselves and living with the unremitting anxiety that results. We will start to enjoy eating for nourishment and without guilt. We will decide whether we'd rather be a size eight or a size fourteen or whether we'd rather let how we feel determine our proper weight and forget about a specific size until we get there (my recommendation).

We will begin to regard what we eat as *Beauty Food*. We will choose what we eat for the purpose of making us feel good and look good.

I know that what I'm saying is not essentially new; however, my personal history with weight control prompts me to harp on the delusional aspect. I know what it feels like to worry about how tight your clothes are getting and not really enjoy what you eat and still not be able to do much about it. Only in the last few years have I been able to quit kidding myself (most of the time) and get rid of the constant anxiety that goes with the problem. There must be millions of people who, like me, don't need to change their weight by a lot but would very much enjoy being ten to fifteen pounds lighter and just can't seem to get there and stay there. "Lose fifteen pounds" is not the good way to think of it. It's all negative. A ten- to fifteen-pound difference in what I weigh a year from now is a lovely and doable ambition. No matter what a person weighs, a modest change in the right direction will lift the spirits.

After my second daughter, Mary Dixie, was born, I returned home feeling sylphlike and hopped onto enemy scales that read 165. That was in July. Three months later I was down to 112 pounds, 6 pounds less than optimum. I can't brag about it, since I didn't do it by dieting; I got a nicely dangerous case of tracheitis about the same time that it was becoming apparent that my marriage was in its pure sense done for; however, I don't recommend tracheitis for getting slim, unless you like coughing every minute. I mention the experience only to tell you that I have been fifty pounds overweight and I know how it feels.

Losing that fifty pounds was easy; you can't eat while you're coughing; staying the weight I like is a different matter. It requires *doing*. Here's how I eat to look good and stay healthy. Before breakfast, when I first get up, I have a cup of warm spring water with a squeeze of lemon and some acidophilus capsules. In a little while I begin swallowing the many vitamins and food supplements that I take every day—some with yogurt before breakfast, the rest after breakfast, with either fresh orange juice mixed with pineapple juice or cranberry nectar. I take vitamins only with a meal; they do the most good when they can be absorbed with digestive juices, which the stomach won't produce unless there's food in it. Along with a good multiple vitamin I take a multiple mineral plus other vitamins

—C, E, A (beta-carotene)—and supplements for my specific needs, including calcium with magnesium, selenium, pantothenic acid, biotin and L-cysteine for hair, manganese, zinc, lecithin, and EPA (fish oil), as suggested by material that I read and how I feel. I cannot overstate my high opinion of the value of these supplements, based upon my experience, but I would urge you to become informed for yourself before you decide to take anything other than a multiple vitamin and vitamin C. I think it's safe for me to suggest that along with vitamin C and vitamin E and the other basics it's very good to keep a bottle of echinacea on the shelf to ward off colds, and to take capsicum by capsule or sprinkled on food instead of black pepper as a good vein and artery cleaner. If I feel a sore throat coming on, I put two tablespoons of apple cider vinegar in a glass of water and sip it. If only I could keep in mind to do it, I'd take some every day, for it's beneficial in general and also does, for some reason, help to control weight.

For breakfast I have oatmeal with sunflower seeds, raisins, berries, and a little milk. That's 2 percent milk; nonfat milk just will not give the thrill. (I know everybody's scared of milk now; maybe I'll switch to soy milk soon, if they don't stop shooting up the poor cows.) I have a little coffee or breakfast tea, sometimes regular, but if it's a performance day, decaf. Caffeine isn't supposed to be good for us, but a little of it isn't the end of the world, and there's nothing better than a really great cup of coffee. My favorite tea is Lapsang souchong; it smells like bacon.

For lunch I have protein—tuna fish if I'm at home, grilled fish or chicken if I'm in a restaurant. I used to have a big salad at lunch but have discovered that a big bulky salad is too much matter and not enough sustenance for a long workday. I am crazy about huge wonderful salads, but I eat them maybe once a week now instead of every day.

For dinner I pay attention to what my system responds to best. I go a bit heavier on meat than most authorities suggest. I don't eat a lot at one time or eat it more than twice a week, but I do eat meat when I need to feel strong, almost always a

few hours before a live performance. (The pasta that is supposed to give all that energy doesn't do it for me.) I do not eat
meat together with potatoes though. I try not to mix proteins
and starches, as I think the combination is fattening. I eat
either a starch (baked potato, pasta, corn, brown rice, black-
eyed peas) or a protein (fish, chicken, beef, beans) and cooked
vegetables, both green and yellow or white, with either one,
and beets twice a week. I have a small salad almost always at
dinnertime, with olive oil and lemon juice or vinegar—tarra-
gon, rice, or balsamic. I prefer lemon juice. When I've put in
a very tough week, traveling and pouring out energy, I have
calf's liver, and when I'm not concerned about picking up half
a pound overnight I have lamb—very full of fat, but to me the
most delicious "flesh," as the vegetarians call it. We used to
have leg of lamb every Sunday night. I had to quit serving it
regularly; Hal Holbrook's cholesterol level would be 400 if we
weren't mindful.

I don't eat tomatoes much anymore; I'm afraid the acidity
isn't great for people with arthritis. It makes me sad, remembering how we used to pull a warm ripe tomato off the vine
and sit out on the back porch with a salt shaker, salting and
eating, leaning way out over the grass so that the juice
wouldn't run down on our clothes. They were wonderful
sliced and wonderful stewed, but nothing compared to the
undiluted pleasure of that sun-warmed and juicy back porch
special.

I don't eat a lot of fruit. I eat some, because it gives a certain
clarity to the skin. Part of staying healthy is figuring out what
our own particular system requires, and if we pay attention to
how different foods affect us and apply some common sense,
it's not hard to do. A lot of people flourish on a diet of mostly
fruit, but it makes me weak and mean, so I have half a banana
most every day, avocado in salads, and cranberry juice or orange juice or sometimes pineapple juice to take vitamins. An
apple once in a while tastes wonderful. Pineapple is good for
you. Grapes are a great dinner occasionally when I want a flat
stomach in the morning. Since fruit is loaded with sugar and I

don't feel strong from eating it, I don't see any sense in forcing it on myself. It's one of the great deceiver foods that we imagine we can eat all we want of and not gain weight. Wrong. Anything we eat a lot of will put on the pounds. I don't know about you, but plenty of fruit, especially bananas, will plump me up like a down cushion. All that said, fruit is an excellent detoxifier, and if you have the willpower to eat nothing but fruit for a day, you will feel the cleansing benefit. Fruit should be eaten by itself, not with any other kind of food. Some people like to have only fruit for breakfast. Good for them.

What about bread, the staff of life? I love bread, good hearty dark bread, and have learned to love it with *no butter*. Isn't that sad? Admit it. It's sad that we can't eat butter anymore, but we cannot. Anybody who picks up a knife and spreads butter on bread is leaving reality for that moment. Better jelly, especially that delicious all-fruit jelly. The best idea is to buy bread, or bake it yourself, that is so good you don't have to do anything to it. (My friend Walter Roszin, who grew up in Russia, says that nothing has ever been or will ever be as good to him as the piece of bread and glass of milk he would be given by his mother.) Another good idea is not to eat bread every day, at least not at every meal. And no sandwiches. As I just said, I try not to combine starch and protein. I prefer to eat them separately so that I can eat more and get away with it, and I can. Anyway, sandwiches have to have mayonnaise, don't they? And mayonnaise is another one of those things we cannot have. Remember, *no sandwiches*. When you look at a gorgeous, enticing sandwich with mayonnaise squishing out of it, train yourself to see it as an unfriendly agent, a saboteur of your well-being, and remind yourself that you can relish some popcorn after supper if you don't let this adversary trip you up. After you get your weight where you want it, once in a great while you can indulge in half a sandwich made with mustard, if that's appealing. I've reached the point where such a treat is luscious and filling.

What about dairy? This is a big and troublesome question for me. There's a history of osteoporosis on my mother's side of the family, so I want to be sure to have plenty of calcium. Some say drink milk; some say that's not the right way to get calcium. I don't know. I love yogurt. I have buttermilk if I wake in the middle of the night and can't sleep. I keep low-fat cottage cheese in the house at all times. I have it sometimes at dinner on my baked potato, or for lunch, or as a between-meal pick-me-up. It's good with a salad or with melon. A little yogurt on top keeps you from missing mayonnaise. Cheese is hardest to stay away from. I put out nonfat cheese sometimes just so I can pretend, but it isn't the same. Once in a while I encounter a gorgeous triple-cream cheese and have some with delight. Makes me hungry now just thinking of it. I allow myself feta or some other kinds of goat cheese, parmesan on pasta, provolone, mozzarella, swiss, and good old sharp cheddar, but not more than once a week. I can't have cheese all the time and neither can you, if you want to stay slim. Face it. It's not on the main list.

In 1981 I sailed from the Tonga Islands to New Zealand with my husband and his mate Robert Rossiter, which expedition I will be referring to again as we go along. I stayed on a week after we got there and ate my way across North Island. In some state of relief to be safely on land again, or letdown that the adventure was over, or elation that I had been accepted as one of the boys, I ate cheese at every meal, along with everything else that was heavy and hearty. I thought I was enjoying the feasting until I realized that the meals were making me feel sluggish and slow. The torpor that overtook me was not alleviated by my ever-tightening blue jeans, so I said good-bye to the stroke food and returned to my country and my senses. (Every time I hear the word *torpor* I think of Dame Edith Evans's unforgettable line in the movie *Tom Jones*, delivered to Hugh Griffith as he lay dead drunk in a haystack, "Rouse yourself, Brother, from your *pastoral torpor.*")

The funny thing is that when we were under sail out in the middle of the briny deep, our favorite meal was canned meat pies, and they served us very well and didn't feel heavy at all. I know that we were burning up a lot of fat moving about the boat, and the body does burn calories just trying to stay warm, but still I couldn't help but feel that I'd gotten away without paying the piper that time. Could it be that happy activity had something to do with it? Gee whiz.

Coffee, tea, juice, alcohol, water? The only liquid we should take in quantity is water. It is especially important to flush out the system with water if we want to treat ourselves to caffeine or alcohol, even though we read lately that a glass or two of wine with a meal is good for digestion. Lots of fruit juice isn't great; it's loaded with sugar and very fattening. Get used to drinking water, bottled spring water if possible. It's getting less expensive all the time and is worth more than any other libation you're likely to imbibe.

Start your day with a glass of water and end it with one. Six to eight glasses a day, and don't let me hear that excuse about not wanting to have to get up to go to the bathroom all night long. Your body will adjust rapidly and you will sleep better than you have in years, I promise. Here's the basic rule: drink water until your urine is clear. Dark urine is not a healthy sign, so keep drinking water until it gets pale, and if it doesn't, go see the doctor. A word of warning: avoid taking diuretics; they are deadly—literally deadly over a period of time. And if your doctor insists that you have to for some reason, be sure to pour down the water. Constipation? Put away three big glasses of water before eleven o'clock in the morning for a few days and say good-bye to sluggishness in the old alimentary canal. (When I was growing up, the term *alimentary canal* was used to cover any mention of intestinal function, if indeed it became absolutely necessary to allude to it at all.)

Lots of people believe that meals should be taken with no liquids, so as to allow the stomach to do what it's supposed to with enzymes. It makes sense to me that if water can take the nutrients out of food in the cooking pot, as we know it can, water might also wash what we're supposed to derive from our food out of the stomach before it can get into the bloodstream.

Certainly it would dilute the digestive juices. Europeans believe that two glasses of wine with a meal aids digestion. Nobody believes that guzzling water with a meal helps digestion, so I drink my eight glasses before breakfast, between meals, and well after dinner.

Let me restate what a lot of people don't consider obvious: drinking a goodly amount of water is extremely important in keeping a person healthy and not overweight. If you tend to retain water, drink *more*, not less, and just watch what happens to those ankles. If you need an energy boost, drink a glass of water. Water, not just any liquid. Don't kid yourself about that can of soda pop. I don't know an overweight person who doesn't live on diet colas. Hardly any liquids other than water are going to do you much good, and they may, as in the case of diet sodas, be bad for you. Bloat, bloat, bloat. If I'm dying to have a soft drink, I go ahead and have the real thing. I just don't do it all the time. When I'm home in Tennessee in the summertime, I go over to Billy and Barbara Younger's grocery store and get an icy cold Coke in a bottle. Oh boy, does it hit the spot, that old familiar flavor and that dewy green six-ounce bottle. I wouldn't give you a plugged nickel for diet Coke in a can. Afterward I drink a glass of water to dilute the Coke.

Now that I've derogated perhaps your favorite refreshment, I must mention a most unusual liquid that I feel is terrifically good for me. It is a tea that is made from the Kombucha mushroom and called, quite sensibly, Kombucha mushroom tea. My aunt Helen got on to it of course; she is always at the cutting edge of the newest thousand-year-old health advance. I've been drinking eight ounces a day for several weeks and I have become a believer. This slightly effervescent brew is a grand tonic and is said to be capable of stalling the aging process, an idea that has a certain ring to it. It's not easy to come by: a certain amount of time and effort are required to make it, and if one buys it in the health food store, it's expensive, but very few wonderful things come to us by magic. Just our children.

So how does it become fun to eat the way that's good for us? How do we change it from a hardship to a pleasure? When I was little, I would ask my mother how she kept her slender figure when many of the ladies did not. (The social pressures in little country towns did not include weight control.) Her answer was always the same. "It's a matter of puhsonal pride, my dahling." We have to see the reward for the effort in terms of our own delight and self-esteem. If we can't visualize it, then there are two chances, slim and none, that we'll be able to enjoy the pursuit of loveliness. However, if we can get a grasp of a picture we'd like to be, a feeling we'd like to have, then we're off to the races.

Let me conclude these ramblings with a few simple rules that can give you lots of assistance in the good health–good weight campaign. My contention is that the less complicated we make an eating plan, the more attractive it will be and the easier to stay with. There are a few rules I try to follow, and I'll run through them again. The big one is:

Everything we eat we should be able to think of as *beauty food*. If we can't think of it that way we'd better not eat much of it, now had we?

YESES

- Water, lots of it. Water between meals is an energy booster, and a large glass half an hour before you eat promotes good digestion and weight reduction. Don't guzzle fruit juice all the time, but do drink a glass of cranberry juice every day; it's very good for the urinary tract, for both men and women. I don't drink much sparkling water anymore since I heard that it's not good for strong bones. Don't drink water with your meals.
- Vegetables, fresh, not cooked too long or too greasy, all kinds, all you want. Broccoli and sweet potatoes seem to be leading the pack in nutritionists' favor right now. I love turnip greens, and the pot liquor.
- Bread without butter. *Without butter*.

- Eggs. They seem to be okay again. How wonderful. I eat about three a week, poached or boiled, not fried. They're great at lunch.
- Popcorn is okay, without butter of course. I am not exaggerating when I say I wouldn't go to the movies at all if I couldn't have my corn. (I don't put salt on it myself, but if the movie house people already did, I feel no remorse.)
- Olive oil has become the great eating thrill for me. It makes everything taste good. Yes, it is a fat and therefore fattening, but I eat lots of it and still my cholesterol is low and my weight stays reasonable. However, I do recommend tossing a salad; you will use much less oil than if you bring the dressing to the table and ladle it on. (Some smart folks spray on their oil to further reduce the amount they're getting on their lettuce, endive, watercress, and cilantro.) Olive oil is high in monounsaturated fat and vitamin E, both of which are good for us. Try dipping toast or bread in it if you're aching for butter. Try it on your baked potato. Use a little olive oil wherever you would ordinarily use mayonnaise, in preparing potato salad, for example, or tuna fish. Try it for popping corn. Deeelicious!

NOES

- No salt. No salt unless you are drinking lots and lots of water, in which case you should take in ¼ to ½ teaspoon a day. I don't cook with salt. I put salt on the table in case somebody just has to have it. I have figured out that the salters are going to salt it at the table whether it was cooked with salt or not, so what's the point of hitting their heart with a double whammy? Any canned food you eat has salt, bacon is loaded with it of course, as is almost everything that's been preserved, and all our favorite condiments, ketchup springing first to mind, have plenty, so suffice it to say you don't have to worry about not getting your share of salt unless you run miles and miles a day or do hard labor on the rock pile.

My father loves to look pitiful and describe how the pioneers would travel long distances on horseback to get to the salt lick and bring some back to their cabin or wagon train, *"for without it they would die!"* He tells me this when I'm reminding him that if he's having a piece of bacon with his eggs, he doesn't need to salt them. He maintains that eggs and fish are two things which are not worth eating without salt, and there is truth in what he says. When I broach the fact that his doctor put canned foods off limits because of the salt content, he counters with an uplifting history of the Campbell's Soup Company and of how Campbell's is to this day *"the greatest soup company in the world!"* The combination of his charm and fervency always works and I relax my principles for that moment, so my advice on salt is just do the best you can with your nearest and dearest, but don't *you* load it on *your* food. That you can control.

- Don't eat protein and starch together very often. Eat protein with vegetables and salad, or starch with vegetables and salad, but don't combine them. We know we're going to have to have a piece of toast under a poached egg, and clam sauce would be pointless without spaghetti, and there will be other exceptions, but try to make them exceptions, and I promise that you will notice a change in your belt line pretty soon.

- No butter ever. No margarine. Don't think margarine is okay, because it's not; it's another deceiver.

- Peanut butter? Don't touch it, even though it is maybe the best thing ever invented and healthy to boot. Well, okay, a teaspoonful with no bread every other month. Or on a boat in the middle of the ocean.

- Mayonnaise. Forget it, and forget those health food substitutes. They're sad and not unfattening. Use mustard instead.

- No cream, and no creamed anything and no cream *of* anything. Cream cheese shall never pass these lips again. Ice cream? Now I'm going to start crying.

- No chips and dips. Forget "nonfat" chips; they've still got calories, and no nourishment. Even salsa dips have calories, and mayonnaise-based dips are truly suicide time. Chips and dips are the epitome of mindless eating. You see them, you put them in your mouth. Afterward you eat just as big a dinner as if you'd had nothing. Chips and dips are big enemies.

- No desserts. If you remove dessert from your mental list of daily expectations, you'll get used to the change very quickly, and you may find as I have that it's easier to do than to torment yourself with something that's supposed to be dessert and is not the real McCoy. Get up from the table. Then an hour later you can watch a little television or read a book with a bowl of popcorn. Sometimes we have fresh pineapple for dessert, when we have company, or low-fat sherbet. And once in a while go ahead and have a real dessert, like chocolate pie or fudge cake or *once in a blue moon* an old-timey milk shake or malted in one of those metal containers they take right off the stirring machine and set down by your glass. Mother McCree! I'd have given a quarter not to have even thought of that one.

TIPS

- There are lots of great suggestions for making nonfat foods tasty in countess cookbooks and magazines, and I'm not setting myself up as a cooking adviser; however, I'm passing on a few of my favorites: Lemon juice and/or chopped onion to take the place of salt. Cilantro, chopped fresh if possible or from the herb rack, to make any salad special. Chopped fresh herbs instead of powdered from a bottle, and if you use the powdered kind, throw it away and get a new bottle every three months. Fresh lemon juice, cayenne pepper, and chopped parsley make everything taste better. My Aunt Helen makes her tuna salad with mustard instead of mayonnaise and you don't miss the mayo a bit. Our neighborhood café, the Gingham Garden, stirs raisins into their tuna and it's scrumptious. They also mix lemonade and iced tea for a treat on a hot afternoon. Salt-free soy sauce added to lemon and oil salad dressing along with a little powdered mustard you will like, I'll bet.

- Never skip breakfast. It's too good an excuse for overeating later in the day. It also throws off your metabolism somehow. Start noticing how many people with weight problems always mention that they didn't eat anything for breakfast, or whatever the meal before the one they're just starting now.

- "Masticate your food thoroughly" my grandmother Hillsman used to say. She thought a person ought to chew each mouthful twenty-five times. We thought that was overdoing it; now they tell us she was right. If we want the food to do more nourishing and leave less fat behind, we should chew until there's nothing left to swallow, practically. One ends up eating less too.

- Start noticing the eating habits of people who have weight problems. You will become aware of similar patterns of eating, and more important, of ways they fool themselves. If you compare and analyze your own tendencies, and are mercilessly honest with yourself, you will notice a boost in self-control and willpower.

- Start noticing the eating habits of people who are in control of their weight. If you distinguish habits or attitudes about eating they have in common, it would not be criminal quietly to steal them for yourself. Particularizing in this fashion will help to make the process an interesting journey to a desirable achievement, as opposed to a drab exercise in deprivation.

The point of all this food talk is that some of us may wish we could be different from the way we are at present, either physically or emotionally, and a great part of becoming what we'd like to be has got to depend upon what we eat. Making such a change pleasant is not all that complicated: we are going to get what we want, and we're going to enjoy the process of doing so. When we begin to feel hungry for the old familiar fat food, we're going to remember that it turned out to be a false friend, and we're going to eat something healthy instead so we won't be hungry, and we are going to think of it and relish it as *beauty food*. We just have to make our resolve and start in with no fiddle-faddling. The Cherokee chieftain told his son, "When the time comes that you must kill a bear, then kill a bear." I feel confident that very shortly, perhaps even the first day you start to change the way you eat, you will be rewarded with a change in the way you feel. If you give yourself high-quality fuel, your system is going to run better. Remember, you're going to start giving yourself *beauty food*.

Goethe said it: "The most important thing is to learn to rule oneself."

≈ *Chapter Three* ≈
GOOD HABITS—RESULTS AND ROSES

The man who wants a garden fair,
Or small or very big,
With flowers growing here and there,
Must bend his back and dig.

The things are mighty few on earth
That wishes can attain.
Whate'er we want of any worth
We've got to work to gain.

It matters not what goal you seek
Its secret here reposes:
You've got to dig from week to week
To get Results or Roses.

—EDGAR GUEST

Nothing is stronger than habit.

—OVID

$\mathcal{W}$HEN I WAS TWENTY-EIGHT YEARS
old, I began to notice a few tiny folds of skin just above my
knee. I remember how old I was because of conversations I
had with my friend Dorothy Emmerson, and how she hooted
with laughter when I would refer to my "elephant knees." I
would laugh too, but not uproariously. I had the uncomfortable feeling that these were subtle little heralds of things to
come, and was I ever on target there. Over the course of the
next fifteen years, that skin on my thighs seemed to develop
an ever increasing curiosity regarding what was underfoot and
became determined to creep down and peek out over my knees
for a good look. I was no longer joking around about elephant
knees. That wasn't all that was going up and down my frame
either. The hideous truth was coming home to me that unless
I was prepared to devote a certain amount of attention to
holding the flesh on the bone, it wasn't going to stay there by
itself. My flesh was headed south. Oh brother.

I had never been, as we say where I come from, "athletically
inclined." I always sprained an ankle running to keep up with
my brother and his friends. I got my fingers jammed playing
volleyball and basketball in school. The only swimming facility
other than Drummond's Slough, where only boys were allowed to jump in and then only big boys, was the swimming
pool in McKenzie and that was a thirty-minute trip. My little
sister and I went a few times in our early years, but because
our mother had us wearing shower caps instead of real swimming caps, we felt that we looked a bit goony. I've seen the
snapshots and we were not imagining things; we looked very
goony, even at six and eight years of age. We waded in the
surf at Panama Beach the summer we went there with Uncle
Leon's family, but that wasn't exactly moving us toward the
Olympics, and then when we were ten and twelve, we started
going with a busload over to McKenzie to take swimming

lessons with Ellis West. Ellis was very tall and slender, blond, and an exciting piano player. It's very easy to get a crush on someone who introduces you to a new wonderful thing, plus he represented getting to go to McKenzie with a bunch of other novice practitioners of the female calling, prancing and preening our way in and out of the changing rooms, flailing about noisily in the water so that he would come save us, and afterward lolling by the pool with that ever-delectable refreshment, a bottle of Coke with a package of Planters Peanuts poured into it. All that and his piano playing. And the fact that he played the trumpet salute every morning as the flag was raised at school, an honor I had my eye on and grabbed the minute Ellis was graduated. I must have had a crush on him. I think so because of a dream I still remember in which the McKenzie swimming pool was Heaven and Ellis West was Jesus.

The next winter when Midge couldn't get over the flu, Daddy and Gina decided that we would have to start spending winters in Florida to keep her healthy. Hal was already off at college, so Gina and Midge and I spent two months every winter in Sarasota until we were out of high school, during which time Daddy bought beachfront property on Siesta Key and put up an apartment motel, the Sea Dream, "so we'd have a place to stay." What fun we had. Daddy would drive us down, then take the plane back home to go to work and leave us with the car. We would sing and play car games and laugh riotously at any silly thing. Once Daddy accidentally backed into a display pile of watermelons at a filling station and was so embarrassed he insisted on paying the man for the whole pile, so we put a bunch of them in the car and stopped at a pretty place down on the side of the road and gorged ourselves. For once Gina didn't object to our eating too much watermelon, which she usually had something against because of the seeds or something, and none of us minded the fact that a soft balmy rain was falling all the while.

Midge's head would clear up about the time we drove through St. Petersburg. Every time, like clockwork, her sinus headache would disappear and her color would change as we drove over the bridge. By the time we got to Clearwater, Daddy would always warn us that the minute we got there he was going to "take a running start and jump right in the middle of the Pacific Ocean," a pronouncement that would be met with squeals and squeezes and protests that he'd have to jump across the entire country to do that.

I wish Gina had written down her suntan lotion recipe. Naturally she eschewed the local tourist emporium where such things were sold at what she considered ridiculous prices. (Robber's Roost we called it, after a name in a Zane Grey novel.) The basic ingredient of her suntan lotion was olive oil and she made sure we applied it liberally, with the result that we smelled like salads. We were afraid no boys would come around girls who smelled so unusual, but thank goodness we didn't suffer that sad fate; as a matter of fact we turned a rather dazzling golden color and managed to keep our beach towels creditably crowded, pretty good going considering the fact that there was hardly anybody around in the 1950s. Once our initial foreignness was hurdled, water skiing was mentioned. No fools we, Midge and I talked our parents into taking us all the way to Lido Key, on the other side of Sarasota, for lessons. We wanted no witnesses. The azure waters of Lido Key were subjected to an ugly roiling for several afternoons, and then one day we could sort of do it, and we let well enough alone, not wanting to put anybody at Cypress Gardens out of a job. We did learn to dive from the board of the Sea Dream pool, no flips or swans of course, but passingly graceful, and that was fun if somebody was watching.

Still my enjoyment of water sports was always more about the suntan and the boys than the water, in which I never quite got to be comfortable, so all in all I'm afraid my go-rounds with the water don't qualify as regular exercise.

I wasn't allowed to take dancing classes until I was grown and then it was too late for dance to become a regular part of my day. Finally, when I was knocking on forty's door, I took myself to Walter Roszin's studio to prepare for my sailing trips with Hal and met up with the first exercise that I every truly enjoyed. Who wouldn't have? Walter has to be some kind of a genius. He can get your best and then some; everybody who went to Alex and Walter's learned to stand on their hands and fly on a trapeze, and I assure you that there has never been a more surprised acrobat than I. When I first met him, I had in mind to take my little girls for lessons in gymnastics and tumbling. He said, "What about the mama?"

I said, "Oh, Heavens, no! I am not coordinated at all and besides I don't like the way I look in a leotard anymore."

He said in his lovely accented English, "You come too. We make up something special for uncoordinated." So I went and he did. I like to believe that I could have joined the circus eventually, but in a couple of years Walter retired. We are still good friends. I dedicated my first yoga video to him as a meager attempt to thank him for opening a heavy door and escorting me through it.

Then all around me was aerobic mania, and none of it seemed appealing. Many of the runners and joggers I saw appeared to be in merciless pain as they propelled themselves forward like stick people, torso rigid, legs chopping at the ground, and anyway running hurts my ankles, so that was out. The frantic perkiness of the aerobics routines I had seen made me feel very outside the experience, if you follow my drift. Weight lifting? Please get real.

As a performer who depends in part upon my appearance, and as a woman who wants my husband to keep thinking I'm the prettiest one, and as a person who has painful back problems plus arthritis, I had to face the need to work at something constantly that I had always dealt with sporadically—my body. My friend Lori Coveillo, who gives shiatsu treatments, suggested that I try some yoga classes. I said, "I don't think so, Lori. I tried yoga in New York in the late sixties. We all lay on the hard floor while the great yogi intoned over us, 'Send your mind to the *blue* skies,' and all I got out of it was a chilly back." Lori persisted, however, and I was introduced to Wendy Merson, and Wendy and yoga changed my life.

Loving yourself is learning to discipline and rule yourself.

I might mention in defense of my bad attitude toward exercise that I do feel there's some legitimacy in not wanting to give over too much time and effort to that part of me that, even under the best circumstances, is not going to Heaven. To point up the fact that I have some high-caliber company, I have stolen one of my husband's favorite quotations from Mark Twain: "Whenever I feel the urge to exercise, I lie down until it passes away." I wonder if Mr. Clemens might have taken to yoga, given that it unites time spent improving the flesh with time invested in the life of the mind.

My childhood friend Publilius Syrus said, "Practice is the best of all instructors." I'm just beginning to realize what practicing yoga can do for my health, and there are two operative words here: *yoga* and *practicing.* Before I got on to yoga, I had been inclined to picture how terrific something would be when I really put my mind to it; I'm learning lately to put the perfect picture aside and do whatever is within reach now. Letting tension build up in the body as the overload builds up around us is a really poor way to spend the day, and it doesn't take going to a gym for an hour to get healing relief. Just ten minutes of yoga stretching and deep controlled breathing one morning will be stimulating enough for a person to want to make it twenty minutes next time and to make the next time the next day. Twenty minutes of yoga stretches and conscious breathing every day will change a person's life.

Before I go on about how yoga changed (saved, in a way) my life, I'll just have to take a moment to tell you about the snake doctor who came through town way back before I was born. He worked the countryside with a clown sidekick, who would start the proceedings with some tomfoolery. The clown wore huge shoes shaped like snowshoes with blunt toes, on which he could balance as if they were stilts; when he perched way up on the tips of those shoes and ran at the children, it scared them to death and attracted them at the same time, grownups too. Once the antic had drawn a crowd, the snake doctor would take over, standing up on the wagon touting his snake oil, reeling off the vicious and deadly ailments that it was guaranteed to cure. When he'd run the gamut of his harangue, bearing down on the dire infirmities from which his potion would save the population of McLemoresville, from rheumatism to rheumatic fever—all the rheums—he'd urge everyone to step up and buy a bottle. If they didn't start buying, the clown would call out, "Let 'em die, Doc. Let 'em die."

Well, that's not quite how I feel about touting yoga; I'm not quite so heartless as the snake doctor's clown. I am eager to get my message across to you, however, because I happen to know how important my message is. Yoga heals. Yoga makes you healthy. Yoga postures, sustained and sweated through, rush oxygen to all the organs of the body, and everything begins to work better, from top to bottom. Good health and good looks are synonymous. Try to think of a robustly healthy person you know who is not attractive. Shining clear eyes, clean strong teeth, shining healthy hair, and clear glowing skin are all attributes of beauty, and we can have them if we get healthy.

A vigorous and supple form is achievable, I promise. Since a supple spine has all to do with good health and long life, most yoga postures, along with whatever else they're designed for, promote flexibility of the spine. As we age, the spine becomes compressed and less flexible; shoulders and back tend to round forward; nerves that serve the internal organs are less able to function properly; the flow of blood and oxygen to organs is impeded. Moving the spine is vital. There are six possible directions we can bend our spine—forward, backward, laterally to either side, and twisting to either side. Yoga practice balances a movement in one direction with another in the opposite direction and returns the body to center. For example, after the Cobra (in which one's legs and torso are resting on the floor, palms pressing down, raising the upper half of the body, head facing forward and up, until the body is touching the floor only from the navel to the toes) one might follow with the Rabbit or the Child's Pose. (Both involve sitting on heels with the body bending forward to stretch out the lower back muscles. The Rabbit pose is active, hands grasping heels and pulling back while the legs are pushing the torso forward; the Child's Pose is passive, arms by sides, body relaxing into itself.)

It is almost impossible to sit and stand straight if we have weak back muscles. Since I was born with a weakness in my lower back, I understand how hard it can be to develop strength there, especially as a lazy or "too busy" adult; however, if we don't, we could wind up shaped like an S viewed in profile or having one hip noticeably higher than the other when viewed from behind. (Spinal curvatures never are as noticeable from the front, unfortunately for the curvee, so for too long we can put off—literally, if you will—facing the truth.) Good posture does not always come naturally, but it can be acquired.

The way we sit and stand has an enormous amount to do with how we are shaped and how fine we look. A depressed or angry person often stands slumped forward. Sometimes changing our posture can actually help to alter our internal state. When I catch myself feeling slumpy, I take a slow deep breath, reach the top of my head toward the sky, and a smile appears. Beautiful posture rises straight up from the earth, as if we were planted in it and newly sprouting from it, or as if the fountain of life were bubbling up through us (and it is). As I sit here on a little wooden stool to write, I have to keep correcting my rounding forward, which is the very reason I elect to spend part of my writing time on this backless stool.

Another defining characteristic of a lovely form is how it moves. A certain amount of strength is necessary for easy and smooth motion, and a good deal of suppleness is required for a person to move with fluidity and grace. Wendy Merson discovered a series of exquisite flowing postures from the Taoist tradition, called Silken Movements. They have names like Holding Up the Heavens and Drawing the Bow. I can't perform them like Wendy, but they are a thrill to do, so I included them in my second video, *Yoga for You*. Whether you're going to make it onstage in a tutu or not, these exercises encourage grace and poise while they intensely oxygenate the blood.

I used to think there was something to that saying, "No woman can be too rich or too thin." Truman Capote said it and it sounds smart, but it's not smart, it's sad. We know that there are degrees of both rich and thin that are not good. We've read the pitiful accounts. Slender is nice; thin is not, except in the fashion industry. What we want is a body that is made of flesh and bone, not just bone. Man or woman, we want some kind of *shape*. I don't care to look like a boy or a stick, or even a decathlon participant, not that I've ever been in danger of getting a discernible muscle. I do want to look like a woman, and if possible one with a certain lushness about her. The practice of yoga changed my shape. As one gets older, the tendency is toward thickening around the middle, *n'est-ce pas?* Yoga stretches, particularly slow side bends that one holds and breathes into, tone the muscles that pull in the waistline, and keep the food you eat from settling around there.

I've always had nice long slender legs, but they didn't go all the way up, if you know what I mean. I mean *thighs*. Not hideous, but there. Now my legs go all the way up. It's hard to believe, but I know it's true because my wild cousin Ann Carter Uhl Gaines from Bowling Green, who will say whatever comes into her mind, unedited and heedless of the cost, said exactly that last May when we were getting dressed to go to the Kentucky Derby. She always gets ready faster than I do and comes into my room to chat while I'm finishing up. She watched me parading around in my underwear for a few minutes and then stated, "Dixie, your legs are better now than they were when you were twenty-five years old. And I remember exactly how you looked that time Tom and I took you out to Jones Beach and you had your eye on that lifeguard, and we nearly didn't make it back into town in time for dinner." Ann's memory for high jinks is alarmingly accurate, but I was thrilled that she passed down the ruling on my legs.

Sun Salutations, a series of positions that are performed in as fluid a fashion as possible, work wonders for a person's legs. The Salute begins standing. Raise arms to meet over the head, then bend forward all the way, arms down to the floor on either side. Place hands on floor and bring one leg back into a lunge position, then the other leg back to join it, to make the body form a straight line, heels to top of head. Push back with hips to sit on heels facedown, arms still forward, then thrust body forward between hands and face up into Cobra position. Lift hips up, hands and feet in place on floor, into Downward Facing Dog position. Step the starting foot forward into another lunge, then bring the back foot forward to meet hands on floor in complete Forward Bend. Lift arms out to the sides as body lifts forward and up to standing. The series is repeated starting with the other foot lunging back, each change in position accompanied by a long deep inhalation or exhalation of breath.

By the time one builds up enough stamina to do ten Sun Salutations in a row, with regular breathing to match the moves, one will notice a change in the shape of the legs, as well as other nice places, or I'll be a monkey's uncle. If you want to practice Sun Salutations along with me, get my first video, the *Unworkout*.

Or get my second video, *Yoga for You*, and do the series of Warrior poses with me. The whole standing series on that tape is very leggy.

The body wants to fix itself. Our own bodies will heal themselves if we can give them proper fuel, keep them clean inside and out, get the blood moving around, and charge our minds with positives. The hardest part of fitness is coming back *after* something—after having a baby, an illness, an injury, depression, a death close to you, financial loss, a move to a new house, even a vacation. An exciting job can be a mixed blessing if, for instance, it takes up all your time so that you have trouble getting in your exercise. And if you've been through a divorce, you'll have had your own set of difficulties. Whether you gain weight or lose it, your health is under siege. Then we add the task of staying fit as we get older, which takes more effort all the time, and if we don't keep our mind in a good place, we feel less and less like expending that effort. Yoga is an encouraging discipline, as tough as one wishes to make it and at the same time forgiving. You don't have to feel that it's hopeless to get back to it if you slack off for a while. From the first moment you return to deep breathing and stretching, your body says thank you, as opposed to "Now I'm going to make you suffer for backsliding."

Loving yourself is learning self-healing and self-government.

Vitally important—irreplaceable really—for good health and good form is walking. First stretch out for a few minutes, especially your hamstrings. My favorite hamstring and general all-around great-feeling stretcher is the Downward Facing Dog pose I mentioned just earlier. Start on the floor on your hands and knees, toes curled under, then take a deep breath in, and as you exhale, lift your knees off the floor and straighten your legs, lifting your behind up, up, up. Spread your fingers apart and consciously press your hands against the floor, pushing your tailbone up and away from your wrists to make the top of an inverted V, neck relaxed, looking back toward your thighs, heels trying to press into the floor. With practice, as your hamstrings release, you'll feel more weight in your feet than on your hands. Try to press your chest gently toward your thighs. *Quelle sensation!* Breathe slowly and deeply. Sense the energy zapping from your hands up to your pelvis, which is pointed skyward. The objective is to look the way a dog does when he gets up from his nap and stretches out, back flat, shoulders down, hips lifting up. This stretch will tingle in the backs of your legs and in your arms and shoulders if you do it with concentration and deep breathing and hold it for ten deep breaths.

Now head out on your walk with long relaxed strides and work up to a nice brisk clip. I walk half an hour or forty minutes, more when I have time. Take the longest steps that are comfortable for you, coming heel down first so as to work the muscles and lift your behind. Be conscious of your breathing as you swing along, keeping it even and deep and as slow as possible, visualizing the oxygen pouring into your bloodstream and brain. Don't think you can count the zillions of steps you take in home or office during the day as *walking;* it's not at all the same. Strolling is pleasant, and certainly better than sitting in the house, but brisk walking is what's good for you. Swing your arms too—big happy robust swings.

These days I'm hoping against hope that the three or four vigorous walks I get in every week will prevent my having osteoporosis. I have yet to get a satisfactory answer from any doctor or health expert. They just don't seem to know. I have read that the answer to that question was determined in my system years ago, perhaps by heredity, and all I can actually do now is try to minimize the devastation. I resisted taking hormones to ward it off because any doctor will tell you that hormones increase one's chances of having uterine cancer. I opted for herbs. When I got to the point that I didn't know if I was awake and perspiring in the middle of the night because of female changes or from fear of shrinking, I decided I'd rather take the risk of cancer than wind up the same height as the hall table; I started on hormones. After I had begun taking them, I found out that I can't quit unless I want many other kinds of unpleasant things to happen. As I said, I do hope these hormones work; if you are watching television twenty years from now and you hear my voice but don't see me anywhere, then you can surmise that they didn't.

Be that as it may, I don't want to wallow around in a negative trough, so let's move on to skin, which is an upbeat subject for me; I want to make it the same for you. Aunt Helen's skin is perfect, and so was my mother's, and I had therefore a good shot at clear skin, but when I was thirteen or fourteen, just in case, I asked for the famous arsenic skin care regime. When Daddy was fifteen years old, he had gotten sick with raging chills that wouldn't let up, and after quinine and all known remedies failed, Papa—my grandfather Carter—had finally gotten worried enough to take him to the doctor for it. Dr. Massey prescribed Fowler's Solution of Arsenic in escalating doses. The chills abated. The arsenic cured Daddy of the chills and threw in an unexpected bonus. To Daddy's delight his adolescent complexion turned "as smooth and clear as a girl's." He never had a chill or a pimple again. So when I thought I might be starting to have a little breaking out, I prevailed upon my parents to give me the arsenic cure. My skin never broke out, ever. Sorry to tantalize you with this story when you can't try it yourself; I don't remember the dosage, and anyway, one dare not try it without a doctor, and the doctors won't prescribe it anymore, the old spoilsports.

Let me repeat how important it is to drink lots of water and eat the right kinds of food if you are interested in pretty skin. Think about how that would work and it will make all the sense in the world to you. Drink water instead of soda pop. Colas are not going to make your skin or anything else about you prettier. Picture it and you'll agree. Drink water by the barrel, stay away from chocolate and fried food, work up a sweat now and again, and you are very likely to be right pleased with your epidermis. Think of your skin as the allover organ that it in fact is, not just the part that's on your face, and treat all of it well from the inside out. No amount of expensive makeup will make unhealthy skin look pretty.

Now I'd like to tell you how I treat my skin on the outside. My regimen is very simple, but very important to me, since I believe that aging skin is hard to disguise and that a person who possesses beautiful skin can appear ageless. Not necessarily young, mind you, but ageless. It's not a bit of good wanting to appear younger than we are by much; it's got to make a person feel squirrelly, that attempt, and ultimately lacking in dignity, which quality would be one of the loveliest rewards of advancing years carried off well. There's nothing undignified, however, in desiring to possess an ageless aspect. There's mystery in it, and beauty, and yes, dignity.

Anyway, here's what I do every morning and every night: I liberally apply a rich gooey cleansing cream that I get from

Aunt Helen's store and gently massage it into my face and neck and chest. (I'm going to start selling it soon. If you want to find out about that and other products I think are extra fine call 901-986-3560.) Then with warm water I wet one of the cheap white washcloths I buy just for this purpose (expensive washcloths are too thick) and ever so gently remove the cleanser. Then I rinse my face and chest in cool water. That's it, except when I'm cleaning off lots of makeup, in which case I do the same thing two or three times. Then I put on whichever face creams I'm currently using (I change every so often to surprise my skin), lots at night, eye cream, neck cream, the whole works, and my skin is happy as can be. I have almost no wrinkles and almost no blemishes. Once in a while, maybe every three months, I get a rich collagen facial.

My message to you, Dear Reader, is this: I use the greasiest possible face cleanser and have for years, and it is fantastic for my skin, so the same thing *might* be good for you too. It's the accepted wisdom now that one should never put grease on the face, that "light" is the word, but I'm here to say that "light" does not get my skin clean, and it leaves it dry to boot. Gooey cleanser (with lanolin) and a cheap warm washcloth—that's my advice. It takes me a big three minutes.

Some of my friends cannot use my oily cleansing cream; they say it makes them break out. My daughters use it and love it. "Everyone to his own taste," said the old lady as she kissed the cow. Each of us must find what does the job best for our particular skin. That said, just remember that all the wrinkle creams in Saks Fifth Avenue and all the makeup on the Hollywood movie lots can't do anything for dirty skin. You've got to get it clean, really clean, at least twice a day.

Also, we may never never never go to bed with our makeup on. That would be extremely naughty.

Back when I was living in New York and wanting to do the very smart things all the Fifth Avenue girls did, I went through the Laszlo routine. It took forever and cost quite a lot, so I thought it must be great; then after about five years I had to accept the fact that my still young skin was as dry as the

Sahara. I asked Aunt Helen to send me some of her cleansing emulsion from her health food store and in a week my skin was dewy again. It's not how much it costs; it's what works for your particular skin. The big reason that expensive skin regimes work for so many women is that when we've paid out all that money, we're probably going to be more diligent about making the time to do it.

I am now beginning to get a few light brown spots on my face and neck and chest, from the sun (even though I do use sunscreen) or aging or both. Another charming newsy item I'm going to mention here, in case any of you have had something similar and fear it's thyroid trouble or something weird, is this: on both sides of my neck from beneath my ears to my shoulders I have tiny freckles. Well, I'm calling them freckles, but they're not the adorable kissable kind, and there are way too many of them. Thank Heavens for our brilliant down-to-earth dermatologist, Dr. Victor Newcomer, who laughed when I asked him if one of my organs was out of whack. He said, "Stop putting perfume behind your ears and rubbing it down your neck, and the skin will eventually clear up again."

"How did you know I put perfume behind my ears? Do I have too much on?" says I.

"I know it because I'm supposed to know it," says he. It turns out that having perfume on that part of my neck for a couple of decades (I was taught that young ladies shouldn't wear "scent" until they're thirty), I have finally gotten sunsensitive to it. (Is there no end to the constant reminders that we are getting up there? Apparently not. Cy Coleman wrote a song called "After Forty It's Patch Patch Patch" that I keep threatening to put in my cabaret act.)

With these off-putting developments occurring right and left, I'm in the process of investigating skin products that use glycolic acid (fruit acid, alpha-hydroxyl). I have just been introduced to some newly researched skin care concoctions that look very promising. I will act as my own guinea pig (Don't take offense, my darling Gretchen Wyler and animal rights friends, to the animal reference) and if it works on me,

I may go into business and start selling it. If I do, it will not be at Chanel or La Prairie prices. I was afraid to try Retin-A, although some friends have gotten wonderful results from it, and no way am I going for a chemical peel (that sounds skeeery), so glycolic acid may be the answer for me. I'll let you know.

I do not use body soap. Call me crazy (or trashy), but I think it dries my skin. I take an occasional milk or oil or bubble bath; that's as close as I get to soap. Don't get the wrong idea; I do at least shower daily. Sometimes I scrub after a bath or shower with a rough towel, one of my personal luxuries. I got two nubby towels from a natural fiber mail-order catalogue, part linen, part cotton, which I keep in my bathroom and do not share. They are great for rubbing up the circulation and they don't take all the moisture off the skin.) Sometimes I just let the bathwater stay on my body, but I never fail to slather on soothing silky lotion. Jergens and Vaseline Intensive Care hang right in there with the fancy ones. I gob it all over. Then I do a little yoga breathing while it dries. What a lovely sensation it is to feel clean smooth skin against clean smooth sheets.

On my thirteenth birthday I was allowed to go to the store and get my first tube of lipstick—Tangee Natural. It turned a pretty scary orange color once you put it on, but what did I care; it was lipstick. I had been waiting forever for this rite of passage. Ever since I could stand up by myself, I had watched my mother brush her thick black hair, put two combs in it just above each temple, screw on her earrings (pierced ears were considered vulgar at that time and clip-ons came later), and finally put on lipstick. She always wore crimson red lipstick, and she always blotted it with Kleenex after she put it on. She didn't like glossy shiny lips, but she did like dewy skin. She didn't wear makeup or powder. She didn't need to.

I imagine that all little girls, like I did, attach mystique to the ritual they watch their mothers perform in their toilette, however simple it may be. I recently turned up a picture of my little daughters sitting in their pajamas on the bathroom rug in our apartment in New York at about one and two years of age, each with a pump bottle of Jergens lotion, just working away on their hands. Cute, cute, cute.

Makeup. Where would one start? We are so inundated with the newest news on the newest look that I'm sure I'm way behind everybody else on this subject, and frankly I don't care. After the age of thirty we should use less paint anyway. That's the irony; one looks best in makeup at the age one doesn't need it. I don't buy much makeup, but I seem to have a lot on the shelf, my practice being to keep whatever I have until it's used up. My girls told me not long ago that at a certain point I have to throw out mascara or it will hurt my eyes. I suppose they plan it that way, the cosmetic companies. If everybody did what I do, sales would be slow. Lipstick is my fastest turnover item, about a year per tube if it's a favorite. (Yes, that's the truth, although I keep seven or eight different shades going at the same time, even though I try not to fall prey to the alarm sounded at the beginning of each season by the fashion magazines that everything we have on our bathroom counter is so out that we must throw it all away and start over if we don't want to become pariahs.) My makeup theory is that the more of it one puts on, the less the quality of the skin shows, so I don't put on much: a liquid base with sunscreen in it, Aida Thibiant or Chanel being my current favorites, a very light brush of powder, and lip gloss or lipstick. When I want to dress up, I pencil my eyebrows and lips, and brush bronzer or blush all around my hairline, under my eyebrows, and across my collarbones. Personally I don't think that big old pinked-up cheeks are the loveliest thing on a woman over forty.

While I'm of the opinion that on some young women lots of makeup can look very good, and that only very young women can look very, very good in lots and lots of makeup, I do believe that everyone should wear a little. (Except men. I'm trying to get used to makeup on men because some of my friends wear it, but that's a hard one for me.) A daily toilette, however simple, is a must for feeling beautiful. Perfectly clean skin with lightly and precisely applied makeup and a hint of fragrance is a subtle gift to one's family and coworkers, and ultimately to one's self.

We are creatures of habit. Eventually we become a composite of our habits. Habits of cleanliness and loveliness will be nice to live with down the line; habits of sloth will not. Longfellow said,

> *Let us do our work as well,*
> *Both the unseen and the seen;*
> *Make the house where gods may dwell*
> *Beautiful, entire, and clean.*

Chapter Four
AESTHETIC SURGERY

Oh wad some Pow'r the giftie gie us
To see oursels as ithers see us!
It wad frae monie a blunder free us,
An' foolish notion:
What airs in dress an' gait wad lea'e us,
An' ev'n devotion!

—ROBERT BURNS

I wish that for just one time, you could stand inside my shoes,
And just for that one moment I could be you.
I wish that for just one time, you could stand inside my shoes.
You'd know what a drag it is to see you.

—BOB DYLAN

Freedom is an inside job.

—SAM KEEN

OWADAYS IN OUR EMPOWERED, EN-
lightened, and high state of consciousness, we all like to say
that we're not getting older, we're getting better. We say that
older is great, that people over forty are the most interesting,
and we try to project the attitude that we don't care about age,
that age doesn't matter. Well, it's a gallant sentiment, but
it's just not entirely true, and I've become convinced that
pretending it is true does not accomplish what it's supposed
to. If it's true, why has every friendly adviser I know cautioned
me to quit announcing my age all over the place? Not feeling
free to mention this very basic fact bothers me, but I don't do
it anymore, because I know it's not good business. It gets
printed, but not because I proudly shout it out the way I did
ten years ago. The word we hear now, "ageism," suggests that
perhaps there's reason to lie or at the least keep mum, and this
message inevitably translates in the subconscious as something
that's wrong with us.

I'm a happy woman, at home, at work, and in the middle of
the night when it's just me and the ceiling, but let me say this:
growing up is hard, and when we think maybe we've started
to get there, all of a sudden we've started aging, and aging
is hard. Many aspects of maturing are quite wonderful and
rewarding, but certain things about the process are, well, uncomfortable, yes? Emotionally and physically. I've seen
enough already of the second half of my life to know that it's
not going to be just like the first half. I will have to keep
getting a stronger prescription in my glasses, and regular
checkups against cancer of one thing or another. I won't enjoy
working in high heels for hours on end. I will have to spend
more time keeping limber in order not to stiffen up physically
or mentally. Least appealing of all, eventually I will have to
put up with the insufferable attitude typified in the greeting,
"How are we today, young lady?" (I admire the way my father

instantly takes on anyone who calls him "young man" or "Daddy Carter." They don't do it twice.)

So what, says I; let's not make the best of it; let's make it the best. Best won't happen by itself. Adjustments must be made, and blessings must be counted. One very attractive aspect of what I see ahead is knowing at last that I'm okay, that my family and friends think well of me, and that I'm respected as a good and professional worker. I consider this knowledge an achievement of sizable proportions, and I intend to enjoy it. I intend also to enjoy the allowance even a ladylike person has to speak her mind more boldly in maturity than in youth. (Strong opinions presented strongly by a young person are often strident and annoying; mature options, even if they're wrong or unwise, have at least the credentials of experience.) I intend to abjure, no matter what the provocation, the pestilential anger that makes any existence harsh. Angry youth may be idealistic, exciting, or romantic; middle-aged anger is just one kind of failure. Happiness is harmony in the place of dissonance. However stormy the music of a lifetime, after forty years of age one must begin to find chords of peaceful resolution. Whatever hardships or disappointments one has experienced, as my friend Maria La Magra says, "Get over it, Blanche." Angry and bitter is not the way to approach the second half of life, unless one definitely wants to rule out the possibility of lovely experience and fun.

Sometimes the adjustment to the over-forty years requires coming to terms with what's past and irretrievable, with where you are and what you are. Sometimes it's necessary to take a deep breath and do a few things that you hadn't expected to be on the program. Like having your face lifted.

Let me tell you about Huntingdon, Tennessee's town inebriate, who had deposited himself on the steps of the doctor's office at the end of a weeklong binge. Dr. Cox found him waiting there, red-eyed, unshaven, unclean, unstrung, and generally in a pretty advanced state of decay, and greeted him with, "Good morning, Marvin. How are you this morning?"

The answer was honest. "Not too good, Doctor Cox."

"Well, you look all right," the doctor said briskly as he stepped over him to get to the door.

Then came those words that put Marvin in Carroll County history: "You know, Doctor, I'd rather not be quite so pretty and feel a little better."

My case was just the reverse; I wanted to look as good as I felt.

When I came home from the first screening of the pilot episode of *Designing Women*, I sat down with my mother and said without preamble, "Gina, I'm going to have to have a face-lift." Although I understood that my mother would want, as she always had, whatever was beneficial to me, I knew this word was bound to appall her, that I would *think* of messing with "the Lord's creation." I had heard her say many times that she would never consider it for herself, just as she had refused to put a rinse on her hair when it started turning grey, and sure enough, by the time this conversation took place, it was clear by anyone's standard of beauty that she had been quite correct in holding her position. I dreaded telling her what was in my mind; I was ashamed to, but I had to.

So I took a deep breath and repeated, "Gina, I'm going to have to have a face-lift." She was in enough physical pain by this time in her life that her expression was often hard to read, and in any case I could hardly expect a big happy smile. She didn't smile, nor did she respond in any way for a long moment; she just looked at me intently and finally she said, "Why?"

I said, "Gina, I am enough older than any of the other three lovely actresses on this show that if it does turn out to be my first big success, after all these years of performing, I don't think I can bear to be identified as 'the older one,' and that is surely what is going to happen, because I have just seen myself on the screen with them."

Now she did not hesitate in her response. She lifted her chin and took my hand, "All right, my dahling, would you like me to go with you to meet some of these types of doctahs?" And then she smiled, my Gina.

It was her place to make it all right with Daddy, and I was to do the same with Hal and the girls. That's how things have always worked in my family, and the system has served us well. Since Gina died, I have had to get used to going straight to my father without her prior intercession, and we miss that part of the decision-making ritual, as we miss her in uncountable other ways, but lucky for me she was very much present for this resolution.

There's something mortifying about what it is we're doing, we who have decided to "improve" what our life has done to our face, to improve upon it by eradicating our own history, in a way. I don't imagine that anybody is glad to acknowledge what the act itself means. I didn't want to, but finally there it was. I was ready to remove a good part of the experience that life had recorded on my face—the what we call character. There's something initially humiliating about admitting that you don't look like you want to. One needs to let this truth sink in, then figure out exactly what the reasons for surgery are, if it's necessary, and if it's worth it. Once we fess up to feeling ashamed of ourselves and logically arrive at why that feeling need not apply, then we may proceed with a clear conscience and enjoy the result. For me the reason was as practical as overalls; I work in Hollywood.

In Hollywood any greeting, business or social, especially business, has to include a mention of the other person's appearance. In the South we gush, "It's so *good* to *see* you!" In New York a variation on that, like "Marvelous to see you again," is standard. Only in Hollywood do you know to expect a head-to-toe survey, then "You're looking terrific," or "You look fantastic," or the terrifying "You look good," delivered with deep insincerity. (One appreciates an awful lot the odd sincere compliment.) Time was when the agents representing me were every bit as scary as the rest of the business; time was when I dreaded that inevitable perusal at the biannual luncheons or breakfasts, with my grade recorded in interest level. This was a part of that time.

So off we went, Gina and I, both of us nervous, but only me showing it. What an education. What an assortment of advantage takers. Still etched in memory is the surgeon who had a mirrored coffee table in his office. He told me to lean over and look down at my reflection. "This is how you're going to look six months from now," he assured me with a grim little smile. I found the interviews frightening and very demoralizing; every time I left another office, I felt older and uglier. Without exception what I was asking to be done— cleaning up my jawline and double chin—was dismissed as not nearly all it was going to take to make me presentable.

Then too there was almost always a seriously phony lecture on my underlying reasons for wanting surgery and how important it was that I not be expecting other problems in my life to be cleared up by changing the way I looked. I don't remember ever getting a chance to say that the way I looked was indeed the problem I wanted to clear up. If I had felt genuine concern on the part of the doctor or had been encouraged to enter into a real conversation and actually express myself, I might have thought there was some point to this tack other than ego stretching on the part of the surgeon. The manifest purpose of the whole rigmarole, however, was to impress me with his grip on the weak and pitiful secrets of the human psyche, in this case mine. By the time he had made sure that I felt both unsightly and neurotic, he would be in complete control of the situation and I wouldn't have the beans to recall what I might have wanted to ask about, even supposing I could have worked up the nerve to squirt the questions out of my wrinkled old mouth. Somehow the psychological part of the session with the great man (it happened always to be a man, no male bashing intended) seemed designed to impress upon me the yawning depths of his apperceptions and indirectly to threaten that I'd better watch out or he might not be willing to operate on me. Har, har, har. Har, har.

Gina and I would drive home after these interviews with me in or close to tears. I felt ever more helpless, undecided, and unprepared, never having dreamed that I would in a million years consider *plastic surgery*, a term I had always heard uttered in a low voice and with a certain tone. Woefully unknowledgeable, I would swing back and forth between going no bones about it for the most expensive doctor and giving up on the whole thing. The latter turned out to be not a possibility because by now Gina had the bit in her teeth and giving up was not in her lexicon. Her little girl needed a certain thing done and it was going to get done, and done properly. She kept insisting that we had to have more information. She was right, but where were we going to get it? Not from the doctors we'd seen so far, who wanted only to discuss how much better they were than all the others.

And people who have had it done do not talk, you know. The great beauties and the rich socialites are not admitting that anything has ever been cut on their head but hair, not even a little mustache waxing, so one doesn't get a chance to read illuminating interviews on the subject given by the people who are in a position to know firsthand. I don't know of anybody except Joan Rivers who has come out of this particular closet, leaving those of us who for our business or for other personal reasons need to have ourselves chopped and sewn, having to resort to hearsay recommendations, unless we happen to be really close to somebody like Babe Paley, and even then our best friends won't always tell. I've had some close friends—ears standing out from the tension of the skin that has been slicked back and zipped up from behind them—look me in the eye and swear they've had nothing done.

If you're lucky enough to have a compassionate hairdresser, you can get some valuable tips and warnings. A person in show business can pick up information in makeup rooms, some of it helpful, like the inside scoop on who's considered the best surgeon this season, and some of it so ghoulish it'll scare the fatal filling out of you—stories about the woman who obviously had one side of her head sewn up by the nurse; or the actress whose collagen injections started to ball up and move around; or the nose that has so little cartilage left, it could collapse at any time; or the eyes that will no longer close all the way; or the mouth that has been pulled into a permanent smile, even in repose. Deliver me.

Almost nobody ever admits to having had it done, and I have never talked about it publicly because nobody ever does talk about it; actually it seems to be considered perfectly okay to tell a point-blank lie about it. (I realize it's a little silly to single out this subject as if it were the only area in which it's okay to lie these days, but please humor me.) Although I've regaled my nearest and dearest with the saga of my fresh frontage and even offered to share some of the early *Designing Women* income with a couple of folks toward the same end, I long ago worked out a public answer as to whether or not I'd "had something done" that went like this: "Well, I certainly have nothing against cosmetic surgery, and I intend to take advantage of it myself when the time comes." I have been advised against talking honestly about it for the same reason that I've been advised against telling my age. Everybody knows that in show business you are supposed to stay miraculously younger than springtime for your entire life, or at least for your entire career, unless you happen to have the gift of an Elaine Stritch or an Eileen Heckert.

Mother Nature offers us many lessons in humility as we advance in years; we don't need a reinforced impression that we're performing some tasteless or offensive action by getting older. There's something wrong with that feeling, and there's something wrong with having to sneak around to get your face lifted. If society, or the great They, demand that we look younger than we are, then we're going to have to be allowed a bit of repair work; otherwise we're damned if we do and damned if we don't. Although I'm still not quite as mad as Naomi Wolf, I am tired of hedging the issue when I am asked about plastic surgery.

It's a procedure that involves taking quite a risk with the Lord's creation, make no mistake about it. My mother's good sense and determination that I not put myself into the hands of someone I didn't trust, and the luck to have a friend who would share his doctor's name, combined to get me to a great surgeon. Not every face-lift recipient has been so fortunate. I have decided to recount my tale to you, Dear Reader, who have put your hard-earned dollar out for this book, in hopes of saving you a lot of grief, not to mention pain and money. But mostly grief.

Having pretty much given up on finding a surgeon in Los Angeles—which I had assumed was the logical place to start looking, home of the movie stars and all—I was about to the point of going to New York and nosing around, no pun intended, and then a miracle happened. A friend of mine told me of a doctor up in San Francisco he thought I should meet. This particular surgeon had originated something called the SMAS technique, whereby the muscles of the neck and chin are lifted and reattached, so that they do all the supporting, then the skin (with what you wanted to get rid of gone) is softly laid back in place and reattached separately, thus relieving the poor skin of the responsibility of keeping all that tired flesh pulled up, looking ever so tight and unnatural while it's doing it, and unable to keep it up for long anyway. I had not heard of SMAS (Submuscular Aponeurotic System), but the concept made sense, and the recommender's judgment I trusted and appreciated, so I decided to go—by myself, since Gina's health wouldn't allow for the round-trip in one day. I went to San Francisco, sat down across the desk from Dr. John Quincy Owsley, and here begins my tale of a very happy and successful experience with what I now call aesthetic surgery.

I am going to give you a profile of what to look for in an aesthetic surgeon, based upon this one gentleman and my experience with him. This is my only frame of reference, but

at risk of immodesty, I say take a look at me, and I believe
you'll agree that some pretty fine tailoring has gone on, especially when you consider that I am now past the three to seven
years after which you are supposed to need it done again.

Dr. Owsley greeted me quietly and respectfully. I wasn't
made to wait a long time so that I'd be impressed with just
how busy and in demand he was. He asked me what I wanted
to change. He passed a hand mirror across his desk and asked
me to look at myself and describe as exactly as I could what I
wanted to look like after the surgery. Every time he asked a
question, he actually stopped talking and let me answer. And
he listened to me. He came around behind my chair and adjusted the skin on my face a tiny bit this way and that as I
looked at myself to show me what was possible, what he
thought I wanted, and to make sure that we were both talking
about the same goal.

When he had established our agreement on the desired
result, he resumed his seat and proceeded quietly and unhur-
riedly to explain the technique he would employ, the one he
had in fact originated. He told me that this procedure involved
lifting and repositioning the layer of muscle and connective
tissue, lying just beneath the fatty layer in the skin, that ex-
tends from the temple region down through the cheek and
neck to the collarbone. The skin would be lifted along with it.
This layer of connective tissue contains and interconnects all
the muscles that move the skin to make facial expressions.
With aging this tissue and the skin sag down together. He
told me that the SMAS face-lift should last at least five years,
but he didn't make promises. (He did not tell me until I knew
him better that the embarrassment he had experienced at having to tell patients, as he had to when he started practicing,
that they could expect to need a redo in three to five years had
goaded him to figure out a face-lift that would last longer.)

He did not seem rushed to get to another appointment. At
no time did he indicate that I needed more work than I had
suggested. Before the end of our interview I asked him why he
hadn't done so, and his answer was "I don't believe in fixing

what isn't broken." At no time did he tell me how great he was. At no time did he put down other surgeons, another first for me in these encounters.

I became relaxed enough to ask many questions: what were the risks of things going wrong, would my face stay loose enough to make funny faces, would there be pain (for which I have zero tolerance and of which I am deathly afraid), and on and on. I asked about the fabulous things I'd heard were being done with laser surgery (no blood, no scars) and found out that contrary to what I had heard, with the laser there is an incision and blood and a scar and that the laser requires exquisite precision, as it is harder to control than the surgical scalpel, that in fact many of his patients came to him for redos after laser mistakes. The laser is a surgical tool, not a way of avoiding surgery. Dr. Owsley's unglamorous comment on the difference between the two methods of surgery was, I believe, "It's not so important which hammer is used, as who is driving the nail."

After a while I began to feel heartened and secure. No question had been brushed aside as silly or unimportant. The business of this meeting, as Dr. Owsley conducted it, was for me to assess the information he gave me and then make a decision. What a difference! When I got up to leave, he gave me some material to take home and read. He knew that I wanted to have my face ready for the new fall television season, but he did not urge me to make a quick decision, as others had done, or hustle me to make the appointment for surgery right then on my way out of the office.

I got back on the plane, went home, and reviewed the consultation with my family. The next day I called for an appointment, flew back as soon as the doctor could schedule me, and got my face lifted. During the interim I had two marvelous conversations with patients of his who had offered to talk with "pre-ops" about their own experience.

The night before surgery I stayed over in the hospital connected with the doctor's office, slept all right even though I was mildly nervous, got up, and washed my hair, still feeling just fine. As I dressed in the loose clothing suggested in the detailed preoperative instructions, it suddenly came to me that I was about an hour away from having my face operated on, and by the time I walked into the office at seven o'clock, I was scared witless, which fact did not surprise anybody there. Everybody is always scared, I learned.

Hal was with me, holding my hand. Once the preparations for surgery began, my anxiety abated enough so that my heart didn't quit entirely. Everyone was most gentle and reassuring. I'm afraid of needles; I both longed to go ahead and get started, and dreaded having the IV stuck in my vein. Then the needle part was done and although a dopey drowsiness began to overtake me, it hadn't quite overcome my trepidation about what was going to happen to my face.

At that time I hadn't learned how completely you can trust Dr. Owsley not to overdo anything. I sat bolt upright on the operating table with one last reminder: "Please, please remember. I don't want to wake up with forty-five-year-old eyes looking out of a twenty-five-year-old face. I want to look good, not to go back in time. Do not make me look one day younger!" The last thing I heard as he gently eased me back down onto the table was "Well, maybe forty."

I spent the first night at the hospital, as all patients are required to do, and Hal stayed with me. He had to get back to Los Angeles, so my sister came to be with me for a few days. She met us at the hospital the next morning, and after Dr. Owsley had removed the drainage tubes and the head wrap, checked the remaining bandages, and given his okay, Hal and Midge tied a scarf around my head, put me in a limo, and took me over to the Huntington Hotel. I hadn't wanted to go to one of those hideaway places; Hal and I love the Huntington and have had wonderful times there, so that's where I chose to recuperate. Hal escorted me through those tasteful portals as if we were there for a romantic tryst. While he signed us in at the desk, Midge chatted amiably at groggy me about what was going on over at her house, what the children were up to lately. The elevator man didn't bat an eye as they leaned me up against the wall, and very shortly I was in bed eating sherbet, happy as only pain medication can make you. Against orders I peeked at myself in the bathroom mirror once and looked away quickly. My impression was of a nun who had been beaten up. That quick glance wasn't terribly upsetting, even so. I had looked like a pretty nun, albeit a black-and-blue one.

I am afraid of pain, as I have stated, so I take painkillers if they're called for. I see no reason for hurting when medical science has come up with something so you don't have to. Bravery isn't the deal here. This is not a testing ground for personal courage; this is cosmetic surgery. Take the pills and be thankful, I say. And I did, so I don't remember the first few days very clearly, except that I lay still and Midge looked after me and read her book.

The second day after surgery Midge took the bandage off my head and put me in the shower. The doctor had said I should wash my hair. I was amazed. I did it and nothing hurt. As a matter of fact it felt wonderful. I could feel the staples behind my ears with my fingers, but my head didn't feel them, if you get what I mean. On the fourth or fifth day I went back to the doctor to have some of the stitches removed. After the fifth day I was saddened by the clear lack of a need for any more pain pills, as I had enjoyed them. Alleviating my sadness was the way my face was beginning to look. Each day the swelling was radically reduced and the discoloration was going from black-and-blue to yellow; I was looking better faster than I had dared to dream I might. It makes me sorry for myself in an odd way that I was so amazed by my appearance. What must I have been willing to settle for? I wonder as I'm writing this. Aren't we pitiful sometimes.

On the seventh or eighth day I went for the last of the stitches to come out. As I was telling Dr. Owsley good-bye, I asked him if it didn't make him feel good to be doing something that made people so happy. He seemed pleased that I had recognized his main motive. "Yes, it does feel good," he said. "I look forward to coming into the office every day because of it."

When I got home, the little girls were beside themselves, Gina and Daddy were overjoyed, and Hal was astounded at how I had transformed in one week from bruised to flower-faced. In another week the bruises were gone. I didn't start putting on makeup for another two weeks, but I could have. One tiny space behind one ear healed more slowly than everywhere else, and then it was all over.

For several months after surgery one feels the nerves that have been cut reconnecting and waking up again, tickling or itching or buzzing a little, and the hair that has been shaved around the incisions in the scalp has to grow back. There is a feeling of tightness for a few weeks that goes away with the last bit of swelling, helped by the natural movements of your face.

The only negatives I have to report about the whole megillah were, first, waking up from surgery. It's not pleasant and there's nothing to do but tell somebody it's hurting and get a shot. I was fortunate to be in the care of an anesthesiologist who concerns himself with waking one up as well as putting one to sleep, so my discomfort was reduced as much as possible. In the right hands you don't have to experience hateful postoperative nausea, and you get an injection for pain the minute you're yourself enough to ask for it. It's good to talk about it before the surgery, so you know what to expect and they know your concerns. Like it or not, they have to wake you up; the alternative isn't desirable at-all at-all. (That's the actor Conrad Bain's representation of an Irish accent. He just says over and over, "At-all, at-all, at-all." He kept me laughing with such nonsense through the time I served on *Diff'rent Strokes*.) The other negative is a postoperative sadness over nothing you can put your finger on. Mortality. Vanity. Transience. Our lovely insubstantial flesh. These are my only quibbles. Certainly it was worth it. I went right back.

The next spring when the show went on hiatus I went back

to Dr. Owsley and had what is called a brow lift. I could have done it at the same time as the face-lift, but I hadn't been sure at that time that I wanted it at all. I was so elated over the outcome of the first surgery that it was no trouble deciding to finish what I had started. I wanted to get rid of the tired look above my eyes without having an incision in the eyelids themselves, and the brow lift does it. The result is less skin hanging down over your eyes, a cleaner brow line, a smooth forehead, and a slightly higher hairline.

I went through exactly the same drill, except that our friend Lee Moorer came up to take care of me. Lee was assistant nursing supervisor of the operating rooms at UCLA Medical Center at the time of her retirement, after working there twenty-four years, and she's a retired air force colonel. She does as she pleases now, and it pleases her to spend most of her time doing nice things for her friends. Hal stayed with me in the hospital and then Lee took over. As we entered the Huntington this time, Lee's smiling and friendly manner suggested that we were probably in San Francisco on a publicity trip, and the colonel in her suggested that if anybody thought we weren't, they'd best keep a lid on it. The management of the hotel smiled at me as if I were Princess Diana. Everyone was wonderful. We stayed a week. There was discomfort after the surgery, and there were painkillers for it; the bruising took longer to go away but the final result was a tremendously happy one.

I will mention again that at first none of this new glory makes you happy to look in the mirror, and one is wise to follow the advice not to do so. Even after such bruising as there is disappears, along with the swelling, and you look just grand, seeing your new face makes you feel strange. I think it was explained that we are so used to our faces in the mirror morning and night, however casually, that we are able to recognize even the tiniest fraction of change, and that although the fresh visage is thrilling, it's "not me" for a while. The number of days or weeks it takes for the new look to become "me" varies with everyone; my postoperative letdown was fairly shortlived, I think because all of a sudden I saw more of my daughters in myself, a gladsome prospect indeed.

Here are some things to watch out for when you're looking for "your" surgeon.

1. If the doctor you're meeting doesn't seem to have plenty of time to talk to you, it's not a good sign.

2. If the doctor you're meeting looks at you in a pitying or sad way, it's not a good sign.

3. If the doctor does not encourage your questions and answer them fully and to your satisfaction, stop asking questions and conclude the meeting.

4. If the doctor says anything derogatory about another plastic surgeon, start putting on your gloves.

5. If the doctor has to tell you how good he is, ask him what this consultation has cost, as you're putting on your gloves.

6. If the doctor wants to do all the talking and doesn't encourage you to talk, he can't be finding out all he needs to know; at your earliest opportunity make a break for it. (You wouldn't want to wind up looking like him instead of you.)

7. If the doctor suggests any procedure in addition to what you think you need, leave by the nearest door. This admonition doesn't only have to do with his being after your money; it's imperative that the two of you share the same aesthetic. If he wants to make you "prettier" by his lights, run like a rabbit.

8. If the doctor presses you to make an appointment for surgery at once, run like a rabbit.

9. If the doctor is patronizing toward you or makes you feel stupid, congratulate yourself on not punching him as you summarily say good-bye.

10. If the doctor adopts an attitude of sophic superiority when he brings up your reasons for surgery, be wary. It *is* important that a person not go into this thing expecting any more from it than physical change, so there is legitimacy to

the question; just make sure a number isn't being done on your head that has nothing to do with your face.

12. If for any reason you just don't happen to *like* this doctor, run like a rabbit. You are putting your face and your life in his hands. You have got to be able to trust this person implicitly. I am talking about a visceral response as well as an intellectual one.

13. Keep looking until you know you have met the right surgeon for you.

14. Once again, make sure that you and he (or she) know exactly what you want the outcome to be. He may have suggested and explained a way to go about doing something a little differently than what you originally thought; perhaps he can give you an idea with a computer mockup, and if you're thrilled about it and very clear about it, great.

By the way, you should plan a way to really rest, as in bed rest, for a week or more after surgery. If you feel discomfort, take pain pills for a few days. Don't try to prove anything. Really rest. Two weeks of rest and a month after that of not going full steam is a realistic game plan. Don't be brave and strong. Lean on your family to let you do nothing for as long as the doc advises, or better yet, if you can afford it, get off by yourself and stay quiet and still. This repose will promote fast healing, a beautiful result, and less postoperative blues than you'll have if you try to get back into the swing of things right away.

I advocate taking pain medication for pain, and I joke about enjoying them; however, *the longer you take them, the longer it will take you to get over them.* There will be a slump in energy and in spirit when you stop, so beware of taking pain pills a moment longer than you need them.

And finally, finally get your mind set to pay for the job you want done. Although the highest fee does not guarantee the best results, this is not the time to budget yourself. Take out a loan, if you have to, to have your surgery done by the person you want. Fooling with your face is dangerous. You can be miserable for the rest of your life if somebody makes you look different from the way you want to or, Heaven forbid, makes some kind of awful mistake. Take it seriously, do your research, put out your money, and delight in the result. I strongly recommend that you make no effort to conceal the fact that you've had aesthetic surgery. You've laid a lot on the line; don't be ashamed of it. Accept congratulations.

May God bless you in this adventure, if you decide to undertake it. I remain very happy that I did it, and happy with the way it's shaking down, as it were. I'm grateful that what I had done was so well done that I have felt like myself all along, and when I see the little lines that are coming in now, they don't bother me. It's time. I don't expect to lift my face again. (Just for the record, I reserve the right to change my mind if my earlobes start getting long, but only if Dr. Owsley will do earlobes.)

The glorious years ahead of me—for I do see many glorious years ahead—will not just happen. I've done what I can with surgery. Now it's up to me to combat the natural slowdown my body is going to experience; it's up to me to deal with our culture's prejudicial attitude in terms of just how interesting it really thinks a middle-aged woman can be; it's up to me to wage my own friendly battle against the law of gravity, to keep aiming for the uphill slopes and to avoid the natural temptation to find an easy downhill grade. I do not want to spend any time going downhill. I wouldn't ever want to give up on e e cummings's "all that juice and all that joy."

Now that I've made my case for aesthetic surgery and encouraged you to do it with your head held high, if you so desire, Dear Reader, I would like to end this chapter with another thought.

Neither my sister, Midge, nor my sister-in-law, Margo, have seen reason to go this route. They have had the experience of one husband, one marriage (Midge to Stephen Smith Heath in 1965 and Margo, Margaret Winchester Heiskell, to Hal in 1962), one lifelong love, and one face for the duration. I look upon that privileged record with frank envy. By way of tipping my hat to Midge and Margo, I would enter here the second verse of Thomas Moore's "Believe Me, If All Those Endearing Young Charms."

> *It is not while beauty and youth are thine own,*
> *And thy cheeks unprofan'd by a tear,*
> *That the fervour and faith of a soul can be known,*
> *To which time will but make thee more dear:*
> *No, the heart that has truly lov'd never forgets,*
> *But as truly loves on to the close,*
> *As the sunflow'r turns on her god, when he sets,*
> *The same look which she turn'd when he rose.*

≈ Chapter Five ≈
PLEASE DON'T WEAR BLACK TO
WEDDINGS, YOU-ALL

Dixie Carter wed in her hometown

By ALICE FULBRIGHT

Memorial Day was celebrated in a big way yesterday in McLemoresville, Tenn., where Hal Holbrook married Dixie Carter in the First Methodist Church of her Carrol County hometown.

The marriage is No. 3 for both Holbrook, 59, the actor-impressionist best known for his one-man show "Mark Twain Tonight!" and for Miss Carter, the actress-singer who celebrated her 44th birthday Friday. But the mid-afternoon wedding had the emotion and freshness of first nuptials.

Guests from as far away as New York and California, arriving in the West Tennessee community about 15 miles northwest of Jackson, drove past a sign reading "Welcome to McLemoresville. Home of Dixie Carter."

A crowd assembled early in the old cemetery across from the lovely old church with white columns and a belfry.

Holbrook, a three-time Emmy winner, chatted informally in front of the church with his groomsmen, occasionally hitching up his gray pants and fingering the pink rose boutonniere in the lapel of his dark blue coat in the nervous way of bridegrooms.

Best man was his son, David Holbrook of New York. Groomsmen were Hal Carter of Memphis, the bride's brother; Don Wolff, Holbrook's agent; and actor Majon McCalman, both of Los Angeles; Richard Wiesenthal of New York, and the bridegroom's sailing mate, Robert Rossiter of Auckland, New Zealand.

All 150 seats were taken in the [...]

ing "until death do us part."

The bridesmaids, all of whom were the couple's daughters by their former marriages, were dressed in white cotton and lace dresses and flower-laden picture hats. They sang "The Lord's Prayer" after vows were exchanged.

"We really practiced," said Eve Holbrook, 14. The other attendants were the bride's daughters, Mary-Dixie, 14, and Gina, 15, and her niece, Jane Wiesenthal of New York. (The Carter children's father was Dixie's first husband, New York financier Arthur Carter. Her second husband was actor George Hearn, star of Broadway's "La Cage aux Folles.")

The bridegroom's oldest daughter, Victoria Holbrook, 31, of New York, was in a front pew. So were her sister, Midge Heath of San Francisco, and Holcomb's sister, June McPherson of Montreal, Canada.

"We've had a big weekend," said the bride's mother, Mrs. Halbert Carter.

"The church is small but we invited the whole town — all 315 people — to the reception," she said.

"But it isn't true that Hal will put on a benefit performance of his one-man show after the wedding, as it was reported. My goodness, he told me once that it takes him four hours to get made up as Mark Twain."

The bridal procession walked a quarter of a mile from the church up a hill and over a wooden bridge that led to the Carter home and the reception for a big waiting crowd.

The new Mrs. Holbrook said [...]

WHEN MY FATHER WAS A VERY LIT-
tle boy, he would go over into town to see his papa and his
grandpapa Harvey (his mother's father) in the family store.
He was his grandfather's pet and loved him dearly, but his
father had already become, as he was to remain his whole life
through, his hero, adored completely with no fault found (and
emulated in every way possible, even to slicking down his own
red curls with Vaseline when he got a little older, trying to
match Papa's straight black hair). His trip to the store, across
the road that ran beside his front yard, took maybe a minute
and a half for a small person, unless he stopped on the way to
call on one of his "poidners" (partners) like Mr. Sam "Po-em"
(Parham) and collect the nickel or piece of candy that his visits
often yielded, especially after he would say what Grandpapa
taught him, "I'm Halbert E-oy (Leroy) Carter, three years
old, redheaded, and a plumb good-un!"

Sometimes when he got there, Papa would be distracted or
too busy to pay attention to the freckle-faced chunk waiting
eagerly beside him, and when the time became longer than he
could endure, Daddy would tug shyly on his father's pants
leg and beam up at him, "Papa, here I are." I say "beam"
because I know the look my grandfather saw on his little boy's
face; I've seen it all my life and it's there still, sunlit first thing
in the morning and anytime I drop into his room to visit;
it's the look of someone expecting that you'll be as glad to see
him as he is to see you, someone who's taking a chance on
love. It's a breathtaking reminder of the beauty in a pure
intention.

Before he was born, there had been a baby boy named
Jamey who died at six months of age, and I think Papa and
Mama must have had a special joy in Daddy's arrival on the
scene—redheaded like his mother and graced with a laughing
winsomeness that could and did charm all who encountered

it, young, old, male, and female, especially female. Boys liked him but girls fell all over him; out of trees they fell.

He enjoyed their attentions until one day in his seventeenth year when he looked across town and saw my mother's long brown legs descending from his cousin Opal's buggy. "Who is that girl with Opal, that brunette?" he asked somebody. "Why, that's Esther Virginia Hillsman from over at Treze-vant." Then, as we say in the South, it was all over but the shoutin'. In Aunt Helen's words, "Halbert was stricken with Virginia." He was wild that somebody else might get her before he could figure out how he would be able to support her. Finally he talked to Papa about it and Papa said he'd make Daddy half owner of the store, so he did get her, and she got him, and I don't know which one loved the other more.

My father resides with us in California since my mother died seven years ago. He's a living lesson in many areas, one of them the rewards of impeccable grooming. Every morning he completes a detailed toilette and comes out for breakfast in a jacket and tie. When asked about dressing up all the time, he will say, "When you get old, you can't look pretty but you can be clean" or "The older a person gets, the more of them-selves they should cover" or "Well, I have to wear some-thing!" But he knows he's good-looking and he enjoys it. He knows too that all of us appreciate his handsome appearance.

Daddy's interest in the sartorial began at a young age, I gather, but did not represent his very earliest attitude. When he was two years old and processed out of the relative freedom of the dresses (aprons, as they were called) all babies used to wear, he resented the restriction of his newly starched bib and tucker. He would commence swinging his arms furiously round and round, crying out, "Don't feeeee jooood!" (don't feel good), then wriggle it off and scamper like lightning out of the house. Mama would give chase only so far as the front walk, too horrified in her extreme modesty to follow his naked flight over into town, so Papa would come home with him presently, declaring that it looked like Halbert was a little wild man and would have to go live in the woods. (Papa never spanked him for these forays, but on the few occasions that he popped him on the seat to get his attention, Daddy would be inconsolable, crying to Mama, "Papa don't *wuv* me," though of course he knew better. Much better. He has told me, "When I was a little boy, Mama and Papa and Grandmama and Grandpapa Harvey and Grandpa and Grandma Carter were my world. They were my whole world. I never dreamed as a child that I'd ever have to get along without them.")

Somehow he got used to the confinement of what little boys were made to wear back then, and as he got older, he became interested in dressing well, probably with girls in mind. He did take advantage of being allowed to go barefoot all summer (Papa was happy to save the shoe money); he took off his shoes the minute school was out in the spring and didn't put them back on all summer except for Sundays. I love the story about how Mama Carter was scrubbing Daddy in the bathtub one night and said, "Halbert, you've been going swimming with the big boys down at Drummond's Slough, haven't you?" He'd been told not to because he was too little; he knew he was in trouble, but he had to go ahead and confess. "Yes ma'am, I did go in with Leon and some of 'em just once or twice. But Mama, how did you know?" Mama said it was easy to guess because he was clean behind the ears.

He would disobey Mama sometimes but not his Papa. However, if his parents argued, he would go stand beside Mama with his little fists all balled up, ready to defy even his demigod to take up for her, an action which they both thought was so cute it would end the argument. Papa's mother was half Cherokee, and Papa definitely showed his quarter strain. He had pitch-black eyes that were almost too bright and coal black hair; he was not tall but powerfully built, devoutly religious, and afraid of nothing on this earth. Daddy remembers getting to tag along one night when Grandpa Carter came into town to see if he could hire somebody to come over to his farm and get a mule out of a well it had fallen into. The mule had stepped on boards left too long covering an old dry well, and the rotten boards had given way under it. Someone was going to have to sit on a board in a rope sling and let themselves be lowered to where the animal was stuck, pawing the air, and get a rope around it to draw it up. Grandpa couldn't find anybody who needed the money that bad. Papa said he was going to do it, and he let Daddy, who was maybe nine years old, come along as they walked, carrying a lantern, out the road to Grandpa's. Daddy said it was a terrifying thing, to look down into the well by the lantern light and see that mule, eyes rolling wild and red, kicking and snapping at anything that came near it. Grandpa hadn't wanted to ask any of his boys to try it, but Papa had made up his mind. They let him down into the well and he got the rope around the mule's head and forelegs, and then he and Daddy walked back home.

Papa had Parkinson's disease and died while Daddy was away in the war. I was still very small, but I remember him well, his authority (when he said frog, everybody jumped), his goodness, and his entertaining manner of speech. One of my favorite stories is how Papa had mentioned at dinner that Brother Mayes, a Methodist lay preacher, had been turned down by the Maccabees, an organization that provided insurance, and how Mr. Robert McKinney had said to Papa out at the store that he didn't understand the Maccabees turning Brother Mayes down for insurance, that with his pedigree (his father was nearly ninety years old then) he was an excellent insurance risk. Mr. McKinney had gone on to say they'd probably "have to shoot him in the head on Judgment Day." A few days later at the dinner table the family heard the report of a shotgun, from a squirrel hunter perhaps, and four-year-old Melba cried out, "Oh, oh! They've shot poor Brother Mayes!"

Another time Brother Mayes had been railing around town about how reading the newspaper made him sick and tired, until one day Papa said, "Well, Brother Mayes, if reading the paper gets you so upset, why do you keep reading it?"

And Brother Mayes came back fast with, "I just want to see what the Devil's up to next."

• • •

It wouldn't have been more than ten years later that Daddy was in white linen playing tennis over in Trezevant at the Hillsman place. The particular afternoon I have in mind it happened that his competitive nature, his wonderful athleticism, and his desire for Gina not to see him beaten by anyone all conspired to put him into such a sweat that his whites were drenched and his underwear shorts underneath were visible. He nearly died of embarrassment. He steeled himself against the fast retreat he wanted to beat, because he wanted even more to hang around for dinner, as the midday meal was called then, and lap up Gina's admiration for his prowess. And since I've heard him tell about it many times, I know that the incident made a mark.

Even though he's told it as humorous, that story has always made me feel sorry, or something, for Daddy. I can picture his excitement and his eagerness to impress Gina and her sisters, and his feeling a little intimidated by her big brothers Thomas and Jack, with their easy gentility, and their friends, all college boys, and his youthful innocence and general hope. I can picture how thrilling it was for him to race back and forth across the tennis court, throwing himself utterly into the game, and winning, winning, winning. And then I can picture how crushed he must have felt when Jeff J. Blanks pointed out with amusement that you could see Halbert's blue-striped underwear through his slacks. This is what I love: he did not stop going over and playing tennis in his white linen pants; he just made sure he wore solid white underwear underneath. And he did not stop winning against the college boys.

He did not stop winning all his life, as a matter of fact, and always fairly, without shortchanging anyone or dealing falsely. He turned down the college athletic scholarships offered him to stay at home and go into the store with Papa, who was sick and needed him there, and out of that sacrifice he made a wonderful life, for himself and for all of us. He has lived by the examples set for him.

When Daddy was growing up, children knew what they could get away with, what was acceptable, and what wasn't even discussable, in clothing as well as behavior. It seems to me that many people have given up on a general standard of grooming, dressing, or behaving, and sadly, on teaching their children how to present themselves properly. By properly, I don't mean primly or richly. I mean cleanly, nicely, or to get down to it, in a way that does not turn the stomach of a person who may be forced to sit next to them on a bus or plane, or at a stool next to them in a coffee shop, or in any situation where the person doing the looking—or even, please excuse me, the smelling—is going to be made uncomfortable. Basic personal grooming and clean neat clothing are simple good manners. Dirty sloppy people are demonstrating, first and foremost, bad manners. (Good manners are actions and attitudes that represent regard for other people's comfort, whether physical or emotional, and bad manners are actions and attitudes that say, among other things, "I don't care how bad I make you feel.")

Taking the trouble to make a pleasing appearance is by all means a friendly gesture toward those people with whom we come in contact, and it turns out to be bread cast on the waters, for the outcome is sure to enhance positive feelings inside us.

Grooming and dressing with care makes you feel good and lifts every aspect of your life.

So what do I mean by grooming oneself nicely? To start with, the aforementioned toilette, just as important for men as for women, begins with brushing the teeth thoroughly, including the tongue (against bad breath), and dental flossing, at least in the evening. Once I asked our family dentist, Dr. Dewhirst, if flossing was really a must. "Only for the teeth you want to keep," he said. I brush my teeth three times a day because I have discovered sadly that *no one* loves you enough to tell you that you have bad breath, and I really truly don't want it for myself. We all know it's awfully hard to take, even if the fumes are coming from a friend, and as for romance— step back, Loretta!

Next we bathe or shower, wash our hair at least every other

day, shave face or legs (or wherever there's hair that looks better off than on, and if I were the Ruler of All Things, the targeted areas would definitely include women's underarms), apply emollients, toilet water, bath powder, shaving lotion, perfume, according to personal taste, never forgetting deodorant. Then last it doesn't take a lot of time for a person to check to see if there's hair growing out of their nose or ears or somewhere else unexpected, and to do a little snipping with some blunt ended scissors. Once a week we have to manicure our fingernails or get somebody else to do it, and once every two weeks we have to work on our feet. We have to. Pretty painted toenails and smooth heels (my bête noire) are a must for women, and men should know that a bad-looking foot can for some of us be as deadly on romance as bad breath. *Clean* fingernails and *clean short* toenails. Essential. I hope these remarks don't strike you as crude. I feel impelled to tell the truth here—my truth, anyway.

I may sound very un-European and gauche, nagging about getting rid of hair here and there, but I have to say, because I don't hear it bruited about, how grateful some of us would be not to have to look at hair in certain places on certain people. I notice chic clients (mostly women) are waxing like mad in the few salons that I frequent; I myself don't have time, am afraid it will hurt, and don't want to spend my money that way, so I use the trusty old razor with creamy lotion. Anyway I'm talking now to the person who maybe isn't used to going to chic salons, who doesn't live that kind of life, as well as to the supersophisticate who, I hope, will be turning these pages.

I should admit the possibility that I've become a little phobic about hair, though. I did Blanche in *A Streetcar Named Desire* last year in Memphis, and in my zeal to give it my all, I stripped the color out of my hair until it was past blond. Tennessee Williams described Blanche's appearance as "moth-like," so it seemed clear to me that she should be pale from top to bottom. I eschewed a wig, afraid that it would limit me physically onstage, and went through the trauma of the bleaching.

Standing up in front of people and using the words of this great poet was a profound privilege. I hope to proceed, before I would have to go onstage using a walker, with a plan to perform the role in other cities farther east. Next time, however, I will be wearing a wig. Within two months of the bleaching my hair started to break off right down to nubbins. I thought I was going to be bald. Thank heavens I have strong healthy hair and my divine Aunt Helen to give me all kinds of vitamins and herbs for growing it, because I'll tell you what: getting on female hormones and going bald in the same year isn't the most fun prospect.

I love long healthy shiny hair; I've even gotten used to long hair on men, finally, sort of; I just think there could be one more law added to the ridiculous number of laws Washington keeps piling up over our heads, and this is it: *Long hair must be kept clean.* Except for Bob Dylan, who should be exempted from all laws and carried around on a palanquin and named Pasha of America.

Grooming and dressing with some care makes you feel good, and lifts every aspect of your life.

I understand from experience that not every suggestion of any nature is received as happily as it's given, and grooming is a touchy subject. I don't mean to be presumptuous. It's just that sometimes over the years I've had these kinds of things which have not been in the forefront of my mind, pointed out by a loving parent or a trusted friend, and the reminders have helped me enormously. I cite unbecoming hairstyles, dingy teeth, lazy posture, unconscious nervous mannerisms, sharp or agitated tones of voice, galumphy walking, unbecoming clothing, and unconscious habits or attitudes that I appreciated knowing about, even if I was sorry to have to hear that I wasn't perfect for that moment. I am offering these not original, not ground-breaking, not state-of-the-art recommendations in the spirit with which they were presented to me on those occasions, hoping that you will find one or two of the notes useful —hoping also that you will not take me too seriously, for I certainly don't take myself that way.

Although my father is indubitably correct about the heightened importance of good grooming as one gets older, it's definitely not the purview only of the older set. Good grief, no. I find it hard to believe the unbelievable garb of the young people I see strolling Melrose Avenue here in Los Angeles; they look even worse to me than the assortment parading the streets of New York. Strangely, people of all ages dress more nicely and seem to be cleaner the farther away from the two coasts one travels. I don't know what's going on. I know that young people still *must* want to attract other young people. I don't get it. Duh. Actually I do have a sprig of a theory, and this is it.

What's wrecking all of us—I'm guilty too, but at least I feel ashamed of myself—is jogging clothes. Why? Because they're not clothes. We think they are, but they're not. I don't hear the smart comedians hitting on jogging clothes the way they used to hit on leisure suits, but there it is; we're all running around in pajamas. Exercise clothes have become big business now, and it's not just because people are buying them to exercise in. They're buying them to wear like clothes, but neither are they clothes, nor do they disguise excess avoirdupois. The person who wears sloppy jogging clothes thinking it's a slimmer look is oh so wrong. On the other side of the coin the person who has gone to some trouble to get in shape is throwing away the result wearing exercise clothes, loose or tight. Yes, even tight. That compressed sausage look cannot enhance any flesh but sausage, I'm afraid. And the practice of wearing tights instead of pants or jeans or slacks or skirts is proliferating in a way most unfortunate for the practitioners, who seem to feel that tights with a big loose something hanging over them are a "look," and who are quite correct about that, but not in the way they imagine, is my guess. Nobody, not even Lauren Hutton, would look good in that rig, unless at the ballet barre, and then the top wouldn't be loose, would it? In my opinion workout garments are basically unbecoming to everyone, slim or not slim. The one exception I can think of is Lee Moorer, my friend the air force colonel, but Lee is unusual in this as in other respects. The rest of us ought to get them *off* when we finish running or walking or working out. Please get them off.

"But they're more comfortable," you may say. "No they are not," I say. After a while in those things the spirit begins to sag, and you feel like changing your mind about what you started out to do, stopping over at the Kentucky Fried Chicken place instead and spending whatever's left of the day supine in front of the television. I speak from experience. If I'm not exercising in them, I'm gaining weight. I have a friend who gained thirty pounds wearing them to work for a year. That shapeless stuff is not really comfortable. It's another deceiver.

Knit clothing, even fitted, even beautifully tailored and elegant, can contribute to a tendency to go ahead and have the mashed potatoes and gravy. I like to wear knits for traveling, because of how wonderfully they pack and shake out, but they scare me a little in the discipline area. I need to make myself take stock of what's going on all the time; for me that's the easiest way to keep myself in shape. If I have a dress or suit with a belt or definite waistline, then I know right where I stand when I put it on.

We need to wear clothing that reminds us of our bodies and our posture and inspires us to be our best. If you have been wonderful enough to do some exercising, then reward yourself with a change into something that allows you to enjoy the result. Even if the result isn't at this point visible, you'll have a certain happy feeling. Sloppy is not as comfortable as it is depressing. And brother, is it ever depressing to the people who have to look at you.

I know I keep harping on the other-people aspect of appearance, but please bear with me. When my girls, who are looking at apartments all the time but who are still actually residing here with Hal and me and their grandfather, flop down after working out as if they mean to leave themselves in that condition throughout the day or even, if it's late in the afternoon, at the dinner table, I have learned an expression to put on my face that communicates my deep desire that they put on *clothes*, and they're good-natured enough to take the hint. Many's the time I have to make myself change out of my yoga or walking apparel, but I know if I don't, I will have taken the shine off my husband's greeting at the end of the day. Hal won't say anything critical if I'm unkempt; I can tell the difference though. My mother used to say, "It's little enough you can do for your husband and your family to keep yourself looking presentable for them." First thing in the morning is important too. My girls are not perfect about leaping out of bed and brushing their hair and getting nicely put together before they come down for breakfast. Neither am I, although I do wash my face and brush my teeth and my hair. We all ought to get dressed for breakfast like my father does. I did back East; I blame California for this one. (Have you ever had someone stay overnight with you and stagger out of bed and straight into your face in the kitchen? Now that sight will make the milk of hospitality run very skimmed.)

When I talk about clothing, I mean garments that you don't have to be eighteen years old and perfectly proportioned to look good in, garments that have a structure of some kind, a shape. Let's get down to it. Big huge T-shirts are not really clothes either; they are floppy posters for messages or advertisements for someone you've never met. Fitted T-shirts are another story; they at least are excellent for showing off a splendid upper torso. Blue jeans are clothes. Blue jeans are great-looking. So are sport shirts, knit or not. Far be it from me to attack casual clothing. We don't have to get dressed up to be well dressed, Heaven knows, and so does Lauren Hutton. And Lauren Bacall. And Ralph Lauren. Quit yelling; I've stopped. But in my opinion we should return to wearing *clothes*, at least.

At the same time we should resolutely refuse to let the fashion industry scare us into the clothes we wear. Jacqueline Kennedy created fashion not because of what she wore but because of how she wore it. It was her style, not her clothes, that women were trying to emulate, whether they knew it or not. The simplicity of the way she dressed strongly evidenced her confidence in what she had to offer as the woman inside the dress. Not all of us could look our best as minimally decked out, but all of us should keep in mind that it is our own habitation of a garment that gives it style.

Do yourself a favor, as they say, and as you can get the money to do so, invest in some articles of clothing; if you buy them with quality in mind and a little thought for the future, you will not have to replace a particular article for several years. The following remarks are predicated on my preferences and lifestyle. Obviously a person who lives a more casual or a more outdoorsy life wouldn't need as much dress-up stuff. Still, I believe that one should be equipped at all times to attend a wedding or a funeral or to accept an unexpected social invitation.

    • Figure out what you're looking for before you go into the store, before you choose the store you're going to, in point of fact; no point in buying something even good-looking and on sale if you're going to let it hang in the closet. Every time I look in my closet to pull out something for a special occasion, I have to glare at the terrific items I bought for when I'd be slimmer, or when I'd want to wear something very colorful, or when I'd be going to some unspecified event that would call for a lot of sequins. Most of these mistakes I made because of sale prices. Just because a suit is 50 percent off doesn't mean it will suit me.

    • Don't get me wrong about sale prices. That's just about the only kind of prices I pay anymore. I always try my best to buy out of season and thereby pay one-third of what I would when the clothes first come into the stores. What I wear isn't going to go out of fashion in one season anyway. My mother taught me that. She also taught me that once in a while the whimsical garment is a wonderful idea. I have two Christmas sweaters with jewelly stuff all over them that everybody has seen for the last six or seven years, but I don't think anybody takes much notice, and if they do remember, they're more likely to enjoy seeing the old thing show up again than to make a judgment on me. My purple sequined New Year's Eve dress I have worn since the year before Gigi was born, and when I came down in a different dress last New Year's Eve, my family made me go back upstairs and put on the old purple.

• We musn't worry about being seen over and over in the same thing if it looks good on us and we like wearing it. (Obviously I don't mean three days in a row.) When somebody says to me, "I've always liked you in that dress," I *think* most of the time it's perfectly innocent, I think so because I say that sometimes myself and mean it in the best possible way. If you have friends who would say something snarky about having seen you wear something before, by the way, you should be much more concerned with whom you've got for friends than with how old your clothes are.

• Underwear that fits is the first order of business. Nice underwear is remarkably influential on your state of mind, and in some weird way, on how easily you can keep your figure the way you want it. Ratty old underwear with rippling stretched-out elastic is a huge downer, and don't forget what they always say: "Better have on nice underwear in case you have to go to the hospital!" Don't you just love the old sayings? I would say, "Better have on nice underwear because you might forget who you are and think you're in the movies and pull your dress off in front of a lot of people." Or, "Better have on nice underwear because you want to feel lovely all over." I don't own matching sets of bras and underpants. I have whites and blacks in both. And although bras with underwire are not particularly healthy (metal on the body never is), I wear them sometimes.

• Socks and pantyhose don't necessarily have to be expensive, but are important for color and shade. Socks ought never to be thrown in a hot dryer; hosiery in too pale or too dark a shade can ruin an otherwise good-looking outfit. I think a healthy flesh color is by far the most becoming to the leg, so I don't fool with white hose; I buy only what I know I'm going to wear, which is nude-colored hose in summer and black hose in winter. I used to wear L'eggs or Hanes pantyhose; now I invest, and I mean *invest*, in Donna Karan. So long as I can afford to buy them, I feel they're worth it, because they fit like a dream and the texture is vastly becoming to the leg. I do wash them very carefully, however, to make them last. (I try to make pantyhose and bras the only nonnatural fabrics I wear. Silk bras and stockings are sadly expensive.)

• After spending years in nightgowns and peignoirs and mules with maribou on the toes, I've turned to pajamas, silk pj's. They're expensive. One day I would like to create an inexpensive line of pajamas made of silk, sleekly tailored and glamorous. And a person could wear them with mules, of course. I'll bet half the divorces that are happening at this minute might have been avoided if both parties had dressed for bed with the other party in mind.

• As for slips, we hardly need them anymore. I prefer camisole tops, which come in handy as a blouse substitute under a low-buttoned suit jacket in hot weather, or under any see-through material. A see-through blouse with a clearly visible bra is not the essence of enticement. Men's see-through shirts depend on the man we're seeing through to.

• Consider investing in two good black dresses and two good black suits. Between them they should cover all four seasons of the year. Even if you're blond, you should have black in your closet, because over the long haul it looks better than anything else. If you are very rich, then you can buy a gorgeous amber velvet to wear to a special dinner party, but if you're not very rich, you're going to have to fall back on what's hanging in your closet, and believe me, you cannot beat black. I have almost only black in my closet, so I'm prejudiced.

A black dress does not have to be expensive if it has a good shape and fit. You may need to change the belt or the buttons if they're of poor quality. The shoes you wear with this inexpensive item do need to be of fine quality, however, no matter what the dress cost. Buy a simple dress or suit made of silk or wool (if you can find simple anymore), and wear it with good shoes, a good handbag, and a pretty silk scarf, and you're in business. Just don't ever touch it directly with an iron. Steam it, or lay a towel on it before you iron it, preferably on the wrong side. If you press it with an iron, it will shine, and that will be the end of it.

Different black fabrics are never the same shade, so don't try to make a suit out of a black skirt and a black jacket of another fabric. Wear them with other things, not together. For some reason it doesn't matter with a blouse and skirt, only skirt and jacket.

Please don't wear black to weddings, you-all. Please don't. It's spoiling the look of weddings, the way the ladies are wearing black to them now. And don't wear red, unless you're a bridesmaid and the bride has chosen red for you. And while we're on the subject, why don't we go back to the polite policy of finding out the color (or shade) the mother of the bride plans to wear and staying away from it for ourselves. The groom's mother has to do it, so we should too. And *please do not wear white.* Only the bride gets to wear white. The closest we can come is eggshell. Can't we try to preserve the notion that we are respectful of the bride's purity? It's a beautiful part of the marriage ritual. Can't we be just romantic enough (don't say hypocritical) to restrain ourselves from flaunting it?

I do love black, but I think white is prettier in the summertime. I know there are some gorgeous black organdy getups, terribly chic. I still think we're all better off with a closet full of white stuff in the summer. And unlike black, white looks fine mixed together in all different shades. All whites and off-whites look good together. Black should not be worn by girls under the age of nineteen or twenty, maybe twenty-one, depending on the freshness of the young person in question.

• After the good black numbers and the good black shoes (two pairs, leather and silk, if possible) I suggest that all the rest of the wardrobe be garments that you would be comfortable wearing to eat out in a restaurant. We know we have plenty of loose stuff and a couple of pairs of blue jeans. Now everything that gets purchased should be nice-looking shirts, slacks, sweaters, or dresses, whatever represents your own preference.

• By the way, if you have purchased a fine garment, be particularly careful not to spill food on it or perspire very much in it, so that you do not have to send it to the dry cleaner, ever. I'm not kidding. Even expensive dry cleaning destroys fabric; it takes out the sizing (body), and unless your brother owns the establishment, your beautiful garment *can* just get squashed flat and shiny under an iron instead of steamed on a form, and then the seams will show through and it's really finished. Totaled. Good-bye to it. So trust me when I tell you that it's better to deal with a little spot the best you can and keep the garment out of the cleaners forever, if possible. With care it is possible. (Just don't forget your deodorant.)

• If you want to take really good care of a piece of clothing, try to hang it free from other things, so that air can get to it all around, and with tissue paper stuffed in the shoulders and arms. Go to that trouble and your garment will stay fresh as a daisy for years.

• I like skirts. If you wear a skirt, you do have to put on hose; that's the hardest thing about wearing a skirt, but try it; you may just like it too. I can guarantee that you will enjoy your day in a skirt, and you might find that you go out to dinner more often; it could be that you're already dressed for it. For my gentlemen readers, don't start up with me; I'm recommending slacks for you.

• Maternity clothes. Just please wear *something*. Less is not more at this particular time, no matter what your age, size, or condition. Wear leotards to work out in, if you're that perfect a person, and then cover it all up. It's all too intimate. It's revealing too much. It's depriving a divine mystery of its sanctity. And may I say that if I were a baby and came to find out after I was born that my mother had had photographs taken with little or no clothes on while she was expecting me, I would say, "How dare you?" I would be really embarrassed. And mad.

• Coats. Living in California doesn't demand much attention to coats; going east a lot, I have to keep something for cold weather. I think a trench coat is the best-looking raincoat for man or woman, and a camel-colored overcoat the best for either sex. Whatever color you choose, get a full-length coat (knee-length) if there's only one to be acquired. Short parkas look good over slacks and jeans but not skirts and not men's suits.

• Shoes should be the best we can afford, both for the way they look and for the health of our feet. Here I must admit a big dilemma. I have worn high high heels since I was fifteen years old, and I love them. I know they're not good for me, but I cannot give them up, because they make my legs look pretty and because they make me feel feminine and alluring. I wear an 8½ AAAA, very hard to find. When I find shoes that actually fit, I buy several pairs, and since I'm always afraid I'll never find any more, I save them forever, so my shoe racks look suspiciously Imelda-esque. The high heels, I discovered very early on, disguise the length of my foot, making it seem as if it's part of my leg, sort of.

(I am reminded of Hal's telling me not too long ago how surprised he was the first time he saw me barefoot on his boat, that he had never before noticed how long my feet were. He said he was bemused by a fancy that it might have to do with my coming from Tennessee. Believe you me, his not seeing these long underpinnings until then was no accident. If I could have stayed on tiptoe all the way across the blue Pacific, I would have, but you know how unpredictable that rascally ocean surface can be.)

Now of course young women seem to take pride in great long feet and seem determined to wear footgear that enlarges the foot rather than diminishing it. Clearly they are not troubled, as I was, with low foot esteem.

There was one kind of flat shoe made when I was a teenager that I liked. It looked like a ballet shoe and was worn barelegged or with bobby socks held up on the leg with a rubber band. We called them flats. "Are you wearing heels or flats?"

would be the preparty question. They were cut very low over the toes and were flattering even to my feet, but I haven't seen anything like them lately. Some of the new flat shoes that I see young women wearing now are very good-looking indeed. Too bad it's impossible for me to visualize them as looking good on me. I wear acupressure shoes at home and ballet shoes in rehearsal to make up for my penchant for *high* heels when I go out. Me and Camille Paglia.

Tennis shoes, Keds, Nikons, whatever you call them, are another question. They are comfortable and good for the foot. They are essential for many exercise practices. Everyone wears them. But do they really need to be worn everywhere, for everything? Are they really *shoes*, do you think?

• When I became engaged to Arthur, my dearly beloved Ellen Carter Wiesenthal (Ellen and her husband, Richard, and I loved each other the same before, during, and after my divorce from her brother) took me over to Rive Gauche on Madison Avenue and bought me a red, cream, and blue Yves St. Laurent scarf that I have to this day. Every time there was an occasion for a gift, Ellen would give me another scarf. She switched back and forth from YSL to Hermès to Gucci and kept doing it. I became taken with my growing collection of silk scarves and with what they could do for a simple outfit, for example, a skirt and blouse. Try putting out the word at present-giving time that you would love nothing more than a good silk scarf. The present givers won't have to wonder or worry what to get you: they will know. Make sure they know what kind of scarf you are hoping for. The great scarves are very expensive, so your givers can always gang up and pool their money, and since these scarves will last literally a lifetime or more, they can be handed down to your children, and it doesn't really matter which pattern is picked out, because any one of them will be so beautiful you will want to hang it on the wall like a painting.

• Jewelry. What jewelry I have is mostly what Hal has given me, and mostly traditional pieces. Several pieces, not gobs. Costume jewelry is not for me, except for publicity pictures. I like wearing my several pieces of the real thing. I would advise caution about piling on jewelry—costume or real, for men or women—except that I happen to know a couple of people who wear the most outrageous and exotic combinations and amounts of jewelry and look superb. Jewelry should reflect your own personality. If you're going to put it on, you'd better be able to carry it off.

• The generation of my daughters' age doesn't remember when everybody still wore hats. It's sad. When I was growing up, we were used to wearing a hat for winter and an Easter bonnet for spring and summer. I loved putting on my mother's hats, and Aunt Helen's and Aunt Mary's. They would let us dress up in them. Everybody looks good in a hat, women and men. I'm crazy about them on men. I wonder why the fashion industry doesn't push hats again. We would enjoy wearing them, I'll bet.

One of the pastimes Midge and I thought up and enjoyed when we were still too little to go to school or have chores was making "hats" from leaves. We may be the inventors and sole practitioners of this craft, which consisted simply of weaving the stem of one leaf into the next. Good luck and patience were required not to poke the holes too big and ruin the leaf. The green leaves of late spring were the easiest to fool with, but the prettiest hats came from the just-turning leaves of early fall, before they got crisp. We would go around town and sell our handiwork for one cent each. Miss Mary Crossett would always buy one, Mama Carter, Grandmother Hillsman if she was there, and Gina of course. Sometimes Miss Audrey Mitchell would fork over a penny. We didn't operate our hat factory very often because Gina wouldn't let us "worry" the same person over and over again.

• I think the passing of gloves is sadder than the disappearance of hats, although the two go together like ham and eggs, and for me, a person can't be elegantly dressed without them. In 1985, the year after Hal and I married, he was invited by the state department to do a world tour of his show *Mark*

Twain Tonight, and when he told me in passing, about to turn it down as he had done other times, I begged him to reconsider if we could take our three daughters—his Eve, and Ginna and Mary Dixie. He said yes we could if I really wanted to, so then I put the question to the girls. Would they be willing to wear white gloves and dresses? They agreed to do it, and we made the trip—Hal, Bennet Thomson, his stage manager for twenty-five years, the girls, and I. Performances in London, Lisbon, Prague, Bucharest, Tel Aviv, and New Delhi, and home by way of Singapore and Hong Kong. What a trip. We'd never have made it if the girls had refused to wear gloves.

• When Midge and I were in our early teens, my mother got her hands on a leather catalogue from Florence, Italy. We were growing up; from now on we would wear white cotton gloves only in the summer. Every year or two we ordered gloves in three lengths: short, four-button or six-button, and very long for dances. The leather was buttery soft and lined with silk. I loved them. Surprisingly, young and dizzy as we were, we didn't ever lose them. Finally when I married Arthur and could buy gloves in New York, I began to lose them, and I'm ashamed that I did. There is one pair left. I came across it last year in a dresser drawer in McLemoresville. It offers one of those delicate trails of touch and smell that lead back to an immediate sense of my mother, and I have all too few.

My little outline of what I wish we still held standard in attire might seem inappropriate, what with the "real" problems going on all over the place. I don't think it's silly. I think we should be noticing and be aware of each other, strangers as well as friends. It should matter to us what we look like to other people, and they to us. The world around us should matter to us a great deal. We've gotten concerned about trees and plants and animals; it's time we took a gander at ourselves.

We're making the picture better or we're making it worse, one or the other, on a daily basis. In Sunday school we used to sing, "Brighten the corner where you are."

Dressing with some care makes you feel good, and lifts every aspect of your life.

Before I get off my soapbox, I want to mention children's clothes. No, I have to get off my soapbox first in order to get on my knees in a position of supplication. Would there be any way we could please go back to dressing babies in white? Poor little things, they don't know what's being done to them, being decked out in all those hard loud colors that do not make them look a bit pretty. Pastels are sweet, but white is the most beautiful thing you can put on a baby, boy or girl. My baby girls wore almost nothing but white until they were a year old, and after that only the palest pastels, and they looked angelic. It's not really appropriate to use my children as an example; they *were* angels and would have looked like angels if they'd been swaddled in black leather, but what I'm saying is the absolute truth. Children should have their dignity preserved for them until they can do it for themselves. Sometimes it looks as if parents have dressed up their helpless baby as an accessory to match themselves or their mood. I believe a reasonable rule of thumb might be this: if your friends laugh when they first see your little one, you haven't dressed him in a proper outfit. The good response is "Ooooooh." You may think it's cute to laugh at him, but the baby won't like it. And believe me, the baby knows what's going on.

White high-top lace-up shoes and white two-strap sandals with white socks. Period. Why do they need gym shoes before they can run around?

Yes, a pterodactyl flew through the centuries into my window and pecked out these last paragraphs. Don't worry; I'm not imperiling the close bonds I have with many darling friends who put their children in the full panoply of peacock hues. My views on various subjects depart from those of some of my dearest, and they seem to take it in stride.

If you are about to say, "I like to let little Johnnie make his own mind up about what he wears; I think it's good for him to learn to make his own decisions," please don't say it. To start with, children should never see the inside of the clothing store. They have to go to the shoe store to be fitted, but not the clothing store, where we all have to suffer the screaming tantrum of the child whose mother doesn't want to buy him something that has caught his eye. Children's clothes should be bought without the child around. Boy, would the store owners be grateful to do without the howling and whining. It is silly for children to pick out what they're going to wear when they have no idea of the range of possibilities, what's reasonable and what isn't. They should be put into the proper clothing until they are old enough to start dressing themselves. At that point they can be given a few options, but not in the store. That way madness lies. When they start to school or play groups, they'll want to dress like the other children and then you'll have to decide how far along that path you're willing to travel, but at least you will have established that the decision is ultimately out of the little one's hands and safely in yours, as so many decisions should be that involve wee tykes. That's how they like it, believe it or not. (You will be subjected to more of my thoughts on allowing children to make decisions as we go along together.)

PS on clothing: Tops on my "in" and "out" list are "in" and "out" lists. I like to see what famous people are wearing, but why do we need the catty comments? Why do we pay out money to publications that are mean to people? I'm guilty too but only for plane rides. I'm so nervous before taking off in an airplane that I buy magazines to distract myself; otherwise I can't keep from dwelling on how unnatural it seems that a great big heavy thing like a plane should be able to get up and stay up in the air. Still I wonder why we can't peek at famous people, if we are amused by that kind of thing, without tacitly joining the kind of cruel little games of exclusion we are supposed to have left behind in grammar school.

PPS on clothing: I haven't said anything about men's attire because—here's a rarity—I don't hold many opinions on that subject. I do appreciate jackets in restaurants. I like tweeds, blue blazers, and dark blue suits. I like seersucker jackets and straw hats like my actor friend Macon McCalman wears. I like a belt that goes around, not underneath, the stomach, polished shoes, pants with cuffs, and shirts with cuff links. I like white shirts the best. I beg my husband to wear long socks so that he doesn't have a strip of leg showing when he sits down and his pants hike up, but so far he's turned a cold eye to me on that.

And please give me a break, gentlemen on airplanes who are traveling alone and therefore might wind up next to a stranger like me: please wear long pants. Those big old hairy legs hanging out of short pants are bad news if you're strapped in right beside them. Might it be possible for you gentlemen to accept as fact that most of you would be doing everyone a favor by keeping your legs covered unless you're in sporty or intimate situations? Don't be mad at me; someone had to say it.

PART TWO

Beauty All Around

≈ Chapter Six ≈
THE SPIRIT OF THE HOME

For there is music wherever there is harmony, order, or proportion; and thus far we may maintain the music of the spheres.

—SIR THOMAS BROWNE

I'M AWARE, AS I WRITE ABOUT WHAT WE see around us, what we hear, and how important our surroundings are to our state of mind, that if we're tired or frightened or hurt and depressed, it can be hard to care about anything, least of all what cup we're using for our morning coffee. All the same, making ourselves care is one step out of depression, and doing something about it is another. Making "small" things significant can help to create ascending steps. I have spent enough time in the wells of sadness to know that what I say is true.

All of us who have been disappointed in love (and most of us have, either in unrequited or, more terrible, requited love) have learned, in Robert Graves's words, that

> *the Dragon is not dead*
> *But once more from the pools of peace*
> *Shall rear his fabulous green head.*
>
> . . . .
>
> *certitude at last*
> *Must melt away in vanity—*
> *No gate is fast, no door is fast—*
> *That thunder bursts from the blue sky,*
> *That gardens of the mind fall waste,*
> *That fountains of the heart run dry.*

We have felt the "cataclysmic anguish" of love gone wrong or awry or against itself. And we have had to drag ourselves on through days that appear like empty rooms with no light in them and no place to rest. Sooner or later we have begun to furnish these bare rooms, these days that have no meaning, with incident and responsibility. Before I had children, I was helpless against the vicissitudes of the heart. The presence of my little girls enabled me, compelled me, to come up from the indulgences of sadness. If we can't put one foot in front of the other for ourselves, we can do it for someone else first, someone who needs us, and then for ourselves. Now at last I understand that there is very little within our control, nor should there be, but what is must be attended to. We can't make things turn out the way we wish; we can do just our part.

The passage of time is one of the things we can't control, but it doesn't have to fly. We can slow it down by living moment to moment with conscious relish. I think of time going by as an incentive toward getting the most from the moment. I like consciously to remind myself here and there during the day that this minute I'm wishing away while I'm sitting in traffic or waiting for the dentist is not one that I can freeze for the future; it's gone whether I'm using it or not. How can I use it sitting in the dentist's chair? By being aware of it and grateful for it, and maybe by taking a few slow lovely breaths and reminding myself that I'm one of God's creatures, unique unto myself and at the same time part of everything around me. Every moment of every day should be as crammed with life and joy as each of us can make it, because why not? What sense does it make not to drink in everything—every sight, every sound, every sweet sensation that adds consequence to "this mortal coil"? We should keep the stakes as high as we can without damaging our health or going to jail.

I believe that we should live in the most beautiful atmosphere we can possibly create. It takes thought, will, and effort. Money helps, but it's not essential. I believe that we should do it for our loved ones and for ourselves. I don't agree with the "you deserve it" slogans. I don't think anybody "deserves" anything right off the bat, just because we exist. We deserve what we earn. We should live with beauty not because it's our right, but because we can. There is much beauty around us if we look for it. It is our moral duty to appreciate and foster it wherever we can, and the place to start is in our own bailiwick.

The level of our existence can rise only so high as we desire; if we treat our bodies or our physical surroundings carelessly, if we live in a bleak environment, there's every probability we'll live a bleak life. The desire for a beautiful environment is not a superficial one. How grand it is to live in beauty, and how vitally important, and how necessary, and how imperative it is for a full life. Fancy trappings are not the point; the austere simplicity of a farmhouse, or the rumpled coziness of the book lover's and keepsake keeper's rooms, or the tidy studio apartment of sanguine singleness can all offer their harmony to the dweller.

One touchstone of a home is whether the children and their friends are there a lot. College friends used to stop in at our house if they were driving between Memphis and Knoxville, and they never seemed eager to leave. We were all proud of that fact and of our home, justifiably so. When a car would pull up and she'd see a crowd piling out, my mother would sail around and produce a big platter of sausage or country ham, eggs, tomato gravy, and hot biscuits with homemade pear preserves; our pals could count on that; conjointly there was a more elusive something that they came for. There was something about Gina and her house, whether it was the old house in McLemoresville or the bigger one in Huntingdon or the stone house in Atlanta or the cottage in Sarasota, that made you want to come in and stay. Daddy used to tease Gina that she made her home so inviting that "nobody *ever* wants to leave," and it was true.

I have often rued the lack of attention I paid to the many and various things that Gina did (some of which she knew how to do and some of which she just decided to do), from making draperies to plumbing to drafting floor plans to carpet laying to bricklaying and stonework to refinishing furniture to painting to carpentry and for Heaven's sake *cooking*. But since I was often assisting in some capacity or other (even, when I was very small, pinning on a sign I made for myself that said "Gina's Little Helper"), I necessarily absorbed some of it. I absorbed the point of it anyway, that point being the spirit of the house itself. Gina believed that being a homemaker, as in making a home, was a laudable career. She believed that being a mother, as in nurturing good human beings to send out into the world, was a laudable career, and that making a good home for these children of hers was going to have a great deal to do with their becoming good human beings. Gina's way of making a home was to put herself into every inch of it. No detail was beneath her interest. Certain things would have been better done by artisans, but after Gina had carefully cut and mitered a joint of wood molding around a corner cabinet, none of us would have wanted to change it for the work of a master craftsman. The spirit of Gina's home was her spirit, and it was beautiful, like she was.

I try, with a little more success all along, I hope, to take a page out of my mother's book and put my own self into our home. I am sorry that for years I had dinner guests for whom I never said a grace over the meal, under the impression that this custom of my home should be omitted when I had guests who might not be used to praying before dinner. When my daughters got old enough to stay up for company dinners, I began to realize the hypocrisy of my behavior and changed it. Since then I have discovered that even in New York or Los Angeles a religious custom sincerely observed is received as germane to the life of the house and is therefore appreciated as inclusive and genial. This is one of our favorite graces:

> Dear Lord, this humble house we'd keep
> Sweet with play and calm with sleep
> Help us, so that we may give
> Beauty to the lives we live.
> Let thy love and let thy grace
> Shine upon our dwelling place.

(After we say this one, Macon "Sonny" McCalman, if he's here—and he usually is, if we have any company—always adds, "And Dear Lord, thank you for this food, which is the point of saying the blessing, and Dixie can't remember it.")

When our family is able to accomplish the aims of this prayer, and lots of the time we are, then the spirit of the house becomes all that we desire. A house develops its own life, its own personality; it protects its family from the rain and cold; it offers privacy from the rude world; if it's been well cared for, it's charming and cozy; if it's loved, it's glowing and cheerful. If it's cherished, the house will greet its dwellers at the end of a day's work or time out of town with an unmistakable feeling of welcome.

By the same token it languishes if its people don't live in it and appreciate it. Our home in Tennessee is always sad when we first get back. One of our friends who works for us there, Bill or Luella or Cathy, has put on all the lights and started the fires if the weather's cold, but the dear old house doesn't warm up to us for a couple of days; it's as if it feels neglected, which is a reasonable thing to feel toward people who stay gone nine or ten months out of the year.

What makes a house beautiful is what it offers the person who comes into it. If it offers a warm invitation to enter, a comfortable place to rest, a haven from the outside world, and a feeling of friendliness, then it's going to feel beautiful. If it looks as if the inhabitants love it, then it will look beautiful. The house or apartment will offer the visitor what it holds for the dweller. If it does so, the visitor will not want to leave, like Daddy said.

Our house is full of color. I like seeing a change from one room to the next. I like making each room look the way it ought to for the function it serves. I have things that my mother gave me, things that came from Hal's family, and things that I've acquired since I've been keeping house for myself, very few of them recently. Everything in our home is dear to me and has been put where it is by me. Once in a while I move it all around. Because I love my home and try to make it inviting, my friends like it and, I believe, find it charming too.

Color matters most. Color that *you* choose because you think it's beautiful and you want to live with it, not because you think it's chic or trendy.

Annie Potts loves white. She paints her whole house white and puts up white curtains and has colorful kitchen and bathroom tiles and pastels in the receiving rooms, and it's an oooh and aaah house.

Margo Carter, my sister-in-law in Tennessee, brother Hal's wife, loves muted and traditional tones, subtly patterned wallpapers, and painted furniture; she often paints it herself. Margo has beautiful things from her family. She doesn't have to create drama, just arrangements that allow for maximum talking and the game playing that she and Hal and their sons, John, James, and Horace, dote on. She's an elegant woman who spent twenty-something years, until John married Un Chu and her granddaughter Margaret was born, with four big raw-boned males, and her homes have always told that very particular story. She has moved as many times as I have. We both know about getting settled and then doing it all over again. Margo helped me enormously when I moved into our present abode in Los Angeles and when I fixed up the house in McLemoresville. Her contributions are impeccable taste and a loving way of encouraging me to hold it more or less in the road.

Ellen Carter Wiesenthal, my other sister-in-law, who has always lived in New York City, is a big chance taker, but she can pull it off. Ellen is, as they say, "not afraid of color," and she uses it to stunning effect. Her apartment on Central Park West is a sensational example of city taste, moxie, and chic. She helped me with my homes in New York. The most fun was when we lived in the very same building on Central Park West, and her children, Robert and Jane, and my girls could be back and forth all the time, more like siblings than cousins. Along with visits to the Decoration and Design Building, where we looked for fabrics and carpets and wallpaper, she took me other interesting places, like John Vesey's to order glass and chrome étagères, and like Ruth Vitow's to order lampshades, and like the fascinating shop of an unusual gentleman named Chris Chodoff, who had a wax ear. We bought several wonderful things from Mr. Chodoff in the late sixties, including a few pieces by Diego Giacometti. Ellen would say, when I got nervous, "Cheap is cheap." She was right; better buy one good piece than lots of junk; over time you'll wind up with several good pieces that you'll live with forever. (I'm still wearing the St. Laurent silk shirts and the Halston cashmere sweater dresses that she made me buy about the same time. Now YSL is so expensive, I don't even walk in the door.) Ellen was scrupulously careful never to push me away from what seemed lovely to me or to push me into something I wasn't crazy about. My apartments in New York were more soft than sleek. If I wasn't enamored of a thing, we'd pass on it, no matter how right she knew it to be. She wouldn't have dreamed of selecting ashtrays or objets d'art for me. (When I was little, we called them whatnots.)

I would add to Ellen's motto, Cheap is cheap, my own: Cheap is too expensive. It costs too much to shortchange ourselves. Let's work on our aesthetic awareness; let's start observing what's around us and set about to make it pleasing. A limited budget puts you ahead of the game in a way. Having to choose carefully what's most important to you might work to the good. You don't absolutely have to lay Aubusson rugs all over the place; you can make an old wood floor look pretty terrific, either natural or painted. Plywood tables covered with long cloths are lovely; old kitchens with new paint jobs can be charming.

If you have lots of money, I strongly advise you not to hand it over blindly for someone else to do your home, unless you want it to look like someone else's home. Your mistakes will be sweeter and dearer to you than anybody else's perfect design. If you're rich and you aren't sure what to do with your house, pay for the best advice from a decorator whom you find personable and simpatico, but work with the decorator yourself all the way down the line. And never, never, never let anyone put anything on any tabletop but you. That's where you place things that mean something to you, because of their beauty, or because they hold memories you love, or both. No one can choose them for you.

The same goes for paintings, pictures, and picture frames. If you want advice, ask the rest of the family; they'll enjoy having a say. I am a fiend for family photographs. I hang them in the kitchen, in my bedroom, and they're all over the library and the music room. I don't happen to care for family pictures in the living room, but I'm sure that's a silly thing. What I'm sure isn't silly is the absence of a telephone in the living room. I dislike a telephone, period, although I recognize that it's a necessary evil. The day will never come when I let one get plugged into my living room; there I draw the line. That would be almost as bad as an exercise machine.

Speaking of machines, my husband and I are engaged in a running battle, albeit a gentle one, over putting a fax machine into the house in Tennessee. I've lost on whether or not we get one; we're getting one, it seems. I'm standing firm on where it's going to go, though. I detest the sight of a machine in a room that's not an office, and I will not give in, because I know I'm right. A machine in a room where people are supposed to sit and be human with one another, and maybe relax, is a noxious presence. It is an offense to the atmosphere. I believe that there's a danger in acclimating ourselves to the intrusion of cold metal or plastic nonorganic materials all around us. Getting used to it requires desensitizing, and correct me if I'm wrong, desensitizing is just exactly the opposite of the direction we humans are supposed to be trying to go.

I will not alter my position on the fax machine; it will go in a closet, where they so craftily put them in the Hotel Carlyle, or it will go in the laundry room with other machines. It will not—will not—find its sneaky and intrusive way into our upstairs sitting room beside Hal's desk. Read this, my husband. No. I am throwing my body across the railroad tracks here. I love you, but no. We have offices in Los Angeles for necessary evils like copiers and faxes. We go to Tennessee to get away from some of those papers flying at us. Every moment of the day some machine is disgorging some more paper, very little of it bearing glad tidings, most of it entirely unnecessary to the accomplishing of anything of importance or value. I refuse to go all the way to Tennessee to sit in a room where without even ringing the doorbell and asking to come in, a communication can bleat out its appearance in our midst and vomit up some document that will surely to goodness engage my husband's time and attention long enough to kill off our sense of cozy privacy.

I resent the way machines are allowed to tyrannize us. Let's keep the wretched things in their place. The fax machine will be relegated to some place where we can go get what we want from it, when it is convenient for us, not whenever the machine pleases.

Machines are supposed to perform functions for us that will enhance our existence or ease our workload in some way, right? They're supposed to be subject to our will, right? They're supposed to be making life more comfortable, right? Are your machines doing that for you, Dear Reader, or do you sometimes find yourself, as I do, overwhelmed and annoyed and even to some extent intimidated by them? Think about it. Every hard-earned dollar we pay out should really be toward a good end, toward a result that does enhance our own particularity. Think about what you want around you.

Is the reason for being born and living and dying so that we can figure out how to do those things in the most efficient way? I don't think so. For example I will not ever be having a kitchen island, although they are great space savers and very utilitarian. You know why? Because I think utility is overrated. I think the most important thing in the kitchen, after the sink, the stove, and the refrigerator, is the kitchen table, and I'm not even so sure the refrigerator comes ahead of it. The kitchen table makes the kitchen a place where the family comes to sit and talk together. Families don't gather together easily around kitchen islands.

A colorful warm kitchen—with a kitchen table in it, if there's any way to squeeze one in—is, to get down to it, the heart of the home. I am not a lover of a chic kitchen. Too sterile. Too cold. (No, thank you, no slate.) When a person gets up in the morning and goes for that first sip of juice or coffee, a cheerful kitchen is a goodly help in starting the day well. If something bad happens or you can't sleep at night or you need to work out a problem, that's where you go. The dogs aren't crazy; they know the kitchen is the happening place.

I am a lover of a separate dining room. If you have a dining area that's an extension of your living room or of your kitchen, I recommend that you go all out to make it feel separate and hallowed. Yes, hallowed. Breaking bread together has been from time immemorial a significant occasion. If your dinner table is in the kitchen or at one end of the living room, turning out the other lights and using a hanging light over the table, or candles, will create a sense of separation. Potted palms and ficus trees make beautiful room dividers, as can folding screens (if they're beautiful). It seems to me that many people don't put much love into their dining room, I suppose because they don't sit down to eat together all that often. Well, of course the first way to make a dining room or a dining area beautiful is to dine in it. Eat with your family, and invite friends over every so often. Although when I was growing up, the meals themselves were cause for celebration, I have discovered to my relief over the years that the food doesn't have to be perfect; it's the breaking of the bread together that lends grace.

Let me tell you how I like to set my dining room table. Don't make fun of me now, for being so literal and simplistic. I'm talking about trying to make ordinary days and occurrences extraordinary. I'm talking about trying to make everything around us beautiful. I'm talking about trying to get to Heaven, in different kinds of ways.

With my booty from *Designing Women* I bought a wonderful table for the house in Tennessee that will seat eighteen when fully extended, and even so at holiday time there's an overflow that I seat at my mother's dining table set up in the living room. I like an old-timey tablecloth. I know it's correct not to have a cloth on the table for a formal dinner; I just rarely get that formal. Leaving aside that it protects, a pretty tablecloth is warm and inviting. I haven't felt expansive enough yet to buy the table of my dreams for our house in

California; here we have a plywood table that Oddvar made for us, which is covered with a floor-length burgundy velvet cloth. On top of the velvet I use colorful cotton tablecloths. In Tennessee I stick with white because it's what that old house is used to.

Years ago, visiting my college buddy Diane Meeks Carden in Virginia, I found an old silver epergne at a flea market, and it has been my dining room centerpiece ever since. It has a removable cover with openings that allow the stems of flowers to be put through. Something about it is just right for me. The flowers stand in it separated and graceful, especially if they're graceful flowers. I like roses and freesia together. I have also four large silver bud vases that took my eye "long ages ago," as Aunt Helen would say, which I place away from the center of the table with the same flowers in them. If the roses are in bloom, I put one rose, full blown, in each. On either side of these small containers I place a crystal or a silver candlestick, making eight candles altogether on the table. If I make the table bigger, I use more candles.

In Tennessee I do the same thing with small vases from the Mediterranean Shop in New York and lots of candles. We have columbine blooming there in warm weather, and it makes an exquisite combination with our roses. And there's a fireplace in the dining room, with a mirror over it, so the candles on the mantelpiece are reflected in the mirror. Simple, easy, and magical.

At each place is a silver service plate, old, from a set I got in a consignment shop years ago, under a green crystal salad plate. I use large white linen napkins, my good silverware, old silver water goblets that I've collected one at a time over the years, and pretty wine glasses. The effect is lovely. My table always look the same. I'm not interested in variety. I like the familiarity of the same way of doing things, the sweet history of my dinner table, the same prayers said over it, the same dishes and glasses and silver. I always use my good china and crystal. It's my credo. When my mother was a bride, she used her best china rarely because if something broke, it would be next to impossible to replace. I don't feel restricted in that way, partly because I have no qualms about mixing patterns of anything. However, I don't use my mother's good china and crystal; that I couldn't be relaxed about. Over the years I have acquired at a bargain odd lots of glasses and dishes and forks and spoons, and now I put out what seems pretty to me and never mind if it's not a matched set. My goal is to appreciate what's there to appreciate.

I believe in candlelight, as does Ronnie Claire Edwards, that most theatrical actress. Trust me when I tell you that those two words are not redundant in the case of Ronnie Claire. In fact many more, and more dramatic, words would be required to evoke this rare creature. She's the one who says all any house needs is a grand piano and an oriental rug and that dimmers are more important than plumbing. She's the one who has written and performs an award-winning and sidesplitting one-woman show entitled *The Knife-Thrower's Assistant, or Life on the Cutting Edge*. She's being encouraged to write the show as a book and is thinking of changing the subtitle to *Memoirs of a Human Target*. She's the one who will remind me with élan, as we stand together in my hallway or hers, going in to or leaving the dinner table,

> *Lives of great men all remind us*
> *We can make our lives sublime,*
> *And, departing, leave behind us*
> *Footprints in the sands of time.*

Both of us vow that in the not too distant future we will dispense with electric lighting altogether and turn to the much more flattering illumination afforded by candle glow.

Nothing that I have described about my beautiful table is out of reach for the person who would like to make dinner an occasion rather than an act of consumption to be gotten through with as little effort as possible. A few flowers are not expensive. Little flowerpots cost even less than cut flowers and last longer. Candles can be expensive, but an eighteen-inch candle will last almost a week. I use linen napkins. (If you hate to iron, switch to fabrics that don't require ironing, but don't give up and use paper ones. Paper goods aren't saving anybody any money in the long run.) It's very easy to make a pretty table, and it's such a lift for those who come to sit at it. It doesn't take an awful long time to garner a nice collection of pretty silverware, glasses, and dishes, if you haunt secondhand stores and keep your eye out. All you need is the desire to do it. What makes the table beautiful is your loving attention.

Now let's talk about the living room. If you want guests to enjoy your home, you have to enjoy it yourself. Every chair should be comfortable and should have a table close enough to put down a glass or a little canapé. If you have a den or library, beside every chair or sofa there should be a good reading light as well as a table. I'm strong on ottomans and footstools because I like to prop up my feet by the fire.

In a perfect world everybody would have a fireplace. As a present for me Hal put one of those little fireplaces that doesn't have to have a brick chimney in our bedroom in McLemoresville. Now *that* is luxury, a bedroom fireplace on a cold winter night.

The place we sleep is as important as the place we eat. No room is more important than one's bedroom. It must be uncluttered and peaceful, the bed linens clean and smooth. The bed shouldn't be used as a repository for anything except coats when there's a party. (A messy room is as depressing as a constant headache. It can give you one too.) I put a carafe of spring water on my bedside table every night. There are lace curtains under the draperies on my bedroom windows because the morning light looks beautiful filtered through them. I try to keep a rose or two in the room. I believe that ideally one would sleep in a room of pristine simplicity so that the time before sleep and the time just after waking could be given over to stillness and tranquil reflection. Therefore I try not to clutter up my nightstand with books and magazines and mail order catalogues. I try.

We have two television sets, one upstairs and one down.

We do not have one in the bedroom. Television, even inter-esting and entertaining fare (*Law and Order*, Hercule Poirot on *Mystery!*), creates an ambience that is antithetical to the feeling a bedroom should have. The bedroom, most of all places in the house, should feel removed from the bustle of the outside world. It should be one's serene refuge. My father has a television in his room because he watches it when he wakes up in the middle of the night. If I start waking up at two in the morning and staying awake until six like he does, I may resort to the tube myself, but not for now.

One word about the bathroom. I just know that when Vir-ginia Woolf wrote "A Room of One's Own," she secretly meant one's own *bathroom*. I don't care about Italian tiles or a Jacuzzi; just the room itself and the privacy it affords are the greatest thing since sliced bread. Ladies (and gentlemen too), forget the high-tech kitchen, the fantastic sound system, the new car. If you don't have your own bathroom, do anything to get one. Work, beg, borrow, or steal; it's an even more luxurious luxury than a fireplace in the bedroom.

When you think of making your home or apartment lovely, remember that fresh flowers make as big a difference as a new piece of furniture, and if you get the new furniture, you still should have the flowers. The poet said, "Gather ye rosebuds while ye may,/Old time is still a-flying," and I take his message literally. I gather my roses while I may, and they make a big difference to me and to my family and people who come to visit. It's no accident that he specified roses: roses are the ultimately beautiful thing. I have them in my yard and in my house. All it takes is your or somebody's strong back to dig the hole and the interest to look after them. Every time, *every time* I cut a rose and put it in its vase, I am made happy.

I would not order floral arrangements for my house, even if I had the money to throw away. First of all it's so much fun to do it myself, and secondly I consider it mine to do. Salvador cooks for us and Eufemia and Zoila keep the house, but I wouldn't ask anyone to fix my flowers, and I'm about as busy as any other working woman, I would imagine. It's such a pleasure to put my own flowers in their vases the way they look best to me and to set them around where I want. It would hurt my feelings to have anyone else do it. It would be like signing my name on a letter somebody else wrote.

If you have your own roses, start cutting them. Cutting makes them bloom more. If you don't have your own, you could start growing them. You'll be amazed at how many roses just three or four bushes will give you. At those times of the year when you have to buy your flowers, the shop owner who gets to know you will often let you purchase full-blown roses at a reduced price. If you cut at least an inch off the ends and lay them full out in a tub of cool water for a while, they'll look perky for days.

I use no more than two colors together in one bouquet, and I prefer them not to be contrasting. For example, I do not like red and white, or red and yellow. I would combine red with pink, or red with purple, or pink with another pink, or pink with white, or make a bouquet of all pastels, yellow, pink, and lavender. I would mix blue with lavender or white. The very prettiest to me is only one color to a vase. The next prettiest to me is a combination of tones close to one another. So if you're planting just a few rose bushes, I suggest all the same color, with maybe different varieties.

A bouquet with an odd number of flowers is prettier than one with an even number. Don't ask me why; try it both ways and you'll see what I mean. After you get past a dozen, of course you can't tell; I like smaller bouquets.

When you receive an arrangement as a gift, promptly pull out all ferns and baby's breath, take what flowers there are out of the florist's vase, cut the stems off a couple of inches, and put them in your own vase. The flowers will look twice as pretty without the padding. If somebody sends you a truly gorgeous arrangement, forget what I just said.

Low vases with short flowers go on low tables; tall vases and tall flowers go on tall tables. A thirty-inch-tall chest or table can look good with either tall or short flowers; however, never put a short little arrangement on a very tall piece of furniture, and never put a tall arrangement on a coffee table. Please do not put on the dining room table a centerpiece that is too tall to see over. I don't care how many you've seen on how many fancy dinner tables. A big huge barrier of flowers in the middle of the table forces guests to talk only to the persons on either side of them and does not foster warmth and conviviality.

Do not overload a vase. If the flowers are beautiful, they will enjoy standing a little apart from one another. Delphinium, tulips, calla lilies, columbine, and roses are the kinds of graceful bending flowers that suit me. These kinds of flowers are so beautiful to me that I like to look at just a few of them at a time. If a vase is stuffed full of flowers, you can't see them. "God's gifts put man's best dreams to shame."

Everything matters. The old "What difference does it make?" or "It doesn't really matter; it'll all be the same a hundred years from now" is a bum philosophy. We can't fix everything but it doesn't help to ignore what we can fix. It just lowers the level of life in us. Acknowledge that it matters and do what you can about it, and then let it go.

All common things, each day's events,
That with the hour begin and end,
Our pleasures and our discontents,
Are rounds by which we may ascend.

—HENRY WADSWORTH LONGFELLOW

Looking for pleasant moments in the common events of the day is a wonderful way to stay interested in the life that either is passing happily or is passing you by. I enjoy my little morning ritual. It sets my mood for the day. I drink a cup of hot water with lemon juice before I get in the shower. In the shower I take the time to breathe and stretch a minute, grateful for the warm water waking up my sleepy back muscles. It's important to me not to feel jerked into the day. Before I put on my clothes, I do a few moments of gentle stretching. Breakfast, however simple, should be taken sitting down and not on the run. Where you eat your breakfast, what you're looking at, and what you're thinking about are important. Throughout the day I look for moments to look forward to again the next day, starting with my good-morning chats with my husband and my father and the way the air feels when I first leave the house to go to work.

Become conscious of what you see and what you touch on a regular basis. Many heightened sensations are just waiting for you to take advantage of them and appreciate them. For example, try being particular about what you eat from and drink from. Food and drink from receptacles that are lovely in your eyes will enhance your enjoyment of what you're taking in (and, believe it or not, will influence against overindulgence). Use a pretty cup or a mug you especially like for your morning tea or coffee. I choose the teacup and teapot from the several I have as if it matters which one I use, and therefore it does matter. The calendar you hang on your kitchen wall or the book you use for appointments should be one that pleases you every time you refer to it, either because it's charming to your eye or because it suits your convenience. The reverse is true also. You may discover that certain fixtures in your day are annoying or even distasteful to you; allow yourself to become aware and do something about them. If you realize that you hate the way the seat covers in your car feel, put something that feels good over them. If your kitchen stool has one short leg, take it down the street and get it fixed. I realized some time ago that my little bedside table was driving me crazy in a low-level sort of way. It wasn't nearly big enough for my carafe of water, calcium tablets, aromatherapy drops, big amethyst crystal, lamp, box of tissues, alarm clock, books, and the two or three pictures that I like to have beside me. So I put that little table beside a chair across the room and shoved a chest of drawers up next to my bed. What a pleasant difference it made. The chest is just a little taller than the table, so it's a better height for the reading lamp. It's big enough for all my stuff to go on top, and it's Chinese red, so it's very cheerful looking. One more minor irritant removed with no expense or trouble.

Don't, don't, don't live with broken things. Fix them or get rid of them, whatever they are. Clocks, radios, tape players, cabinet doors, piano strings, lamps, and sticky windows. They're depressing and also trashy. Fix them or throw them out. Same thing for clothes that don't fit anymore. Try to save only those things that are of real significance to you. If we save a thing long enough, we can become sentimentally attached to it for its age alone and then we're stuck with it. I'm a sentimental fool myself, but I have found out the hard way that lots of excess baggage isn't cheerful.

If you're not completely happy with your own home, I encourage you to start getting rid of what you don't like or change it, in accordance with your own particular preference. Be brave about getting rid of whatever you're living with that isn't aesthetically pleasing to you—towels, a lamp, a light fixture, or the headboard of your bed. Get it out. You'll find a way to make do or replace it. Insist upon living with only what you like, including other people.

When we were first living in California, I was taken to see "Ramtha," a thousand-year-old spirit who supposedly speaks through (is channeled through) a lovely blond woman. Don't say a word; it was California, it was the eighties, and it was interesting. I'm not sure what Ramtha was, but he (or she) certainly gave me some great advice. He said I had bad "mirrors," and he was talking about the people I was spending time with at that point. When we're trying to improve the aesthetics of our surroundings, we should take people into account. We all function best around others who think well of us, and truly all it takes to make good friends is to be a good friend and to expect the same in return. If we give and get back good positive experience, then we've got a friend, to paraphrase a gorgeous song. If you're lucky enough to have a true friendship, cherish it and not just with lip service. (I was taught that you ought to give your business to your friends, if it's at all possible, even if you can get a little better deal somewhere else. The difference in what it will cost you is probably negligible, and the continuing friendship will be much more valuable as time goes by than the money saved.)

A great part of Marcel Proust's artistry was in writing about the beauty in "what lay around him" in his childhood home. The beauty of a home has very little to do with market value. The beauty of a home to the children in it has all to do with how objects are invested with their family history and mostly with their mother's love. The beauty of her home to a mother has to do with how successful she is in making her family comfortable and happy there, and as time goes by, with the memories that live in every nook and cranny. When brother Hal was six or seven years old and in the first stages of a big love affair with whittling wood, he methodically carved a small round hole in the top of Gina's favorite little rocking chair. It was in a most obvious place; you couldn't miss seeing it. Gina was heartsick about it, but since she knew Hal didn't mean to do anything wrong, that he was just in the throes of carving madness, she scolded him and let it go. By the time Hal was grown, she would say that the rocker meant more to her because of the hole her little boy had carved in it than it ever could have in perfect condition, that his mark on it made it precious.

We make our environment beautiful only when we make our mark on it. We must record enough of ourselves in space and time to recognize where we are as our own place, or we won't have a place, and that's not a good feeling. If you don't trust your own taste, ask somebody you do trust for a little guidance, but you have to make it your very own. Whatever we do with our own hands and heart becomes lovely, especially to our children and our spouse, who will appreciate it whether they ever say so or not.

We don't necessarily "deserve" a beautiful existence to start with. We will deserve it when we've made it our goal and accomplished it.

• • •

One of the most splendid and beautiful manifestations of civilized life is language. A lot of people actually find the dictionary interesting reading. I don't sit down with it in the evening like my grandmother Hillsman did, but I find it hard to resist browsing a while after I've looked up a word. It's also fun; I was brought up to enjoy word games, crossword puzzles, and playful arguments over meaning and spelling. (There's a great game called Dictionary that we used to play until dawn when I was on the road with *Carousel* in the mid-sixties. Benay Venuta, Reid Shelton, Joe Pichette, Jerry Orbach, Ron and Lynn Carroll, Dorothy Emmerson, Tom Barry, all sitting around playing Dictionary in the Touraine Hotel in Boston. We were some wild show folk.) I love the English language. We can't take it for granted; if we don't go to some pains to protect it, and *use* it, the beautiful tongue of William Shakespeare will languish and die. Ezra Pound got wrought up about the "betrayers" and "perverters" of language. He died over twenty years ago. Boy oh boy, I'll bet he's whirling in his grave by now.

The Bible is great literature—the King James Version. So is the Book of Common Prayer. Why has that language been changed? Why deprive ourselves of its beauty? Why make it more commonplace? Why excise aspects that elevate and beautify? Shouldn't we at least hold on to what has been achieved before us, if we can't—and in this case we can't—improve upon it? Other languages are beautiful also, but if we can't be linguists, we should try to do our best with the one we were born into.

The sixth-grade class in Huntingdon, Tennessee, had a great teacher in Edith Carter Merrick. She and I were third cousins (or second cousins once removed, depending on which way you count kinship), so I had to call her Cousin Edith instead of Miss Edith like everybody else did, which embarrassed me to the ends of time, besides which being kin to her and being fond of her didn't keep me from being as scared of her as everybody else was. She demanded absolute attention and concentration, and she had ways of backing up these demands that worked. She didn't feel like explaining infinitives or objects of the preposition too many times. One listened and learned. If I were named Ruler of All Things, I would put a stop to pouring money into new school buildings and equipment. I would search out great teachers and pay them very high wages and let them teach. Education has to do with pupils and teachers. It has to do with the transfer of ideas and information from one human being to another. Technological aids can be useful somewhere down the line, I'm sure, but the point is that children must learn to think. Government funds cannot confer upon a child the capacity for abstract thinking.

Cousin Edith; Cousin Lucille; Miss Annie Mae Nesbitt; Mr. Leroy Tate, who taught both math and band in high school; Miss Ludie Franklin; Miss Vivian Finch; Miss Audrey Mitchell, who taught Latin; Dr. Adams, my English literature teacher at UT—all were dear and memorable teachers. Dr. Benish at Rhodes College was a great teacher. He began the term by writing the final exam questions on the blackboard and telling us he saw no need to be tricky in this course. These questions represented what he hoped to teach us about nineteenth-century poetry in this semester, and if we could answer them in the final exam, we'd get an A. I don't remember my grade, but I came out loving the poetry.

The best teachers are the most important people in the world. One of them taught my daughters. Her name is Kit Wallace and she taught first grade at the Spence School in New York City and was the head of the lower school. I believe she teaches at St. John's Cathedral now. When I think of Miss Wallace, I want to sit down and cry with gratitude. I remember how "tough" she was, how fast the downy little chicks under her care became disciplined and interested and focused. They were reading a mile a minute. In the first grade they learned basic algebra. They learned geometric concepts. They were pleased with themselves and eager to learn more. I loved to see her lining them up to march in for school assembly. No nonsense, no gushy gush. Her love for her students was of a higher kind. She was helping them get ready for the rest of their life. There were other wonderful teachers at Spence: Miss Roberts, Miss Dobson, Mrs. Lehman, Mrs. Williams— great teachers in a great school. Kit Wallace made her mark on me. When one day I go back to live in Tennessee, I'll pursue another dream, stumping the countryside to plead for a less expensive and more effective way to educate our children.

(Children now are often encouraged, with the best of intentions, in ways that are to their disadvantage. I wince when I hear parents talking about young children "making their own decisions." What a foolish propped-up idea to put into a little head. Little people can't make decisions until they know something. Young children should be doing what they are told to do, obeying their parents, and behaving themselves. They should be listening to their parents, getting information, talking with their parents, and learning to converse. Ideas should be opened to them—ideas and games and playful states of mind. Children between the ages of two and eleven are learning something every instant, whether information, agenda, attitude, or imperative. William J. Bennett's gratefully received *Book of Virtues* is a most welcome compendium of ideal material for young noggins—older noggins too. At the ground base of any knowledge that will be of any value whatsoever there has to be a sense of modesty and humility. Teaching arrogance is awful. I feel so sorry for children whose parents encourage smart mouthing; nobody's ever happy to see them coming.)

Back to language. The language we use and hear drastically affects the aesthetic of our environment. I believe that we should speak as nicely as we know how, and thus by example encourage young people in the same direction. Slang and buzzwords are going to be around and in use, but we don't have to speak only in slang. And I vote for thinking a moment before we reel off the latest overworked "in" word by rote. It's easy to grab, but does it really express what we mean to say? Here in no particular order are some words and phrases I wouldn't mind not hearing for a while.

Like. I think it started in California, and now it's everywhere. It devolved from, "She's, like, really nice" to "He was like 'Do you want to see a movie?' and she was like 'Which movie?' " Since it's all gotten very tiresome, and since the blight has spread from California teens to everybody all over the place, we can only hope it wears itself out before it wears us out and we accept it as, like, okay.

No problem. Many very sweet people use this expression and mean the best by it; however, it's not saying what they think it is. When I say "Thank you," I appreciate hearing "You're welcome" in return. What "No problem" seems to say, unfortunately, is "I did not go out of my way for you." The speaker thus denies having made an effort to be helpful. Unless I've asked specifically about how much trouble something was, turning away an honest "Thank you" with "No problem" just isn't very gracious, and it reduces the good of whatever it was I was trying to express gratitude for.

Validate, validation. Mercy, please. Can't we all just do our best and not have to have "validation" for being alive, for pity's sake? How unfortunate that the same word used to describe stamping a parking garage ticket is used constantly these days in connection with one's individual worth.

Respect. Pronounced "respact" in California, and used mostly in California, by scantily clad young women in television programs who play characters demanding it without regard for their own behavior.

Issue. Let's return to using this word in reference to a magazine or newspaper, or to currency, or in reference to a real point of dispute. It would be a relief to hear people in the public eye describe their ideas, interests, and beliefs without using this word to death. It would be nice to hear newscasters use the word *subject* instead when that is what they mean.

Hopefully. Ten or twelve years ago my friend Benay Venuta took me, Gigi, and Mary Dixie over to meet Mr. and Mrs. Danny Kaye. Mr. Kaye wasn't well and went upstairs after a quick hello. We sat down with the missus. Sylvia Kaye didn't waste too much time on idle chitchat. She rang for some white wine and launched right into what was uppermost in her mind, the abuse of the English language. She hit *hopefully* first, and hard. I don't think any of us had used it; she just pulled it out of the air. *Hopefully*, she warned me with blazing eyes, is an adverb that must never, never, never be used in the way we so often hear, "Hopefully she will feel better tomorrow." Now Mrs. Kaye's voice rose to an angry pitch. "That does not make any sense at all! It can only be 'I hope she will feel better.' She's not going to *feel* hopefully, is she? No! *Hopefully* does not describe how she is going to feel! She can smile hopefully and hope to feel better; she can look hopefully at her doctor and hope for the best. *She cannot hopefully feel better!*" I don't know whether she was sure when she started that I was one of the villainous people guilty of perpetrating this onerous wrong. I do know that by the time she finished her tirade, she knew she'd found her mark. Benay and my daughters made a good show of innocence; my shamefaced blush gave me away. She had a few more heinous grammatical sins to discuss. When she had discharged her duty, she seemed relieved; her spirits lifted and she insisted, I mean *insisted*—and who among us was going to say a word against it?—that we stay for a bite to eat. She led us past her splendiferous formal dining room into her special Chinese dining room, which was only for eating Chinese food in, and had her Chinese cook prepare us a few simple thousand-year-old dishes. A big hooray for Hollywood on that evening. Since that meeting with Mrs. Kaye, I've tried ever so hard not to misuse *hopefully*. Hopefully I haven't. (I'm so sorry, Mrs. Kaye, God rest your soul. The Devil made me say it.)

Parenting. It's in the dictionary now. Too bad. They've made it a legitimate word, such a functional way to describe raising a child. It sounds bloodless and technical to me, but hey! Looks like it's here, and we're going to be hearing it lots more.

Prioritize. Impact. Both are verbs that should have remained nouns, made-up words that got themselves into the dictionary when half the 450,000 words in the English language have become almost obsolete. We know why they're becoming obsolete too, don't we? Because we don't have time to learn them and use them; we're too busy making up these great new words.

Empower. We ought to be careful how we hold this word out as representing something desperately important to do or to be. Yes, it's good to feel strong and reasonably sure that we're up to the task we're tackling. I'm just nervous about throwing that dangerous word *power* into the hopper constantly. Power is one thing none of us should be trying to grab. Remember "Power corrupts. Absolute power corrupts absolutely"? *Power* and *strength* are synonymous, so why not use *strength? Power* has another meaning that has to do with controlling not only ourselves but other people, and that's really not a good ambition. Plus power does not make people happy. It just makes them crazy for more power.

Entitled. Entitle is listed in the dictionary as a verb that means "to give a name to," as to entitle a book, or "to give a claim or a right to a person." The word is so greedily and wrongly overused today that it would be a joke except that it's not funny. We are all entitled to a chance, maybe. Then, on the other hand, maybe we're just lucky if we get one. Maybe instead of being so quick to yell about what we're entitled to, we should first bow our heads and think about what we have to be grateful for. Maybe a shot of humility and hard work will improve our picture more readily than dwelling on our "entitlements."

Love. This word is so overused and ill-used that it doesn't mean anything anymore. I'm going to talk about it in the next chapter.

Passion. This is a very strong word, one of the strongest to denote intense emotion, yes? Well, businesspeople have gotten hold of it, and now lots of people are using it to describe keen interest in a business deal or whatever, and it's a little embarrassing. Not as embarrassing as a good number of other words businesspeople may be heard to use, but enough to put on my list. There are always words coming along that get invented by business hotshots, usually by changing the part of speech; a new verb has appeared from an old noun: books that are best-sellers now "best-sell." Cute.

Have sex. This expression sounds pretty grim to me—drab, clinical, biolab-ish, test-tube-ish, analyzed, researched, not at all private. It's been a long time since I've heard anybody say "make love."

Anyways. There is no *s* on the word; it's *anyway.*

With regards to. In regards to. Here again there is no *s*. It's *with regard to.* No *s* when you make reference to or hold in esteem. The *s* comes into its own when you want to give your regards to Broadway.

With he and I. With Hal and I. Here's one where Sylvia Kaye did not catch me napping. I was just as appalled as she. Come to think of it, this could be the one that got us into the Chinese dining room. Personal pronouns used as the object of the preposition should be objective, to wit: "He gave it to Hal and *me.*" "He gave it to Hal and I" is awful and you hear it all the time, from well-educated people. Take away the first name and you'll see how wrong it is: "He gave it to I." Would you ever say that? So don't say, "He gave it *to* Hal and I," or "He went *with* Hal and I," or "He called *on* Hal and I," or "This is *for* Hal and I," or "It's a gift *from* Hal and I," or "They sat *behind* Hal and I," or "You go *before* Hal and I," or "It flew *above* Hal and I," or "It buzzed *around* Hal and I," or "That's enough *about* Hal and I," and I'm sure it is. The same goes for "He" and it should be "Hal went with *him* and *me,*" not "Hal went with he and I." One would never say "Hal went with I." No more than one would say, "Hal pinched I," which I'm quite sure Hal would feel like doing if I talked that way. I have to wear a tooth guard at night to keep from grinding my teeth because of listening to this day after day. If I didn't have to work for a living, I'd go around preaching just this one thing until it stopped.

Sit. There are many instances which call for *set* instead of *sit,* but there seems to be some fear that *set* doesn't sound nice enough, so *sit* gets used incorrectly. For example, one sets an inanimate object, like a teapot, on the table. It can sit there afterward, but it has been set down. A person or a dog sits.

Commit. Committed. Mercy me. This poor word is anemic, it is so worn down. We have to be committed to everything from our face cleansing routine to private time with the dog. I just hope I won't be committed to an institution for committing a crime against someone talking about commitment.

I hear you. This is what people have figured out to say so that they won't have to say, "It will be taken care of immediately," or "You're quite right. The management apologizes," or "I agree" or "I disagree." It was invented by people who are tired of commitment. This is a dismissal in disguise.

You got it. This is what people have figured out to say who want to get rid of you quickly, and at the same time give you just a little more than "I hear you" offers. This is another dismissal in disguise.

Aks. In New York City this mispronunciation of *ask* seems to be in full flower. I have performed a John Wallowitch song, "I'm aksing you," at the Café Carlyle that poses this question: "Could you love me too, as I love you? I'm *aksing* you. Tell me!" The difficulties that are being experienced with this one-syllable word make mentioning *asteriks (asterisk)* seem pointless.

Supposably. Undoubtably. Yes, I have heard people say these words instead of *supposedly* and *undoubtedly.*

I just have to add a couple of uncommon cases of word mangling that I cannot stand to let go unobserved and unnoted.

Ordherbs. Wendy Merson knows people who say this instead of *hors d'oeuvres.* I guess her friends are thinking healthy. Wendy herself confessed to me that since childhood she had thought the Yiddish expression *abi gezunt,* as in "wealth, schmelth, *abi gezunt*" (translated, "wealth, schmelth, so long as you have your health") was "a big gezunt," and until recently was using it like this: 'Yoga, schmoga, a *big gezunt!*" I happen to like the idea of a big gezunt a lot, and have taken up using it where Wendy left off. Worry, schmurry, a Big Gezunt! Thank you Wendy.

For all intensive purposes. I saved the best for last. My daughters have heard, on the Harvard campus, the phrase *for all intents and purposes* turned into *for all intensive purposes.* Seriously. Would I prevaricate with you, Dear Reader? That's as far off, but not as cute, as the little boy who came home from Sunday School and told his mother he loved the new song they sang today about the bear, "Gladly, the Cross-Eyed Bear."

Show business as a career, for all its exciting moments here and there, does not necessarily engender food for the soul. (I do wish sometimes that we weren't treated to so much hypocritical bad-mouthing of businesspeople, people who work in corporations, and of the corporations themselves, from show business people, the people in the business of show, in which arena there are plenty of self-satisfied poseurs and unprincipled dealers, like everywhere else. "Let him who is without sin cast the first stone.") I'm talking about television. I don't know what it's like to do movies. This is less true in the theatre, where, depending upon the play, rich and beautiful experience may be encountered. My husband has, in the last few years, performed the roles of King Lear, Shylock in *The Merchant of Venice*, Vanya in *Uncle Vanya*, and Willie Loman in *Death of a Salesman*. He has done new plays with the Seattle Repertory Company and at the summer festival in Williamstown, Massachusetts. *King Lear* had three productions, in Cleveland, New York, and San Diego. Next winter he will tour *Death of a Salesman* across the country and hope to go into New York. (Hal performs his famous *Mark Twain Tonight* between twelve and eighteen times a year, depending on what else is going on.) He does the plays to push himself physically and intellectually and to grow. He does them at significant financial cost; he has to make the money ahead of time to be able to go off and earn very little for several months. But he does it with a glad heart.

For these opportunities Hal is grateful to the National Endowment for the Arts, as these productions are supported in substantial part by it. Of course the public is confused about the National Endowment for the Arts go-around, and I'm confused as well. The idea is to support worthy artistic endeavor that might not be commercial enough to support itself; isn't that it? Isn't the point that it's been decided to allot a certain amount of my money and yours, that has been taken away from us in taxes, to the financing of classical revivals as well as promising art and artists? And when we're given to understand that no judgments can be made on what's worthy and what's not, that we shouldn't have any say in that part of it, it's bound to make us feel funny. So those of us who are grateful for the fine work made possible by the NEA, but who really don't want to support obscenity, whether it's called art or not, are still likely to get one of those bad-sounding labels if we raise a hue and cry. I'm in the arts, and I believe in government subsidy of the arts, but I'm really mad that any of my money has gone to the Mapplethorpe exhibit. If Mr. M. just had to do it, I'd rather he'd put that show on without my help.

How do we resolve this problem? Surely the artistic community could put various of its sagest heads together and figure out a way to monitor some of this stuff so that we don't get the tap shut off entirely, which in my opinion the public has justification in demanding, if they don't like what they're paying for. The people who pay taxes are supposed to have some say in this, aren't they? I don't feel that I have lately, and apparently a lot of folks feel the same.

It's discouraging to go to the movies or the theatre these days hoping for an experience that will exalt and lift. Once in a while a movie like *A Room with a View* or *Forrest Gump* comes along, but all too rarely. Blood and sex are the theme, not ancillary elements, of the movies getting made now. Beautiful or worthy ideas are all too rarely put forward by the entertainment industry. Intelligence as an ingredient seems to be avoided. I cannot understand the broad definition of what constitutes art at this time. I cannot agree with what seems to be a lowering of standards by critics as well as creators of entertainment. When I read high praise for a motion picture that is pointlessly vulgar and boring as well, I can't make out what to think. When I read a great review of a play, go to see it, and find it offensive or tiresome, I don't get it. When I read interviews with people putting on television shows who sound as if they're dealing with Schopenhauer, Spinoza, Ibsen, Shaw, and Marcus Aurelius, as if their show is going to be very fine, philosophically perceptive, morally challenging, or even actually about something, and then watch the shows and find nothing clever, entertaining, or even bearable, when there is absolutely no semblance of what I've read about in what I've seen, I don't get it. We keep right on paying for self-congratulatory vapidity and dishonest trash. We are looking at the emperor's new clothes. And we don't summon up the fortitude to admit it. Are my husband and I the only people in America who really would appreciate less dramatizing of the lower functions and more of the brain and the heart? I don't imagine that we are. Hal's children Victoria and David, whose mother is the actress Ruby Holbrook—brilliant intellectuals, independent thinkers, the farthest thing from stick-in-the-mud mentalities, Victoria an internationally recognized scholar, writer, translator, and teacher of Turkish subjects, and David about to finish medical school—agree with us in this matter, and it heartens me to be encouraged that my opinion of this stuff doesn't consign me to the ranks of the old fuddy-duddies. When David recommends a movie, I know I won't feel betrayed twenty minutes into it, as often happens. We weren't put on earth to slog around in the mire for a while and finally expire with our faces in it. We're supposed to be on the lookout for beauty and truth. Truly interesting entertainment has to be elevating and, in its way, beautiful. When Noel Coward wrote the elegantly self-deprecating line in *Private Lives*, "Extraordinary how potent cheap music is," he was being funny. He never would have dreamed how cheap "cheap" could get.

The level of language in entertainment has gotten sick. Even dear old *60 Minutes* let a few four-letter words go unbleeped not long ago. Seven o'clock on a Sunday evening. Why? We seem to have gotten used to it and accepted it as "reality." Well, it ain't my reality, baby. After we agree that it's plain bad manners, let's acknowledge that the constant use of obscenity indicates either hostility or stupidity or a combination of the two. The only reason anyone with more than a room temperature IQ uses it is to attack. Cursing used to be recognized as an attack mode; people used to take offense and get in a fight if someone cursed in their face; now it's supposed to sneak by as funny. Well, it doesn't sound a bit friendlier to me from stand-up comics just because the audience they're abusing is dumb enough to sit there and laugh. Maya Angelou, in her collection of little essays, *Wouldn't Take Nothing for My Journey Now*, writes in the one called "What's So Funny," "When we as audience indulge them in that profanity . . . we not only participate in the humiliation of the entertainers, but are brought low by sharing in the obscenity." I don't enjoy being around it. Cursing is always angry, always an attack, even when the speaker doesn't seem to be aware of it. It's not pleasant to feel that one is receiving invisible little slaps that can't be warded off or answered. I don't spend a lot of time anymore with people who use foul language, no matter how much I like them and how much fun they are.

There is a very old saying, "Speech is a mirror of the soul. As a man speaketh, so is he." Hearing high-minded ecologists and lovers of every single plant and being use polluted language to put forward their ideals, one notices a dichotomy; the dirty language is just another poison in the atmosphere.

There's many a wonderful person who has felt compelled to resort to strong language in extremis. My husband reminds me sometimes of Mark Twain's famous apology, "In certain trying circumstances, urgent circumstances, desperate circumstances, profanity furnishes a relief denied even to prayer." And a Tennessee gentleman named Carl Orr, who could be counted on to rise to an occasion with a meaty insight dramatically presented, backed Mr. Twain up out in front of our store one Saturday afternoon, with appropriate gestures, 'I *tell* you, gentlemen, there comes a time in *every* man's life when he's just got to *cuss* a little!" (Maybe Mr. Orr was thinking back to the time when he had finally gotten back alive from the war in Europe, and they told him in Huntingdon that Beaver Creek was too swollen for him to get across and get home. At that time he had said, gesticulating violently, *"Hell fire!* Do you think a man who has just made it back *across the Atlantic Ocean* is going to be kept away from home by a little thing like *Beaver Creek?"*) If indeed Carl Orr and Mark Twain both had a point, which I guess they did, my point is that not all that long ago strong language was shocking or at least noticeable.

One of the Ten Commandments requires that we not take God's name "in vain," but eight-year-old children now say "oh my God" like we used to say "gee whiz." We're inured to it. "Jesus Christ," a most profane expression to a person of the Christian faith, has become a repetitive and unremarkable punctuation used in all movie scripts, and by everybody all over the place. The name is used as an expletive, which means it's recognized as profane, and yet nobody seems to care anymore. It's all very casual. It would seem to me that a friendly or well-meaning person would not use an expression that boldly insulted his or another's religion. Four-letter words that were not used in the presence of a lady when I was growing up are now used in the presence of and often by the "lady," and let me tell you, it's not making anyone more attractive. It's not improving the atmosphere. Aristophanes said that high thought had to have high language. Shakespeare proved that it doesn't take long words to create high language. None of us can put together words like Willie the Shake, but we can appreciate those who make words mean something fine, who can make the language sing.

Many of us are parents of young people for whom we would literally die if it came down to it, yet we passively submit to the infestation of their atmosphere. Why do we give our children money to buy tickets to see movies and plays demonstrating behavior we would be sickened to see in them? Why inure them to it? There's something terribly wrong when my daughters are unperturbed by scenes that are so offensive I am ashamed to watch them. I am very sure that the aggregate amount of movie and television footage they have been subjected to in their lifetimes has done harm to them; the question is what harm and how much. The other question is what a person can do about it.

Television sets have become essential machines. People put them in every room, even in their bathrooms. It's so pathetic that we've all become willing slaves to the TV, especially since much of the fare ranges from bad to stultifying. And why do we the people (they say we do) applaud producers who are always talking about "pushing the boundaries"? What boundaries? The boundaries of good taste perhaps; certainly it couldn't be boundaries of light and understanding. Furthermore, even if every broadcast moment were something very fine, television should not be watched hours and hours a day. It numbs the brain. It destroys conversation. It deprives children of an atmosphere in which they can learn how to converse. It preempts family dinners. It isolates.

Some people even put TV sets in their children's rooms, "so they can watch what they want to." Oh please, get the televisions out of your children's rooms, if you love them at all. If the machine doesn't actually hurt their health directly, it will indirectly, because they'll be missing out on healthy exercise while they're in front of it. We are seeing an alarming increase of obesity in youngsters, and television viewing's having replaced active play is the reason. My sister dealt with the problem by simply refusing to have a TV in her home, and even so, she says, it's the strangest thing how her children have always known all about what was on it anyway, as if they absorbed it by osmosis.

Television for education makes sense only if there is serious deprivation in the home, that is to say, if the child's parents are illiterate or absent. If there's anybody at home who can read to and talk to the child, that's so much better than *Sesame*

Street that there is no comparison. The happiest and most successful learning takes place from one human being to another. There's more. Television makes children lonely. It's an artificial and false friend to the children who grow to depend on it, and they all do, if left to watch it as much as they want to. When the television is finally turned off, what is the child left with? Nothing. Nothing and nobody. All gone. What a letdown. Television is a companion that doesn't really exist. It's deadly. Children can't be expected to know what's good for them. The adults are supposed to. Please figure out how much time you believe you should allow your child to watch TV, make sure you know and approve of the programs, and do not bend your rules. You and your child will be glad in ten years.

At the very least families should watch television together. Parents should know just what kinds of influences their children are receiving via the tube. Most parents have no idea, I'm afraid, or they don't want to deal with it. I have developed a real aversion to smart-alecky children's characters on television shows, and almost all are written that way. Why should any of us be surprised so often to encounter rude children when that's the example put before them? I'll bet my hat that the parent chuckling at a crude sitcom joke would be appalled if his or her child turned around during the commercial break and came out with the same line. I must admit that at this point with my girls, when they turn on certain programs, I just go upstairs and read, because they're too old now for me to tell them what they can't watch. I did my best during their growing-up years, and now it's out of my control.

About fifteen years ago my daughters gave me a wonderful take on television. They were allowed to watch for one hour on school days and two hours on Fridays and Saturdays, unless there was something special. (I felt that was too much, but they were such conscientious students and straight A makers, and so hard to say no to about anything, that by the time they were nine and ten, they did get to watch that much.) One Saturday afternoon late I was sitting with them at the end of

Now, Voyager, and after we'd finished sopping ourselves up with Kleenexes, I idly inquired why with their limited viewing time their choice usually turned out to be, I had noticed, something that was in black and white. I asked them how come at their ages they didn't pick new shows that were in color. This was the answer:

"Well, Mama, the shows that are in color are mostly just about transportation. People are just getting into cars and driving away, or getting on motorcycles and driving away, or boats or airplanes, just transportation. But when you are watching Bette Davis, you know something is going to *happen*."

I make most of my living working in television, and I don't mean to bite the hand that feeds me. It's now the most powerful influence in the world. It has the potential to do remarkable things. It is a great resource for people who are confined at home or in the hospital. It is terrific for sports fans. It can allow us to share the thoughts of the world's brightest people. It can allow us to witness events as they take place anywhere in the world. It can bring us the understanding and wisdom of centuries past. It can bring us an understanding of people far away and different from ourselves. It can, *if* we ask such programming of television producers and networks. It can, *if* we require it to move to another plane, just a bit above this one.

Bertram Ross, the great modern dancer who partnered Martha Graham and choreographed with her for twenty-five years, has always lived on this plane. My favorite way to see any kind of performance is with Bertram, for afterward he is able to remember the entire thing—lines, lights, costumes, sets, and characterizations—in minute detail and to talk about it in depth. He loves the theatre and is discouraged and angry with mediocrity or worse but always eager to go and see again. His observations are like he is, perceptive, witty, and clear-eyed. You can't fool Bertram, not on stage and not in life. His is a compassionate nature, but his compassion does not extend to the degradation of the theatre's sacred ground. It broke his heart and came close to wrecking his career when he smelled corruption in the Graham company in the early seventies and resigned. I think Vera Maxwell was credited with saying about Bertram that it was a case of the ship leaving the sinking rat. The action was an almost suicidal one in the world of modern dance, but my great friend could not accept contamination in his artistic family, any more than he could have in his art, because Bertram and his art are one and the same thing. At awful personal and professional cost he made his decision. Bertram is that rare animal, an artist. I am shy about using the word. I certainly would never presume to apply it to myself. Bertram represents the word *artist* to its finest power.

Good manners are "happy ways of doing things," so Ralph Waldo Emerson, with whom I share my birthdate, excepting the year, said. (He also said, "By necessity, by proclivity, and by delight, we all quote.") When we're talking about adding beauty to the life around us, we might do well to begin with good manners. Treating people with whom we come in contact deferentially and pleasantly and even kindly is not hard to do, is in fact quite enjoyable once we get used to it, and makes a humongous difference in our little spot in the universe. That's the easiest kind of good manners, the being respectful of others part, the "good morning" to a fellow passenger on the elevator, the "excuse me" to the person you walk in front of getting on the airplane. John David and Mary, and Roselyn Espey, who worked in the store with Daddy all those years, still speak about Mr. Johnson, a well-to-do farmer who was one of our favorite customers, and his enjoyable way of winding up a purchase, "Thank you, thank you, thank you, and much obliged besides!" We use Mr. Johnson's thank-you with each other all the time, and we appreciate it.

Then there's the good manners that require knowing how to behave in certain situations, which we used to call etiquette. Realizing that not much emphasis is placed on that area anymore, I'd still like to make a case for it. There's a lot to be said for performing ordinary acts with a certain grace and style. Why not? Why shovel food into our mouths like animals when we can eat without turning the stomach of the person across the table from us and even, with our pleasant conversation and good table manners, increase his enjoyment of his meal?

We could return to teaching children lovely manners, starting very young, as a gift to the child, so that he will be welcomed out in the world, a pleasant person to be around. It's time-consuming and a bit of trouble, so the parent has to be prepared to make it a priority; otherwise one lets this and that slide, and time flies, until one day you notice that Junior, who is now fourteen years old, is holding his fork and knife as if they were ski poles, which he may be more adept with than his eating utensils, because somebody actually taught him how to ski.

I like it when a person of the male persuasion stands up as I come into the room, holds my chair and opens the door for me, and carries my heavy suitcase to the car. It's nice being called Mrs. Holbrook or Miss Dixie by my daughters' friends, and it's nice when they wait for me to sit down before they sit down.

I like to hear a proper introduction. I do not like "This is my mother." It's sloppy and it's not respectful and it makes me angry. I like "Mama, I'd like you to meet Joel Kaplan" or "Mama, I'd like to present Joel Kaplan. Joel, this is my mother, Mrs. Holbrook." There's really no need to say the last part; if Joel has any sense at all (and he has plenty), he'll figure that out from hearing me called Mama. It's safer to say it though, to guard against his coming back with "Hi, Dixie." This introduction respects my being the senior and the female, by telling me first who the other person is. The younger person is being presented to me.

Introductions now are usually a mess, and that's if anybody even bothers to try. Here's the way it's supposed to go:

The person who gets told who everybody else is, is the oldest or the most revered member of the group, as, say, my father would be if he were present. If he's not present, I would come next as the senior female and lady of the house. If the new person is a lady about my age and a guest in our home, she takes precedence. If I am not present, Hal Holbrook is next. If everyone is of the same generation, the ladies get to be told the other people's names before the men. As I said, if there is an older generation or a person of high office, like a governor, that person gets to be it. All you have to do is look around and figure it out. Call out the person's name you want to be most respectful to, and then tell him or her who everybody else is. And please use last names also. First-name-only introductions are the true pits and a plague on any house. I resort to them only when I don't know who's who, and it's a dead giveaway.

If there are short clues about people that you can include along with their names, do so quickly, to save whoever they are from that awful conversation opener, "What do you do?" At least if everybody has heard "This is Stephen Kempf, just here from Hong Kong," maybe somebody will jump in and break the ice with "Hi, Stephen. How is it in Hong Kong?" before they get around to the inevitable question. The implication of the what-do-you-do query to certain people can only be "Do you have any money and if so, how much?" I once heard my living room go dead as a doornail when a guest answered the livelihood question with "Nothing. I live off my mother." We should not ask that question. It is bad manners. If somebody wants to talk about his job, he'll get around to it. If he's not in the same earnings bracket as the rest of the room, of if he just got fired, he might appreciate not being put on the spot.

Donald Charles Richardson, the writer, whom I have known a longer time than I care to add up, finds it annoying that people often comment on his being mannerly and polite, and Donny's got a point. Ideally, good manners would be taken for granted, not subject to undue notice, and would be built into the daily experience of children along with brushing their teeth and saying their prayers. Sometimes my mother had someone to help her and sometimes not. It didn't change the program at home one bit. Every day my sister and I were bathed after our naps in the afternoon, given a glass of freshly squeezed orange juice, and put into clean starched dresses and freshly polished shoes. Every day three hot meals were put on the table and we all sat down together to eat. The meals were served nicely and we all behaved nicely or got sent away from the table. I don't remember that any of the three of us ever had to go without a meal, but we might have had to take out our plate and sit away in another room, the punishment being not getting to enjoy the company of the rest of the family. The family meal was ceremonial; there was no being late for it. More than one spanking was settled on my behind for lingering up in Martha Jean and Charlotte Mitchell's bedroom next door, looking at their comic books and forgetting mealtime. Another spanking could come for being at anyone else's home when they were having their meal. Interrupting any family at their table was a cardinal offense; the only thing worse was actually accepting the obligatory invitation to sit down and have a little bite with them. It was a perfectly wonderful rule, and when someone lingers in my home at mealtime, I wish that more people had learned it in as strict a fashion as I did.

Although nice manners can be taught, and improved, and defined and redefined, the truly polite and well-mannered person need not have had the benefit of a polished upbringing or any particularly effete training. I am fortunate to have crossed paths with individuals who, without a background of fancy schooling in etiquette, possess the heart of gentility in their honest desire to behave decently and thoughtfully toward others. That will do it every time.

There are gentle people everywhere. I'm going to quit complaining about the rude ones. We have good friends, true and well intentioned. And fun, for Pete's sake. Good form can't be oppressive; it wouldn't be good form.

. . .

There are the joys of a comfortable house loved and fussed over and made into a beautiful home; there are the joys of hard work and a successful outcome; there are the delights of warm baths and early morning coffee and a crackling fire when it's cold and stormy; there are the luxuries of delicious food with happy conversation and good books to read into the night; for the rich there are silks and satins and fine champagne and trips to Europe and Rolls-Royce cars and downy pillows and diamond rings. There are all the fantastic and desirable places to be and things to own in all the picture books and magazines in all the world. There are all the things that money can buy. And then there is music.

Music. Our direct connection to the divine. Mozart, Bach, Beethoven, and Handel. Schubert, Chopin, Puccini, Debussy, Ravel, Saint-Saëns. Gershwin, Porter, Berlin, Kern. Wallowitch. Of the countless ways that one can cultivate the garden of life, none could be more felicitous than living close to music. I can't imagine getting through without it.

I have always liked all kinds of music—classical, rock, folk, and lately country. I'm a big fan of Bob Dylan, and of course we all loved Elvis, and the Beatles. Rock music is fun at parties, when a person can dance to it. The new rock sound I don't get. Today most of what is playing if I turn on the car radio will make me feel anxious and grumpy in short order. Since I was a child, the strains that make life better and more beautiful for me have been the complex mathematical arrangement of notes that we call classical music. Its effects sometimes thrilling and exalting, sometimes calming and healing, and always restorative. This great beauty I find in the works of classical composers and sometimes, but less frequently, in modern popular composers.

I've read that alternative healing research is turning up remarkable results with music, especially in treating Parkinson's disease, Alzheimer's, dyslexia, and depression. There has been success in using music to reduce the anxiety and vomiting experienced by cancer patients after chemotherapy. Interestingly, neither rock nor pop nor even "new age" music works.

Classical music, which apparently comes closest to the "harmony of the spheres," has the most profound influence. An article by Richard Leviton describes one patient's "ineffable experience of light" in a guided session while listening to Wagner's *Lohengrin*.

The summer that I was two years old I had been taken next door in May to stay with Mama and Papa, because my mother's heart was acting bad and she was put to bed, flat on her back, not to move. Grandmother Hillsman was looking after Gina, as well as Midge, who had been born in January, and Hal, who was seven, and Daddy too. Daddy called and asked his younger sister Melba to come home and help Mama take care of me.

Melba came from Atlanta, where she had been a piano student at the Atlanta Conservatory. The conservatory had tragically burned, but not before she met Winfield Scott Morrison and fell endlessly in love. By this time she and Winfield were married. She was twenty-four years old, hadn't yet had children, and was very spirited. She did not want any of us to call her Aunt Melba. I called her Bebba. Mama was the only person I'd let bathe me or feed me or put me to bed, but I did allow Bebba to take care of me a great deal of the time. I was restive at this strange turn of events, with having been removed from my house to Mama's while both my big brother and my baby sister (whom I called "Doll" at first) remained ensconced in our house. Much as I loved Mama and Papa, I felt exiled because I didn't understand why I was there. I guess I must have thought I'd done something wrong. Maybe I thought it was my fault Gina was so sick. I don't know, and it doesn't matter after the fact, because that summer Bebba, always happiest at the piano and knowing no better way to keep us both amused, taught me to sing. Even out of temper, I had to notice that she was fun. She looked like a redheaded Barbara Stanwyck, with beautiful white teeth and a wild reckless laugh. Daddy says that laugh made many a boy nervous. (Not Winfield, who married her when she was nineteen and has relished her sauciness ever since.)

She had that laugh, she was tantalizing, and she had some very fascinating things in her room when I could get in there and peek around. Especially alluring were the shiny and exotic articles on the white lace doily on her dresser. I watched enthralled when she applied them here and there. She had mirror, brush and comb, hairpins, perfume and powder, lipstick and fingernail polish. I had seen only lipstick and hairbrush on my mother's dressing table. Melba and Mama told me not to fool around at that dresser, but it drew me like a magnet. I remember the day when I seized my chance and stole in to do a bit of fixing up of my own. Turned out it wasn't nearly as easy to manage those magic bottles and things as it had looked to be. Melba could get to them better, for one thing; with my nose just clearing the dresser, reaching my elbows up and over proved tiresome. The tops were very hard to get off and impossible, actually, to get back on, and when a person tried to, the bottles turned over. The powder was just a mess, and the red fingernail polish didn't glide nicely on the fingernail for me like it did for Melba. It spread out over lots more than my fingernail, and the little stick dripped all over the lace doily and my hands and dress and everything. After a while I realized that things had taken a raw turn and I had best absent myself from the scene of the crime. When Melba discovered the mess, she rushed furiously to tell Mama and demand punishment, but she lost her steam on the way and got tickled. Being her mother's daughter, she was always inclined to get tickled instead of mad. I didn't get spanked. Even in exile and out of sorts as I was, I had to love her. So when she wanted me to learn a song, I liked it. I liked her paying attention to me and wanting to play with me, so long as she didn't want to boss me around, and she showed absolutely no interest in doing that.

The trick was in getting me to be still enough to learn the words, as I was a very "doey" (Mama's word for me) child, so she arrived at setting me on the staircase and blocking my way down until I had assimilated that afternoon's verse. Our very first number was "Put on the skillet, put on the lead, Mammy's gonna make a little shortnin' bread." She'd sing the line through and wait for me to finish with the last word, "b'ed." As soon as I caught on to the game and would sing all the words with her, she'd set me up on the piano bench beside her and play while I sang. Believe me, getting to sing while Melba played would have been incentive for anyone, two years old or not. (I have a dream that Melba and I will make a music video together. Other dreams have come true; why not this one?) Then we'd learn another. "Give me one dos-sen ros-sess" I remember, and "She'll be comin' round the mountain."

There were two great wonders about that summer with Melba. One was learning music from an unusual musician who by kismet happened to be my aunt; Melba just had it and has it still, at the piano or away from it.

The other wonder was this: every day after my nap Mama would put a clean sundress on me and I would get to go down the front walk over to my house and see my mother. I remember going into the room and standing by her bed and looking up at her, lying there still and pale. She would become cheerful and smiling when she saw me, and she would ask me this question and that, and somebody would hold me up to kiss her. The glorious new thing that happened was that after Melba got hold of me, I was able to sing to her. I could make my mother feel better. Gina said that I would lean against the arm of the rocking chair and cross one leg over the other, then deliver up the song for the day. "She'll be comin' round the mountain when she comes. She'll be drivin' six white horses when she comes. We will all go out to meet her when she comes." She loved it and I loved it. Gina wasn't musical herself, but she always dreamed of learning to play the piano. She was drawn to music, although she was very shy of trying to sing, even in church along with everyone else. She sang lullabies to her children, quietly and privately; that was all. I thought my songs were doctoring her up, and I'm sure that in their way they were. In any case that summer's experience obviously intensified what was a natural-born love of music and to it added a deep emotional connection. Melba had given me music to give to my mother, to make her smile, to make her well.

At two years of age I had never heard of Kahlil Gibran or that he had written, "The song that lies silent in the heart of the mother sings upon the lips of the child." But even then I understood that when I was singing, we were both singing, my mother and I.

The next year Melba was home for six months while Winfield was in basic training in Biloxi, Mississippi, and we took up where we left off. Now we were cooking with gas: "Cuhdle up-a lit-tle clo-ser, lovee mine." I think we had been working on "Put your arms around me honey, hoold me tight. Huddle up and cuddle up with aall your might" when Mama told Melba that after supper Papa had asked, "Why on *earth* is Melba teaching that baby those *awful* songs?"

These days when she and Winfield come for a visit, late and soon, with Scottie and Kay, and Christie, and in recent years with grandchildren, but usually just the two of them, we get to the piano and go through our repertoire of old favorites, church songs, and hymns. Daddy sings a while ("You Must Have Been a Beautiful Baby," "Always," "Ain't She Sweet," "How Deep Is the Ocean"), and I sing a while ("When Day Is Done," "Hello Dolly"), and we all sing a while ("The Church in the Wildwood," "In the Garden," "Whispering Hope"). Every song is redolent of years of being together and being apart and coming together again, and the other voices that we still hear singing with us.

Shelley said, "Music, when soft voices die, vibrates in the memory."

Hal (brother Hal) never wanted to have piano lessons after his early ones with Mama Carter, but Midge and I did. Gina took us to Huntingdon, starting when Midge was five and I was six and a half, for lessons with Miss Nettie Dilday. Her husband, Mr. Robert, owned and ran the Dilday Funeral Home. Usually we had lessons at their house, where we were allowed to jump up and run to the window when a train passed by, and where Miss Nettie almost always had treats for us, the best being her unbelievably good tuna fish salad, which she made with eggs and chopped dill pickles and pickle juice. While one of us was having her lesson, the other got to play with Diane, the youngest of the four Dilday children and the one our age. Bobby was the oldest, then Betty—Hal's age—then Barbara, then Diane.

Sometimes if there was a funeral that Miss Nettie had to play for, we had our lesson at the funeral home. We enjoyed that too, even the unusual smell, which we didn't associate with anything somber. We played hopscotch out around the ramp the hearses drove up. It wasn't quite as much fun, though, because you couldn't see the trains go by and there wasn't much to eat.

Miss Nettie was blond, blue-eyed, and buxom, a fine pianist, and a loving and lenient teacher. I remember how she laughed when she told Gina that Midge had fooled her for months, playing by ear and not learning her notes. Midge and I took lessons all the way through grammar school and high school. We practiced especially well when it would get us out of washing dishes after supper. The recitals were nerve-wracking and thrilling. Miss Euna Smith would make us long dresses in complimentary colors. The afternoon of the recital we would take a nap, and when we woke up Aunt Mary and Aunt Helen would have come from Memphis. We would have poached eggs on toast before we got dressed; for some reason Gina thought poached eggs were the only appropriate thing to eat at those times. At our first recital, everyone loved how Midge, who was only six by that time, flipped one of her long braids back over her shoulder with one plump hand while she kept the music going with the other. Miss Nettie would recount it with delight: "Never missed a beat. Never missed a beat."

Our last recital was just us two, Midge and me, and Janice Ragland. I played the "Moonlight" Sonata, and Midge played the "Pathétique." I can't remember what Janice played. I do remember that I couldn't get out of the first movement of the "Moonlight" and kept circling around again and again, dah-dah-dah, dah-dah-dah, until Miss Nettie nearly had cardiac arrest and perspired completely through her dress. Then we played duets. Janice and I played the "Poet and Peasant" Overture as a duet, and Midge and I played Liszt's Hungarian Rhapsody as a duet, and I can't remember what they played. I was a big one for making sure we all lifted our hands exactly together, with a flourish, after the last note. Midge thought that was a little phony but went along with it to please me.

When I was fifteen, a new couple came to town, the Robersons. Margaret Roberson gave singing lessons. For the last two years of high school I took singing lessons with Mrs. Roberson. She and Gina drove me to Nashville, where I sang "Oh, Had I Jubal's Lyre" in the Grace Moore Scholarship Contest. I didn't win the scholarship, but I did win the West Tennessee part of the contest, and it was great fun.

From the first summer I got to New York City until he passed away five years ago, Robley Lawson was my singing teacher. He and his beloved Jean, like my great singing coach, Jimmy Quillian, worked with me as if I were a grand diva. My years of studying music with them were joyful and rich, though we all knew by that time that I was doing it for love. Then finally, in L.A., what do you know, I met a heartmate in Michele Brourman. She started playing the piano for me (more like getting the piano to dance around the room for me) and encouraged me into a cabaret act. Tommy Rolla let me sing at his Gardenia, and six years later I was spending the month of April at the Café Carlyle in New York. No effort of love goes to waste, and sometimes it even bears observable results. Now I take lessons from Marge Rivingston, with whom I am learning to sing again from the beginning. It's hard to face what has to be done sometimes; for a person who doesn't mind work, doing it can be easier than facing it. Marge, a master of observable results, works for both love and money and expects her singing students to do the same.

Now I will make this tiny excuse for my lack of discipline at the University of Tennessee. While there as a music major I was thoroughly discouraged by the faculty. It was suggested that if I must major in music, piano would be a wiser choice for me than ."voice," as the course was called. Right there I should have known I was in with the wrong crowd. "Singing" is what I wanted, not "voice."

The summer after my sophomore year at UT I agreed to represent Huntingdon in the Miss Tennessee pageant, then merrily sallied off to Europe on tour with the UT chorus, took advantage of every refreshment proffered, and brought fifteen pounds of European souvenirs back with me on my hips. My mother looked at me with undisguised alarm and put me on a very strict diet and exercise regime. There was another concern. Maybe I could get to swimsuit size in the three weeks before the contest, but what on earth was I going to do for my "talent"? Sing, of course, but what? And how? Nobody had been telling me lately that I was a standout in the field. I hadn't been given one little solo during two years in the UT chorus.

My friend Diane Meeks from Jackson, Tennessee, with whom I had shared a hotel room on the tour, told me that her mother, Miss Hazel Meeks, before she married had accompanied piano lessons for a great singing teacher in Memphis named Jerome Robertson, and that she'd be happy to call him and ask him to see me. This was such a big deal that Daddy took off from the store and drove Gina and me to Memphis to see if this teacher that Miss Hazel thought so much of would accept me with only two and a half weeks left now before I had to enter the contest.

We drove around to the east side of the Second Presbyterian Church, where he was choirmaster, and walked under the canopy to his studio. Jerome Robertson, a dapper grey-haired man with secrets dancing in his eyes, bade us a friendly hello, passed the pleasant southern time of day, asked my mother and father to make themselves comfortable in the waiting room, and took me with no further preamble into his inner sanctum. He then proceeded to put me through about ten minutes of the most exhilarating vocalises I had ever experienced. I couldn't believe how easy it was to fly up and down the scales. Next he jumped up from the piano bench and halloed to the hall, producing the instantaneous appearance of a petite young blond lady whom he introduced as Sara Beth Causey, after which he called in my parents to listen. Sara Beth, a luscious contralto and a pupil of his, sat down to the piano and started playing the one piece of music I had brought, "Summertime," which I always sang at parties.

Mr. Robertson stood across the studio from me, behind, then to the side of, then around in front of his desk, singing with me or sometimes mouthing the words, breathing, smiling as if this moment were happier than any moment he had ever lived before, reaching into me with his eyes, understanding me, understanding how I felt doing this, willing me to thrill myself, willing me to let the music soar out of me, putting wings on me. Every so often he'd stop and start me on a phrase again, every time with more energy, more joy. I was in a state of transport.

When the song was over, way too soon for me, Mr. Robertson shot me a toothy grin that bounced light all around the room, and said, "Pretty girl, you can sing!" Oh, my heart. My heart, be still.

On the way home Daddy said, "Didi, this Mr. Robertson is a great man. You are fortunate to have met a teacher of his caliber."

I did sing "Summertime" in the Miss Tennessee contest and came in second to Mickey Wayland from Knoxville. Rita Wilson from Humboldt came in third, then entered again the next year and won it. Billy Moss was there, and when I didn't win, he did the right thing and swore that the contest must have been "fixed" and jumped in his car in a fury to go off and have a fight with someone about it. That helped to assuage my sorrow.

With my parents' encouragement I left my friends and the parties at the University of Tennessee and transferred midyear to what was then Southwestern and is now Rhodes College, in Memphis. My mother arranged through Mrs. Wolf, head of admissions, that since there was no dormitory room left at the last minute, I was to stay in the home of Dr. and Mrs. Peyton Nolle Rhodes, Dr. Rhodes being the president of the college, with their nine Siamese cats (four cats, five kittens), their rose garden out back, and their dear, dear kindness to me. (The following summer I stayed with Aunt Mary, Gina's pretty, baby-faced older sister, who was called "Sister," who wore high heels and stockings at all times, morning to midnight, and who always waited up for me until the famous "all hours" to offer me cottage cheese and strawberries and work the crossword puzzle with me before I went to bed. The next fall Gina helped me find a garage apartment that I thought was great, which was where I lived until I left for New York.)

In the spring, without warning me beforehand, Mr. Robertson invited a man named George Touliatos, whom I had never clapped eyes on before, to one of my lessons. This dark and intense-looking young man listened and left, after a brief exchange with Mr. Robertson, who asked me after he was gone if I would like to be in a musical. He said Mr. Touliatos ran a theatre downtown in the old King Cotton Hotel and that he was going to offer me a part. The musical was *Carousel*, and I got to play Julie Jordan opposite George Hearn as Billy Bigelow. Macon McCalman, my friend forever since, played the Starkeeper. When George Hearn sang "If I Loved You" for the first time in rehearsal, I couldn't get my breath. I got on the pay phone in the hotel lobby and called home, where I happened to catch both Gina and Daddy having "dinner" (lunch). I told them in a voice hushed so that I wouldn't be overheard and laughed at, "You-all, I don't know what they sound like up in New York City, but I tell you what. None of them can possibly be as good as this boy that's singing Billy Bigelow. He makes the hair stand up on the back of my neck." And sure enough when they heard George sing, they had exactly the same reaction. As did the Memphis audiences. As have New York, Los Angeles, and London audiences. There followed two and a half years of wonderful singing leads at Front Street Theatre, the most joyful experience in the theatre that I have had to date. There was *Brigadoon, Oklahoma, The King and I, The New Moon, Babes in Arms,* and my favorite, *The Student Prince.* Glorious solos and choruses, and the most thrilling of all, *duets.* Duets with George Hearn. Duets with Pat Walker, the silver-throated Memphis tenor. I was singing, all right. I didn't know that I was learning to act too.

While I was working at Front Street, I was going to school, a year at Rhodes College and then a year and a half at the University of Memphis (I transferred to get finished sooner), singing at Temple Israel on Friday nights and Saturday mornings when I wasn't in a show, singing every Sunday, show or not, in the Second Presbyterian Church choir, and attending choir practice Thursday nights if I could make it. The choir job at the Temple paid well and I was grateful for it; singing in Mr. Robertson's choir nobody got paid for and nobody had to; it was glorious. But the highlights of the week were the two singing lessons I had with Mr. Robertson. I loved them even more than the performances at the theatre. I would often get there early to hang around and enjoy the high spirits and playfulness between him, other students, and Sara Beth, or Mrs. Robertson, or Gloria Dick, who all accompanied lessons at different times, and to slip in and listen to Patsy Welting's brilliant coloratura when she had the lesson before me. Every lesson was a short period of undiluted and intense joy, the joy of singing, magnified by the intoxicating effect of being with Jerome Robertson, hearing his pithy and hilarious accounts of times and people in New York back in the forties, taking in bits of advice that came from a prescient quality he possessed, feeling the magical release of my voice from places it had been hiding, and knowing *sometimes* that I was truly singing like a bird—singing, spinning, sailing, flying like a bird. I particularly loved lessons at lunchtime; Mr. Robertson was such an elegant gentleman that something about the sight of him urging me on from across the room with a mouthful of cheeseburger, lettuce, and tomato tickled me so that my heart would threaten to split open with happiness.

Three years after I met him, Mr. Robertson died suddenly

of a heart attack. I lay in bed and cried for a month. I thought my life was over, and in a way it was. I hadn't learned enough to take with me what I could do in his studio. I wasn't ever able to sing that way again. I had tea with Jane Robertson, his beautiful wife, over at Sara Beth's house last year, and we talked about him and cried. I miss him still the way I have for more than thirty years, still see his beguiling bad-boy smile, and still hear him, clear as a bell, promise the way he did that first day, "Pretty girl, you can sing!"

> *Blossoms will run away,*
> *Cakes reign but a day,*
> *But Memory like Melody*
> *Is pink Eternally*
>
> —EMILY DICKINSON

We must all draw from what we have, to find what is beautiful in our lives, to explore and to nourish it. For me the prime source has been my family. The family can be the repository of a mutual trust that, cherished and protected, will offer a sustaining metaphysical connection through the years. (This meaning of the word is not to be confused with "family" as in "We Are Famileeeeeeeee," that most casual and insincere popular song, which people seem to feel obligated to jump around to while they're dishing their new in-laws at the wedding reception.)

I'm grateful that I was born before television took over. The members of my family were our own entertainment. My mother and father were my movie stars. Hal and Midge and I thought they were more fun to be with than anybody. And they were so good-looking. I've told you before, my mother and daddy were so beautiful they were shiny. They were crazy about each other, always laughing together, having a good time, Daddy grabbing Gina in the kitchen, singing to her like Bing Crosby and waltzing her around, and of course they were crazy about us. Daddy used to tease and say that he had the easy part, because my mother was the disciplinarian during the day, and he got to come home from the store in the evening and pet us and spoil us. He was often the one to read us our bedtime stories. Our favorites were the Uncle Wiggly stories, which Daddy would read quite dramatically, using different voices for different characters. When the "skillery scalery alligator" was about to get Uncle Wiggly, and Midge and I would be yelping in fright, Gina would protest indulgently, "Halbuht Cahtah! Don't be so *graphic!* These children will have nightmares!"

Then Daddy got drafted into the Second World War. He could have avoided it, with Papa being so sick and all of us dependent on him, but he didn't think it was right not to go. So at thirty-three years of age he went off to the war. I didn't understand it, nor did my little sister, but we knew something very serious was happening when, the night before he left, after he had read us our Uncle Wiggly story, my mother took all those books, and put them in a box, and put the box under their bed, and said to us, "We won't be reading these stories while your daddy's gone. He'll take them out and read them again when he gets back."

The next day, the day he left, must have been a Saturday, because my brother wasn't in school; he was out at the grocery store, where Daddy went to tell him good-bye. He was white as a sheet, Daddy says, but he didn't cry; he stood with a pencil behind his ear, trying to look grown and businesslike at nine years of age, and assured his father that he would look after everything and everybody while he was gone. He certainly tried his best to do just that. He brought in the wood for the fireplace and the coal for the grate, milked the cow sick or well, and had the cornbread made by the time Gina got home from the store in the evenings, so all she had to do was take out what she had started in the deep-well cooker that morning for our supper.

My brother Hal was good to his two little sisters. He was our champion, taking us on outings in the woods that we thought were the height of extreme adventure, riding us on his bicycle, Midge in the basket, me sitting on the seat, while he stood up to pedal. If he got a good enough start going down the hill by our house, he could make it all the way up the hill by Miss Arbie McKinney's with both of us on, no mean feat for a ten- or eleven-year-old boy. He would even let us be western waitresses when he played cowboys in the empty henhouse with John Curtis Sloan, our participation being to present the two of them with pieces of broken crockery that were supposed to be beans and coffee. John Curtis left Hal tied up late one afternoon with a rope around his neck and went home to supper. Hal nearly strangled. After that I was delighted when Hal got big enough to knock him down. Martha Jean and Charlotte and John Curtis were older than Hal and took pleasure for several years in tormenting him every way they could think of, including siccing their dog on him. Their dog was a mean German shepherd named old Nick, who in his meanness, refused to obey his mistresses and left Hal unbitten. The tide turned the day Hal discovered he was strong enough to defend himself, and the terrible threesome left him alone afterward, and became friendly playmates. (My brother learned as a very little boy that "revenge is a dish best supped cold.") During the time that Daddy was gone to war, he matured beyond his years, and the seriousness which was always part of his nature became reinforced.

My brother sends me letters of advice and encouragement every so often, all of which I save. He often includes a poem by his favorite, Rudyard Kipling, or some excerpt from a thoughtful person's writings, something he divines might be applicable to my immediate situation. When I have been in trouble, I have called him and he has always come.

While Daddy was in Europe (where his one prayer every night was that he'd get home to his family once more), Hal even devised his own defense system against the Germans, one I believe must be unique in WW II history. He went out in the middle of the tennis court and dug a big hole—a pit, you could call it—maybe three, maybe four feet deep, and four or five feet square. He covered it with branches and then laboriously dug out and dragged up great big pieces of sod from the back of the pasture and covered it over. I asked what he was doing at that stage, and he answered, "I'm camouflaging this deal." I remember that as the first time I ever heard that word. And then he affixed somehow in the center of it a periscope of his own design and making. So at the end of his labors he had arrived at what you might call a kind of tennis court–submarine. You could tell when Hal Carter was on guard against enemy attack; all you had to do was look out the window across the tennis court, and if you saw that periscope turning, slowly turning, you knew he was in there, on the alert. One day he crawled in and found a black widow spider already on watch at the periscope, crawled right back out again, never to crawl back in, and that moment more or less dismantled the McLemoresville, Tennessee, defense system.

Daddy was gone nearly two years. Not too long after Hal saw the black widow spider, a strange man came into town. I had never seen him before and don't remember ever seeing him again. (In a town of two hundred people, you know when a stranger has arrived.) This man walked into the middle of town with a bullwhip, which he started cracking across the highway. It sounded like a cannon going off. Then everybody started running out of their houses, yelling and crying, "The war is over! The war is over!" A few people shot guns into the air. It was scary and terribly exciting.

It wasn't very long after that that Midgie and I were sitting side by side in the kitchen, piddling with the breakfast Gina had put out for us before she went upstairs to make the beds, when all of a sudden, without a sound, there in the kitchen doorway stood Daddy.

He looked so young and handsome in his uniform, and he seemed boyish as he held his finger up to his lips and said, "Shhh!"

We sat in a daze, open-mouthed.

Later he said, many times, "Sweetest sight I nearly ever saw, two little girls with their mouths full of egg."

He whispered, half-frightened in his eagerness, "Where's Gina?" We pointed silently upstairs, still transfixed.

He crept up the stairs; we heard her scream; then it was quiet for a little while. That night the Uncle Wiggly books came back out again.

Thank you, Daddy, and Gina, and Hal, and Midge. Thank you for our home. Thank you for the delicate golden threads of trust that have never been broken between us.

PART THREE

The Essence of Beauty

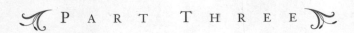

⨳ Chapter Seven ⨳
TRAILING CLOUDS OF GLORY

OWARD THE END OF TENNESSEE WIL-
liams's play *A Streetcar Named Desire*, Blanche DuBois makes
a last attempt to explain herself to Stanley, and to us: "Physical
beauty is passing, a transitory possession. But beauty of the
mind, and richness of the spirit, and tenderness of the heart
. . . aren't taken away, but grow, increase with the years."

It's never too soon to apprehend the truth of that statement and to begin our own search for the quiddity of beauty, the real essence of it. Here's my list of the elements inside us that show through and make us radiate with what we are moved to call beauty:

> Nature's wellspring
> A life of the mind
> An upspringing spirit
> A kind heart
> A growing soul

NATURE'S WELLSPRING

In addition to the cosmetic results of a healthy system, there is another kind of benefit, not so easily defined, a sense of wholesomeness and wholeness that emanates from a healthy person, which is the source, and ultimately beauty itself. We don't suck in our breath when we stand next to a giant redwood tree just because it is exactly so tall or so big around; we don't feel our heart skip to see a colt long-legging it around the pasture just because of its exact proportions or color; we are responding to the fountain of life, the life force, when it is pouring unhindered through any part of God's creation.

The summer after my mother died in March of 1988, I started planting trees at our home down in Tennessee. Gina and Daddy had renovated the house I was born in (Daddy, Uncle Leon, my aunt Melba, Hal, Midge, and I were all born in it, in the same downstairs bedroom) and had moved back into it from the house in Huntingdon where we'd lived since I was twelve. The place had been rented out all those years in between, so everything had run down, and lots of the trees were gone.

First I had thirty weeping willows put in down in the back of the pasture. Then thirty more. Planting them and watching them grow seemed to ease the bottomless grief over my mother's death. Oak trees were planted along the driveway. They took hold and thrived, most of them. My husband was watching the trees along with me, and in the second year he got the bug too and started a beautiful pine grove over by Mrs. Forrest's house. I asked Miss Annie Mae Buck if she'd sell me the pasture that connected with ours and she did, and that gave us room for more willows, swamp oaks, and more pines. We have a cotton gin across the road; Hal got the idea to screen it off with pines and hemlocks. Now we have blue spruce, hemlocks, pines, magnolias, and oaks on that side of the house. We have maples, pears, pecans, pines, and hemlocks on the other side. There are the old walnuts, choke cherries, oaks, and giant catalpas, and the volunteer catalpas we have transplanted from the fencerow into the pasture. There are holly trees and dogwoods, a tulip poplar, an ash, and a sycamore.

The first thing we do every time we go home is to tromp all over the place, even if it's dark, and look at the trees. We love to watch how they're growing, to stand and look at them. When we lose a tree, it's sickening. When one comes back after a bad time, like the young oak that got split almost all the way down the middle during last winter's ice storm, we rejoice. Last winter's ice storm was really awful on the trees. At least two dozen of the willows along the creek were laid completely over on the ground, with their roots sticking up in the air. How Joe Harper managed to lift the dear things back up, get their roots back into that frozen ground, tie them so they'd stay, and save all their lives was not much short of supernatural. There they were this summer, green and growing as if nothing had happened.

Years ago there was a boy in McLemoresville who was a little simple and made himself famous for creating new words from old. He came back from Huntingdon one day talking about how the people there all smoked cigarettes nonstop. He was striking at "fiends" when he labeled them "cigarette femuses." Hal Holbrook and I are tree femuses.

Our favorite is not one that we planted. It's a volunteer elm that sprang up in the fencerow when Daddy was a little boy.

Now, having survived cyclones, tornadoes, and Dutch elm disease, august in its eighty-year-old wisdom, it's an imposing presence. Before we go to sleep at night, we often stand on the little balcony outside our bedroom and look at it looming against a sorcerous night sky, its giant arms stretched over us, royal and primitive.

When I'm drinking in what that old elm tree has to say or commending our young pine trees on their beautiful new needles, I think, Wouldn't it be thrilling to feel the way those trees look and to give off that kind of beauty?

There is no gainsaying the power of a beautiful spirit shining through and transforming physical deformity or terrible illness; what I'm describing is another kind of light. Only those people born with or struck down by infirmity are excused from the duty the rest of us have, as citizens of the earth, to keep the fountain of life bubbling up through us. Those of us who do not act as good caretakers of "the temple of the soul" ought to be ashamed of ourselves. Ashamed or not, we'll pay some kind of price, and we surely won't have as much fun for as long as we might like to.

Taking care of our body and keeping it healthy is the first and most rudimentary means by which we can attain beauty.

A L I F E O F T H E M I N D

The essence of beauty, true beauty, is in great part created from an energetic intellect, what George Hearn used to refer to as the life of the mind. A listless mentality is boring. A person who is bored is boring. A nimble mind is attractive and attracts others like it. We want to keep ours tuned up and in good running condition. Arthritis of the mind is a bad disease and it doesn't take an X-ray to figure out whether or not we're in danger of it. A first testing point could be whether we read anything that requires concentration. Reading is an obvious place to start fueling up the mind.

My earliest and fondest memories include being read to and told stories. When three generations make up the family unit,

there's a good chance the children will have plenty of storytelling to listen to. One-on-one stories, afternoons and bedtimes,
will start a little person's mind dancing. Then along with the
storytelling comes the wonder of books—picture books with
words that you begin to recognize because you already know
the story by heart.

My father does not remember learning to read. He was
reading before he started school and says all he remembers is
that he just knew how. I remember learning to read. When I
caught on, it was like flying in dreams.

My mother's brother Jack Hillsman followed in his father's
footsteps and did not marry until he was forty-nine years old.
Like his father he had had a heartbreaking romance at an early
age, and so he stayed away from the altar for the next thirty
years. Uncle Jack was a gentle man, athletic though slight in
build, very deliberate in manner, and by the time I was born a
schoolteacher. He had done various things, including working
up in Canada in a logging camp for a while. There was that
thing about him that some quiet men have, a hint of mystery,
a subtle aura of warning, but where Hal and Midge and I were
concerned, he was a pushover. He spent his summers with us,
along with his and Gina's mother, Grandmother Hillsman,
and he was happy to watch over us when Gina asked him to,
and so we got to spend a big part of every day with our sweet,
loving, and beloved Uncle Jack. Sometimes he would take a
break to practice his putting out beside the tennis court or to
write a letter or to try to read a book, but we didn't let that go
on for long. "Push *mo* [more], Uncle Jack! Push mo!" brother
Hal was said to have urged from his baby play car. He would
push us on the swings, or pull us in our little red wagons, or
swab up a skinned elbow, or read to us, or tease us at our
meals, with his crinkling blue eyes and slow chuckle. One
evening he addressed me in my high chair with a favorite
question: "Dahling? Dixie? Have you been a good little girl
today?" My three-year-old riposte, "Don't bov-ver me, Uncle
Jack. I am eee-ting my tin-ner," sent him into tears of laughter.

The summer I was four, he set up a little blackboard on an easel and gave me a crayon and taught me the alphabet. Then he taught me to make words. He taught Midge too, because she had to do everything at the same time I did even though she was eighteen months younger. I like to think I did better than Midge that summer, but I can't be sure. The next summer he taught me to read, which was easy by then. "See Mac run. See Muff run." Oh brother, this was the big time.

By the time I actually started to school, Miss Ethelyn Taylor asked me to help her "teach" the class. She asked Midge too. I started to school when I was seven because I wanted to wait until Midge was big enough to go too. I didn't want to go without her. When we started, we both went to first grade, she at five and a half years and I at seven. Then Gina told Miss Ethelyn she thought I should just go on into the third grade, so I did. I was pretty bored except when I was teaching, because I knew all the words and numbers already. Actually the teaching got to be pretty boring too, but it did chisel the available information deep in my brain. Midge and I taught by holding up cards with words or with short arithmetic problems on them in front of the class and drilling our fellow pupils. This we would do while Miss Ethelyn was engaged with one of the other grades she taught in the same schoolroom. Then when she was teaching the class we were in, we would have to sit there and learn what we already knew. Miss Ethelyn wasn't into teaching the concepts of algebra and geometry to first graders the way my girls learned them up in New Yawk City.

Be that as it may, my siblings and I grew up loving to read. Reading was cleverly presented to us as the reward we got after we'd done our chores; then we could sit down with our book. *Tarzan of the Apes*, and all the rest of the Edgar Rice Burroughs books, *Little Women*, *Treasure Island*, the Nancy Drew mysteries, the Edgar Wallace mysteries, the Zane Grey westerns, the "youth books" belonging to my father and my brother, and eventually of course, *Gone with the Wind*, which put me out of commission for a week after I finished it. (When Gigi was filling out her application to Harvard, she answered

the question about what her favorite book was and why,
"Wuthering Heights, because it is almost as good as *Gone with
the Wind."*) From the time I sat in my mother's lap as she read
"Wynken, Blynken, and Nod" and I looked at the pictures, I
was hooked. I wanted to find out what happened to the Gingham Dog and the Calico Cat, even if I'd heard it over and
over. Reading still feels to me like a great luxury. A few years
ago Hal took my sweet and beautiful stepdaughter Eve Holbrook and me for a short getaway to Cabo San Lucas. I started
Out of Africa as the plane took off, read it for the three days
we were there, with breaks at mealtime, and finished it as our
plane landed back in L.A. A perfect holiday. Hal and Eve were
reading, Eve listening to a Walkman as she sunbathed in her
long blondness, terrifically enhancing the scenery poolside.
That was it: lying around reading and eating. Sublime.

When Hal and I were first married, Daddy introduced him
to the western writer Louis L'Amour, and Hal took to those
books like a duck to water. He was missing his sailing trips
and here was another kind of romance. Often we would wake
to the smell of bacon frying in the middle of the night and
know that Hal, reading very late, had succumbed to the appeal
of some campfire grub. We've read all of them and probably
will again; next Hal is on to the sea stories of Patrick O'Brian,
and I just finished John Berendt's *Midnight in the Garden of
Good and Evil.* Nowadays it's harder to read a lot of what I'd
like to. I have scripts to get through, informative material to
cover, and there's mail and paperwork to contend with, so
absorbing novels don't get first priority. One of these days
they will. I'm not complaining.

My all-time favorite book is *Precious Bane,* written in 1924
by Mary Webb. My singing coach Jimmy Quillian gave it to
me to read when Arthur and I were having a bad time of it,
and I never stopped thanking him until the day he died. *Precious Bane* takes place in north Shropshire, in the country of
meres. Mrs. Webb wrote only a few books, all of them set in
the English countryside. She wrote of the countryside, of its
people, and of the past. "There is a permanence, a continuity

in country life which makes the lapse of centuries seem of little moment," she wrote, and she described the past as "only the present become invisible and mute . . . its memoried glances and its murmurs . . . infinitely precious." The "memoried glances" Mary Webb offers her readers are privileged. *Precious Bane* is out of print, so keep an eye out in secondhand bookstores, and ask your friends to do likewise, if you want a reading experience of unforgettable sweetness.

Reading keeps us learning, and we need to keep learning all our lives. Life teaches life lessons; reading exercises the mind in another way; it literally stimulates the brain and keeps it healthy.

Along with reading we should challenge our minds in ways that are different from what we're used to. It's being discovered that our brain doesn't quit on us as we age if we continue to challenge it. Arnold Scheibel at UCLA says that new research gives evidence that we can continue to build brain circuitry into advanced age. He says, "The important thing is to be actively involved in areas unfamiliar to you." With that idea in mind I suppose I should consider taking up watercolors or bridge.

Do you ever try to write a poem for somebody's birthday, or just because you want to remember a certain moment in a certain way? Try it. If you feel silly doing it, don't let anybody see what you've written. I have many poems that nobody will ever see. My family has always been big on writing birthday poems. In July Mary Dixie was twenty-four years old. I gave her a little red leather purse and I wrote her this poem.

> *I wish for you dreams without ending*
> *I wish for you joy without cost*
> *I wish for you peace without boredom*
> *I wish for you love without loss.*
> *May your magical mind keep expanding*
> *May your health never suffer decline*
> *May the rose that you are go on blooming*
> *O beautiful daughter of mine!*

It's not easy for those of us who aren't poets, but it's extremely stimulating and actually lots of fun, and after a while you may find yourself doing one up for a wedding toast. That'll get the old blood flowing!

While we were all still at home, my brother gave Midge and me for one of our birthdays (I can't remember which; we both got birthday presents on both of our birthdays) this poem in an envelope with two new twenty-dollar bills:

> *Your birthday's upon us;*
> *My poor heart is weeping;*
> *Your present is absent;*
> *This isn't in keeping!*
> [some lines I can't remember, then]
> *So in lieu of an item*
> *Of dubious attraction*
> *I'm delivering to each*
> *A picture of Jackson.*

All these years later I remember that birthday present, not just because it was a huge gift for our brother to be giving as a teenager who took it out of his own stash, but mostly because of the poem. The time and the thought that went into it, and the wit and affection that came out of it, has kept half of it in my tired brain for all these years. That is a really fine kind of present, wouldn't you say, Dear Reader?

Buy a book of poems, any poems, and read them. Read them just one a day, very slowly and three or four times. If you don't have a favorite poet, ask for a slim volume called *One Hundred and One Famous Poems*. After you make your way through that, bearing in mind that there's nobody remotely modern in it, you'll have an idea of some poets you like, and you're off to the races. Do it, and you will thank me for telling you to. You will want to sit down and write me a letter one day and tell me what a rich tip that was. I love Emily Dickinson, Wordsworth, Yeats, Keats, T. S. Eliot, Millay, and Poe. Then there's Tennyson. And you cannot beat Longfellow. Not to mention Shakespeare. (For our wedding anniversary three years ago Hal gave me a richly bound edition of Shakespeare's sonnets, his inscription on the flyleaf, "Dixie, my wife, For thy sweet love remember'd such wealth brings . . ." and it's just about my favorite present that he's ever given me.)

Albert Einstein played the violin for a pastime; I'll bet nobody had to tell Albert it was good for his brain. A few years ago I went back to piano lessons, the first lessons I'd had since college. I didn't last long; *Designing Women* started and my second career as a pianist ended. It was an exciting, if frustrating, experience, very worthwhile and very telling. Any activity or skill that requires extremely rapid and precise mind-to-body response is accomplished only by practice. Hours and hours of practice create little roadways or channels in the brain that make it easier and faster for the messages to travel, so that a piece of difficult music can eventually become routined into the system, and the fingers fly almost unbidden to their proper notes. At that point the mind is free to play the music in the piece, not just the notes, and interpretation is possible. What I found out during my resurgence as a student of the pianoforte is that if practice is discontinued, eventually the brain will eliminate connections that are not being used, so those nice grooved-in patterns of a Chopin waltz will fade away, and the process for a lapsed piano student like me will be almost like starting at the very beginning again, but with slower responses.

Before I went into rehearsals for a production of *Pal Joey* three years ago, I had a go at a few tap dancing lessons. I couldn't make my feet do what was being asked of them nearly as fast and easily as my daughters, who were joining me. It was tantalizing, even though I didn't get much accomplished before rehearsals started, and fun to meet Patrick Swayze's mother, Patsy, who has the dance school. I desperately want to take tap classes again, especially now that I know I'll get to play like I'm Ginger Rogers, lift my behind (a side benefit), and beef up my brain at the same time.

Another example of how neural pathways function might be

the routine motions that we make driving the same car for a long time; driving a different car, we find that our hand flies to the wrong place to change gears unless we consciously stop and think. After we get used to the new car, we develop a new set of automatic motions.

Sculpting, plumbing, painting houses or canvases, doing crossword puzzles or jigsaw puzzles, sailing a boat, making a dress, keeping a diary, playing the banjo like our chiropractor, Rodger Phillips—whatever we might really delight in that's different from our norm will add richness, texture, and zest to our regular week, and it will keep the light turned on behind our eyes.

Dreaming—night dreaming and daydreaming—is as important as consciously working the mind. Dream analysts tell us to keep a pad by our bed and write down our dreams the moment we awake, but I'll bet not many of us do it. It's a shame too, because sometimes questions get answered, whether symbolically or literally; sometimes creative ideas form themselves; sometimes people we miss and should call on the phone show up in our dreams to remind us. Although I can't manage to stick with a habit of writing down my dreams, I do try to lie very still for a few moments before I arise and allow a review of the past few hours to bubble up to the surface of consciousness. This practice can provide an excellent guide for approaching the day; the unconscious mind is usually a canny adviser.

Bad dreams serve their own purpose. Every so often ever since I can remember, I have waked in a paralysis of terror, unable to move a muscle or call out for help, with a feeling of weakness and horror. When I was little enough still to be in my baby bed, I dreamed that there was a giant and fierce dog, a boxer, standing just beside my bed, looking at me. I cried out to my mother to make it go away, and she said that there was no dog there, that I'd had a bad dream. That dream has remained clear to me all these years, maybe because I was so sure the dog was really there.

All our dreams, someone pointed out to me, are our own

concoctions. Ever since I realized that I'm making up my own dreams, I can come out of the scary ones a little easier, but I still have them. They're pretty much variations on a few stock themes:

Something is after me, something monstrous; it's gaining on me; it gets me. Just before it does whatever it's going to do to me, I recognize it as someone I know very well. The whole dream is terrifying; the moment of recognition is horror.

Something is after me, a lion or a tiger; it's climbing up the stairs and is about to get me; I begin slowly to move my arms like wings, pushing the air down under me, and I feel myself rising above the beast; I fly up and out of harm's way. I fly a long time.

Something is after me, something I can't see; I don't know what or who it is, but it's malevolent and terrifying; I wake up trying to call out for help and unable to make any sound.

I am together with a group of people some of whom aren't necessarily related to one another in time or place. We're usually going somewhere together, often in a car. They change back and forth into other people as the dream progresses. Sometimes there's someone I was once in love with. I can't find the right words to say what I feel; the moment is gone; I wake up in melancholy.

I am getting ready for a performance; I do not know my lines or what the part is. I do not have the proper costume or even enough of a costume to wear onstage; it's awful. I wake from this one happy as a bird, heigh-do-deay-dee, because it was only a dream.

During low times I have waked squeezing my eyes shut
and hoping that I was still asleep, only to realize that the
nightmare was in the waking world, not the dream world.
That's a *bad* dream.

My father had a real night-mare that recurred all the time
in his youth. He would dream of a killer horse, wild-eyed and
evil, chasing after him, following him into his house and even
up to his room. He has described how the horse sounded
snorting and pawing on the stairs. He stopped having the
dream after he was grown, he says maybe because cars had
taken over and horses weren't part of everybody's life like they
had been.

We make up our own dreams, no matter how horrible they
are. Whether we can remember them or not, they're releasing anxiety. If we're able to remember them long enough to
think about them, we can sort of figure out what's really
bothering us.

Just before you go to sleep, tell yourself you'd like to have
some good happy dreams, and like as not you will. I love to
dream of flying (sans airplane), not necessarily to get away
from a monster, just for the transcendent feeling. I love to
dream of singing beautifully; it's much like the flying dream. I
love to dream of fantastical or lovely things, dreams that I can
wake out of with sighs and smiles.

The deepest level of sleep, when there is no dreaming, when
we are drowning in soft space, sinking ever softer and deeper
into the great bliss of complete senselessness, is the most felicitous state possible. In these times I am almost aware of slip-
ping away from myself into the breath of the universe. Almost
aware, but never quite. I am reminded of how, when I was
very young, I would try to catch the mirror off guard, in order
to see what I *really* looked like, by standing nonchalantly (as I
thought) for a minute with my back to it, and then wheeling
abruptly, before the mirror had a chance to get set with the
reflection it wanted me to see. I never could catch the mirror

doing what I *knew* it was doing, but I'm still not convinced I was all wrong. In a similar way I've never floated up from one of those bottomless wells of sleep able to remember where I went, but nothing can convince me that I haven't been somewhere beyond imagining. And the sense of well-being, healing, and recuperation that rises up with me is remarkable.

Persons who can feel their best, perform at their peak, and look terrific on very little sleep are rare; I can't. I have to have Shakespeare's "sleep that knits up the ravell'd sleave of care" or I can't make it. And in order to refresh, it has to be *good* sleep. I never know when I will experience one of the deep slumbers, although there seems to be some correlation between them and my nighttime yoga routine. A clear conscience is a great sleeping pill; that we know. Children sleep like the dead and feel good when they wake up. Those of us who are no longer children—just childish perhaps—do well to leave off caffeine in the afternoon and perhaps sip a little chamomile tea before beddy-bye. The word *retire* means literally "to withdraw and seek seclusion"; praying or meditating just before sleep is the best way to ease ourselves into restorative, untroubled repose. Most successful for me is a few minutes of quiet breathing and stretching, a few minutes of reading, and a few minutes of reviewing the efforts of the day in order to conclude that I have done the best I could and to leave the rest in the hands of the Almighty.

If I don't fall asleep easily, I lie on my back, resting one hand on my stomach and one hand on my solar plexus or over my heart, and taking long slow breaths, I send my mind to travel ever so slowly with my breath, first to where my hands are, then all the way down to my toes, releasing and relaxing as it goes, ever so slowly, ever so gently, then gradually back up to rest in a spot in my forehead between and behind my eyes. Usually I'm asleep before I travel back up to my forehead; if not, I continue conscious breathing while I let beautiful pictures form behind my eyes, and that way I sail off to dreamland like Wynken, Blynken, and Nod.

Let us not forget dreaming awake, daydreaming. We know

a lot technically about alpha and beta waves and states; I don't think we have to hook ourselves up to a machine to get there. Edgar Allan Poe didn't have a machine attached to his head when he wrote, "They who dream by day are cognizant of many things which escape those who dream only by night. In their grey visions they obtain glimpses of eternity, and thrill, in waking, to find that they have been upon the verge of the great secret. In snatches, they learn something of the wisdom which is of good, and more of the mere knowledge which is of evil. They penetrate, however rudderless or compassless, into the vast ocean of the 'light ineffable' . . ."

Take or make the time, and find a certain kind of place, a private place. Daydreaming is awfully good for a person. When we were little, our mother would tell us not to dawdle on the way to school, but we did, because something else was telling us it was okay. Back when everybody ate out of their gardens, snapping beans or capping strawberries was a perfect time for letting the mind take flight, to sail back and forth between this world and some other, coaxing part of the unconscious out into the daylight, letting the eyes lose focus so that the dreamer could see with other eyes. Fantasy is a beauty builder for everyone, of every age. We can learn to turn our thoughts from bothersome, energy-sapping targets to plans for the future, a favorite place or person, the words of a song, or a good turn we hope to do a friend. Don't get too dreamy driving the car though.

AN UPSPRINGING SPIRIT

Somebody said, "Happiness is difficult to find within, impossible to find elsewhere." Emily Dickinson said,

> *Exhilaration—is within*
> *There can no other wine*
> *So royally intoxicate*
> *As that diviner brand.*

Once in a while I get weary or sad or in some way off my feed, and I want to quit. I want to pack in my exciting life and my exciting plans for the future and settle into a corner with books and chocolates. There are a couple of circumstances that seem to trigger this sagging of the spirit.

Any misunderstanding with my husband is debilitating. When one of us is hurt or angry with the other, I feel like an elephant is standing on my chest. It doesn't matter if I feel that I'm the right one or the wrong one; either way is unbearable. He feels the same, so we never let it go for any length of time; that much we've learned in our years of making mistakes with each other and with others. We talk to each other as soon as we get through sulking, which is usually within the hour. There's nothing that eases hurt feelings like the words "I'm sorry." If for some reason we remain estranged for a full day, it's a lost day for me. I take no pleasure in work or food or friendly conversation. Nothing's any fun. My spirit flags.

Oddly, the area in which I feel the most confident and take the most pride is my most vulnerable: motherhood. Most all the time it's an ongoing thrill to know that the business of nurturing one's child is never over and done. Ninety-nine percent of the time I relish the fact that my children still value my opinion, still want my time and attention, still need me. Once in a long while, however, I am lost for an answer to a serious problem, or almost as bad, my answer is not one they want to hear. Difficulties I can't resolve and pain I can't help or prevent are distressing indeed, but that is life, and every mother has to accept her children's troubles as part of life, indeed as ultimately essential to their growth. That I can do. What I can't do is carry on when we're mad at each other. If there is discord between my children and me, I can't stand it. At these times I'm likely to feel incompetent to mother or guide my daughters anymore, and I resort to sinking thinking: "Just give it up. They're grown. Leave them alone and let them find out on their own. It's better for them anyway." Over these past twenty-five years, with their gentle sounds and silences, my daughters have let me get used to the idea that I can be wrong and still retain their respect. It's such a relief, acknowledging that I'm wrong when I am. Still not the easiest thing though; not exactly rolling off a log, being wrong, right?

Sometimes the smog, if that's what it is, over Hollywood becomes stifling, and I long to find cleaner air, to opt out of the race and the pace. It doesn't happen often; I've almost gotten adjusted to living and working in California, and that fact surprises me whenever I stop to think of it. I've lived here fifteen years now. Twenty years ago if you'd told me I'd wind up in Los Angeles with a television career, I would have said you were telling me a story. But then again if you'd told me twenty years ago that I was going to be happy someday, I would have said the same thing.

In the summer of 1973, to get away from the horrible Hamptons, I rented a tiny house at Snedens Landing. My coach and friend Jimmy Quillian knew about Snedens from the song "Did You Ever Cross Over to Snedens?" which his friend Alec Wilder had written for Mabel Mercer. He had never been there, but when I told him I had to go somewhere away from the beach scene, he at once instructed me to go searching for "the place in that song." His advice was definite, his directions vague, "across the George Washington Bridge and up Route 9W," but I followed them and found Snedens Landing, and Mr. Quillian was proven right. When I stopped in the road and asked if there were any houses to let, somebody said, "Go over and ask Mrs. Tonetti." Ann Tonetti, exhibiting the "kindness of strangers," suggested that I get in touch with Peter Grey in Martha's Vineyard and ask about his place. A week later Gigi and Mary Dixie and I were in it, snugging together on furniture we'd hauled from the secondhand stores in Nyack. It was the place for us, lots of trees and the Hudson River. I read *Precious Bane* there and kept a house there as long as I could pay the rent, even after we had moved to L.A., first Peter Grey's, then the "house in the woods" that Laurence Olivier and Vivien Leigh had once rented, and last and best, the Ferry House right down on the river.

I spent that summer secluded at Snedens Landing with the little girls, cutting back overgrown ivy and cleaning trash out of the brook. I didn't want to see anybody except my mother, who came for a short visit, and Midgie, who came with her three-year-old daughter, Hillsman, and one-year-old Stephen. Her youngest, Christian, had not yet arrived on the planet. (That was one of the times Midge and I discovered that miles apart we'd both bought exactly the same dresses for our little girls. She came back the next summer and it had happened again. The same print fabric. Also Hillsman, Gigi, and Mary Dixie started noticing that they couldn't tell whether it was their aunt or their own mother touching them, if they weren't looking. They said our hands felt just the same, which sort of spooked them and tickled them both. At this time Stephen was two and had started coming up with his famous sayings, like "Mama, you're wreckin' my business," when Midge helped herself to a spoonful from his ice cream dish, and "Aunt Didi, will you run away with me?" stage-whispered at me while his mother was holding him and Hillsman still in their beds to get them to sleep. After Christian was born, so many famous sayings got uttered that Midge and I keep vowing to get down to it and make a little book of them.) We had just gotten two black Labrador puppies, Gilbert and Sullivan, who added to the liveliness in that teensy little house. I promised that I was all cheered up, so they left after a week of splashing in the pint-sized swimming pool that you had to fill up with a hose, and picnicking on quilts in the yard ("pallets" we always called them when they were on the ground and not the bed). Then it was quiet again.

One day my friend Joe Pichette came swinging down the lane. He called out, "I took the bus over here. Are you receiving?" I told him that I was if he'd jump into the brook with me and start throwing out soda pop cans. He did that for a while, then he said, "I came over to find you because I have important news. Our lives are going to change. Dale Davis is back in town."

Joe and I were close friends and he knew that I was in

distress. Apprehending that my marriage to Arthur was going to fail, I had been trying to go back to work, in a diffident kind of way. I couldn't get an agent interested. I was almost thirty-five years old. "Too old" was the message, the wisdom being that I had only five years left to amount to something; forty was the dropping-off point. Joe spent the afternoon and evening bolstering my confidence and left the next day, after extracting a promise that I would call this Dale Davis woman and make an appointment. I had given my promise, so reluctantly, nervously, and therefore a bit resentfully, I called, made the appointment with the much heralded Dale Davis, and drove into town to meet her. Her friend Michael Thomas had gone off to Europe for the summer, leaving her, Jerry Martin, and Annette Sheer to mind his theatrical agency. I found it, a small fancy address in the east sixties, and walked into the receiving room. Through the open doorway to Michael's office I saw behind his desk a person I felt as if I had known forever. Dale Davis and I looked at each other and burst into laughter, both of us realizing at once that we were going to be friends.

Thus began the resuscitation of a career I had put on hold before it got going. Seven years back, Rod Steiger had come into the Upstairs at the Downstairs, seen me performing in a review there, and offered me a part in the movie *No Way to Treat a Lady*. Arthur Carter had talked me out of going to Europe to do the job. I had said no to the job, married Arthur, and that was the end of that.

So at thirty-four I met Dale, asked for her help, and got it. Dale was indeed all Joe had said she would be. She was a teacher when we first met, and that quality carried into her theatrical career. She was inspiring; she was very kind, very intelligent, a South Carolinian, and fun. And funny. She's the one who reminded me that we southerners get away with murder using the phrase "Bless her (or his) heart"; we can say any awful thing about someone and tag it with that phrase and keep a sanctimonious face. ("You know she never has quit taking those Demerol pills she got on when she had her [whispered] *plastic surgery*, or she's started drinkin' again, is pro'bly why she keeps sideswipin' Ralph's car in their garage, *bless her heart.*") Dale is the one who coined the phrase "overlooking the majestic Hudson" to delight the little girls when she and they were sitting in the kitchen at Snedens, about to begin one of their important breakfast conversations. I put my trust in her and felt good about that, but still I was almost unbalanced mentally from the feelings of inadequacy and shame that haunted all thoughts about my floundering marriage, and I couldn't think of anything else. I felt weak all the time and sick. Margaret Anderson, the dear real estate lady through whom I rented at Snedens, told me the last time we were together, she had thought when I first came there with the little girls that I had something wrong with me, that I was dying. Well, I had something wrong with me all right, but as it turned out, it didn't kill me.

Dale had me sing an audition for Jered Barclay, who was directing a Broadway musical called *Sextet* (because there were six characters, nothing to do with Mae West). I sang "Send in the Clowns" and, miracle of miracles, got the part. Then Jered, with whom I've been friends ever since, sat me down and told me I looked weirdly pale and I'd better start wearing more makeup. *Sextet* lasted only one week, but since Jered had tried to help the material with lots of inventive business, I had been given a chance to play the trumpet, imitate Groucho Marx (which I had learned from Jerry Orbach while we were on the road), and whinny like a horse, along with my other duties as a singer and actor, and Clive Barnes gave me a headline in *The New York Times*, which is framed, hanging on the wall in the music room, precious, the first signal of positive possibilities. I have always been afraid to write to members of the press and say thank you for the kind comments that I have received along the way, afraid that it might appear as if I were expecting more praise the next time or something, but I have wanted to. Having been fortunate in this respect, I have wondered if the person who is tippy tap typing out a review has any notion of how powerfully important encouragement (or

its opposite) can be. On a life, I mean, not just as a temporary
ego adjustment; I mean on the course of a life.

Next Dale sent me to read for the soap opera *The Edge of
Night*. It was the part of an assistant district attorney, and I
tried my best to imitate Bette Davis, and lo and behold I got
that job too. It was very lucky for me that these first two
attempts to get work were successful, because they gave me a
meager measure of confidence, and it was catch-as-catch-can
after that. Wanting to work in the theatre as well as on the
soap, I kept trying with much difficulty to get reinstated in Joe
Papp's good graces. In 1963 Joe had hired me to play Perdita
in *A Winter's Tale* in Central Park two weeks after I arrived in
New York from Memphis, and hadn't been pleased when I
left his realm to go work for Mr. Rodgers at Lincoln Center.
Because of Arthur's success (I believe) Joe regarded me as a
dilettante and wanted me to suffer before he let me back into
the fold. I was cast in one play at the Public Theater by the
director and playwright, only to have Joe uncast me when he
found out about it. Another time, after I had auditioned for
him with an aria from *La Périchole*, he said, in the presence of
a gentleman from the press—whom Joe had insisted stay to
listen to me, knowing that if I weren't nervous enough already,
this would polish me off—"You know, Dixie, that's the kind
of singing we make fun of down here at the Public." I felt as
if he had kicked me in the stomach, and I think that's how he
wanted me to feel. I'm sure the writer from *The New York
Times* was as embarrassed as I was humiliated. I would have
appreciated having the nerve to call Joe on what he was thinking and tell him the money belonged to Arthur, not me, but
nerve was not my strong suit just then. Grim as the fact was,
Joe Papp's was the only game in town, except for Broadway,
where I was having no luck either, and I became determined
to take his punishment until he recognized that I was serious,
and I did, and he did. He relented at last and we became
friendly, employer-employee friendly, as we had been when I
was first in New York. I did five plays at the Public altogether,
four during that period. My mother would come to help take

care of the little girls; I was gone from early morning until midnight. (One of the plays, *Gogol*, had a shorter run than *Sextet*. Joe closed it at intermission on opening night, and he should have. It was three and a half hours long. I savored his explanation: "There is no need for so much high-flown language to be accompanied by so much high-flown acting.") My friend the great Dr. William Hitzig mentioned to me once that he had said to Joe, who was also a patient of his, back when I was trying to start working again, "Joe, you should give Dixie Carter something down at your place. Her husband has money; it might be good for you." I didn't have the heart to tell my well-intentioned friend that he had perhaps both caused and now explained a painful mystery; Joe easily could have supposed Dr. Hitzig's suggestion came from me.

After two and a half years on *The Edge of Night* my part got written out, and a fond farewell was said by all. Then Jean Guest at CBS cast me in the TV series *On Our Own*, shot in New York. It lasted one full season.

During the run of a Thomas Babe play called *Taken in Marriage*, Bob Boyette and Thomas Miller, in from "the Coast," invited Dale and me to join them in the Palm Court of the Plaza Hotel to talk about costarring me in a new situation comedy of theirs. They had seen me in the play and were very optimistic about my future on the small screen. The show would of course be shot in Los Angeles. I had never dreamed of leaving New York and would never have gone looking for a job in California. It wouldn't have occurred to me. However, now that an opportunity was staring at me, I had to face facts. It had become all too clear that good reviews in Off-Broadway plays weren't going to build up to the kind of independence I was going to need. Here was a chance.

My girls were remarkable soldiers about it, as they have been about everything. They agreed that it might be exciting to live in California for a while, and we shipped out on the train. I had the nutso idea that it would be good for the three of us to travel across the country the slow way, so that the enormity of what we were doing would sink in on us. Why I thought it would be good to press that fact into the consciousness of these two little girls I do not know. It didn't do a lot for my consciousness either. The day we left New York, a few friends came to the station to see us off. Arthur was there too, sick at heart. I could see misgiving in all their faces. They all knew, even ever positive Dale, that I was too old to go to California seeking my fortune. I knew it too, but I didn't see any other options.

The Messrs. Boyette and Miller were unstintingly kind to me while I was working for them; they are gentlemen to whom I am happy to be indebted. That particular show did not turn out to be one of their hundred million hits. Be that as it may, Gigi and Mary Dixie and I were on the West Coast, and we weren't going to give up right away.

There is a wonderful song the Gatlin Brothers recorded. I did it in one of my first New York cabaret appearances, by which time we'd been living in California about five years. It's called "All the Gold in California," and it warns the newcomer that he's not likely to win in this gambling place, no matter how big a hot shot he is. Listen for it on the radio.

California made New York City seem like a Sunday school class. Money. Power. And what people will do to get it. And how pleasant everyone is while they're doing it. In New York you get a frontal attack; in Hollywood no one ever attacks; everybody keeps right on smiling; one rarely sees the knife. I have never adjusted to the bad things about working in L.A. I just try to keep going down my line and behaving the way I was brought up. So far I'm still working, which in its way is a miracle. Well, it is and then again it isn't. I have examples close by to inspire me and give me strength. There's my father of course, and there's my Aunt Helen.

My aunt, Helen Hillsman, is who and what I was thinking about when I used the expression "an upspringing spirit." Aunt Helen is my mother's sister, the baby in the family, the horsewoman, the one the money ran out on before she got to go to college, the one who took herself to Memphis fresh out of high school at sixteen years of age and got a job in the cotton business. When Mr. Charles Schlemmer, her partner at the Southern Pickery, died, she lost her heart for the business, sold it, and went into the health food business. She's had Good Life Natural Foods for more than twenty years now, and she's going full tilt. She's a sight to see as she pulls out of our driveway in McLemoresville, driving like Jehu in the Bible, white hair, black car, black leather gloves of course, and her boxer dog Tempest sitting in the front seat beside her. (Aunt Helen has been known to make the two-hour trip from Memphis to McLemoresville with three people squeezing together in the back seat and Tempest enjoying the view from up front.) She has a great business in the health food store because, as with everything else she's gone about in her life, she's worked at it like a dog. (No offense, Tempest.) She has read and studied and researched her products, and she is vitally interested in whether or not each customer is receiving benefit from what he's taking. She herself is walking testimony that whatever she is doing is working.

In my childhood when Aunt Helen came to see us, it was the big time. She would drive up in a long-finned Cadillac, dressed to kill, smelling special, and bearing surprises. When I was two, she gave me a fancy little strawberry chintz sundress that remains the favorite garment I've ever owned and the one I felt my all-time prettiest in, barely winning, however, over the diaphanous white strapless evening gown she bought me my senior year in high school. (When my babies were two and three, Gina surprised Midge and me with strawberry chintz sundresses for our little girls; I've never known where she found the fabric.) Aunt Helen would let Midge and me climb up into bed with her on Sunday morning and "read" the funny papers together. Nothing we did annoyed her. On Christmas Eve she would sweep in out of the snow covered with furs and laden with exquisitely wrapped presents. The wrapping was enough to make the occasion all by itself. She was the epitome of glamour. I never dreamed that she had problems or troubles. She didn't broadcast anything but good news.

When we went to visit her and Grandmother at their apartment on Peach Street, everything smelled like Aunt Helen's own special smell, which was better than good. We were allowed to play with the beautiful music boxes on the coffee table in her living room and with the glass dishes that must have been ashtrays. (I didn't know about ashtrays when I was little. We didn't have them in our house, except three brass ones that Daddy brought back from Europe.) When we got to spend the night, we could hear the lions roaring from the zoo in Overton Park. We half enjoyed the scary imagination that they were loose and prowling the streets; we always begged the next morning to go to the zoo.

Once every year or so Daddy and Gina would bring us for a holiday at the Memphis Zoo; Aunt Helen would manage to slip away from the cotton plant to join us and would walk the whole zoo in her high heels, buying us popcorn and making the event superduper. Going out to the plant was superduper also. Aunt Helen would sometimes be in the office, but sometimes she'd rush in from the gin, still wearing her funny little cap to keep the cotton out of her hair, sailing around a mile a minute, but always happy to see us. During those years she had two boxer dogs, Mr. Murphy and after him O'Brien. Tempest is the first girl dog she's had and the first one I'm not afraid of.

One fall Midge and I saw a picture of gorgeous alligator high-heeled shoes and determined that we had to get some for Gina's Christmas present. Our plan was simple; we'd take our combined savings (a little over eighty dollars) and ask Aunt Helen to do the buying for us. The next time we saw her, we covertly gave her our money amidst much important whispering. Sure enough, when she arrived on Christmas Eve, Aunt Helen had our fabulous gift with her, wrapped and ready to go under the tree. We were beside ourselves with excitement. When Gina opened her present Christmas morning, there were the shoes and, of all things, a matching alligator shoulder bag. She nearly fainted and so did we. Then she kissed Midge and me, and hugged us, and then she kissed Aunt Helen and cried a little, and spanked her a little too. We had no idea that our little cache wouldn't have bought either the shoes or the purse.

Aunt Helen has been taking care of herself (and a few others) all by herself since she was sixteen years old, and I dare say there's been a moment here and there when she might have felt just a bit peaked, but you wouldn't know. When I get crummy and demoralized, I can think of the last time I've spoken with her or seen her, marvel at her tireless enthusiasm for the great new things she's up to now, the latest in organic foods, some new project she's got up her sleeve, her constant reminders that I have a whole life yet ahead of me, and find myself ashamed to feel down one instant longer. I am humbled when I think how she, a generation ahead of me, stands with head high, all five feet plus of her, and relishes being the loner that she is, never leaning or imposing on anyone for anything, facing whatever comes without a whimper, and always ready to come to the aid of her loved ones in the bargain.

When I was a college student in Memphis, late for class one day, I slid my car around a rain-slick corner into a telephone pole, and in a moment of supreme irresponsibility got out of the car and went on to class. It got towed away of course, and I didn't have the money to get it back and didn't know what to do. Imagine my surprise when Aunt Helen called me up and wanted to talk to me about my car. I could tell she was mad, and I was all prepared to take my licking, just hoping she wouldn't tell my parents of this gross negligence. To my amazement she wasn't mad about my wrecking the car. She was mad that I hadn't called her for help. She said that she had already bailed the car out for me, and we'd forget it, but this was her warning: "If you *evah* get 'in a tight' again and don't call me, there'll be trouble, my dahling, do you undahstand?" (I still don't know how she found out.)

At certain times when I was first making my way in New York, I would have a lean spell and just not see how I was going to come up with the rent. Invariably—and I mean without fail—an envelope addressed with familiar green ink would arrive and a check with a note saying, "Just had a feeling you could use a little help right now."

I suppose nothing about having an absent husband—not even parents' evening at school or Easter egg decorating the night before Easter—could be quite as bleak as Christmas Eve after the children go to bed. It's just the loneliest time. When I was by myself in New York, Aunt Helen came flying up like Santa, bringing a merry Christmas with her. I remember how one night we were trying to finish the tree trimming at umpteen o'clock, and we encountered the well-known problem of getting the angel on the top. My heart could attack me right now as I visualize Aunt Helen in a black velvet gown, up on the stepladder, paring off interfering branches with a butcher knife and triumphantly affixing the angel.

If you, Dear Reader, don't have someone like my Aunt Helen to pull you out of the doldrums, then look around you and open yourself to somebody you may not know yet. A positive state of mind is not an accident, believe me. Not after the age of seven. Because of my gratitude for the good cheer from those with whom I live and work the closest, I take it as my responsibility to keep sunny in return. Annie Potts told me that she's held to only one unbreakable rule with her children: they have to be cheerful. To quote Annie's friend, Joseph Addison, "Cheerfulness keeps up a kind of daylight in the mind, and fills it with a steady and perpetual serenity."

The amount of good we can do with a glad heart and a smile is incalculable, and the good of it goes out to others and stays with us at the same time. Thirty-second encounters in a coffee shop, at the airport, waiting for a traffic light to change, on an elevator, or at the grocery store checkout—no moment is too fleeting for a friendly attitude to make its mark. There's a lovely lady at the cash register of the Thrifty Drug Store who is able to make a person feel good while she's taking your money, no mean feat. I can't tell you how tall she is or describe her features, but I remember that she's lovely. Beauty of the spirit.

Here I go, about to toot the yoga horn once again. Well, it's made such a difference for me that I feel impelled to keep talking about it. It does so much. I've already bragged on how yoga can reverse health problems, reshape your body, clear your head, and make you as pretty as a speckled pup.

Can you remember how you used to feel as a child when you woke up on a summer morning? Do you remember what a happy prospect it was to greet the day when anything was possible and you had no aches or pains? I try to remind myself, when I forget it, that a healthy person has a big edge in staying happy, is beautiful to see, and is wonderful to be around.

I have learned to connect a low mood with the need for exercise, which for me is yoga. (My learning how to control my eating at about the same time that I started doing yoga is more than a coincidence. It still seems miraculous to me. Yoga just might have the same effect on you, Dear Reader, if I may be so bold.) The practice of yoga is exercise made wonderful, especially for those of us who don't like even to hear the word *workout*. My two yoga videos I pointedly entitled *un*workouts, as a matter of fact. It's amazing when I think about having made two exercise tapes. Me, whose most developed muscle is in my jaw.

One day when Wendy Merson was giving me a class in my dressing room at *Designing Women*, I was moaning a little with pleasure as I could feel a particular stretch relieving the tension in my low back, and Wendy said in her dulcet fashion, "Dixie, you have to make a yoga video. You have to share what you get out of this with other people." I stayed in the stretch a little longer; it felt too good to stop. By the time I sat up, I had decided to do it. I had to bear witness to as many people as I could. I had to show at least some of the good that yoga could do.

The first video MCA decided we should not call a "yoga" tape, as there was concern about yoga being viewed by lots of people as a religion, one that would disagree with Christianity, for example. So right off the bat I made it as plain as possible that I, a Methodist, found nothing contrary to my religion in what I was doing. By the time we made the second video, Jane Fonda and several other beautiful specimens had jumped on the bandwagon and put out yoga tapes. I am proud to claim the distinction of being first to take yoga from the esoteric into the mainstream fitness arena.

In just about every form of physical activity I've experienced, the prevailing wisdom is "If it hurts, keep going until you don't feel the pain anymore." That palliative has never made sense to me, and thank heavens it doesn't apply in yoga. Yoga encourages us to explore the sensations we experience, to let the mind focus in the area of discomfort, to "breathe into" it, and never to force the body past a point of painful resistance. Almost all the poses are challenging for me, but the challenge is in testing and stretching one's endurance rather than in pushing through pain.

Let's discuss pain for a minute. As I have said, I don't like it, I'm scared of it, and furthermore I don't believe we have to sacrifice ourselves on that altar to look good. Yoga is a way of exercising that reduces and even eliminates pain, and I am living testament to the truth of that claim. I am not talking crazy flaky stuff; I'm telling you what I know from my own experience. I have arthritis. I was X-rayed and diagnosed as having it thirteen or fourteen years ago. Ten years ago I dreaded the act of getting out of bed in the morning because standing on my feet hurt so bad. Feet, ankles, shoulders, back, neck, and hands. It jumped around from here to there to surprise me, but it was *always* there to greet me in the morning when I put my weight down on my ankles and feet. Not long after I started to take yoga classes, the pain started to get better. Now, today, I am pretty much pain-free. It doesn't hurt to get out of bed. I have almost no discomfort anywhere except a bit in my neck, which is complicated by two whiplash accidents that have left it with no arch in it. (I know I could have sued, but I was brought up to believe that suing is ignoble.)

This business of hurting someplace or other all the time gets old after x number of years, doesn't it? Are we tired of it enough to do something about it? That's the question. Allow me to reiterate this amazing fact: *I do not hurt from arthritis anymore* except when I get derelict occasionally and miss my yoga stretches for a few days. Then my body reminds me.

It is possible to become acquainted with your body, fingertips to toes, in such a gentle and friendly way that you do pretty well know what's going on. It is possible to learn how to coax muscles to let go tension enough to start building strength. It's really rough to start putting pressure on a poor weak knotted-up muscle, and what many of us don't realize (I didn't) is that lots of times that painful cramped muscle is very weak. Hard doesn't always mean hard and strong. Sometimes it means needful.

Make friends with your body; your body will love you for it. Make friends with your back and it will stop punishing you.

And then there's this new and revolutionary thing called *breathing*. Learning to be aware of and control our breath is the beginning and the end in yoga; it's the ground base for physical fitness, weight control, and stress management. We can learn to send the breath to the part of our body that's hurting and ease the pain. We can heal a lot of things that get out of whack. We can get well. We can stay well. We can be healthy and vigorous and enjoy a well person's state of mind. I can't believe that I'm the rah-rah girl for anything that requires physical exertion, but amazingly enough that's what I've turned into. While I'm working up a sweat, so many lovely things are going on in my head that the exertion is a joyous one.

I try to perform my yoga postures and movements with the investment of seeking to make all of it beautiful, which of course it is when a great yogini or yogi is doing it. I allow myself to believe that I am a true yogini, capable of drawing forth the mystical beauty inherent in this ancient ritual. When I can sincerely and without self-consciousness hold on to this fancy, a heightened experience and result is possible.

Now I can appreciate Grandmother Hillsman's oft-repeated reminder, "The body is the temple of the soul." In my mind's eye I can feel fresh oxygen perking through my blood vessels as I'm doing a Sun Salutation; I can feel my waist getting smaller and my low back muscles releasing as I breathe into a long side bend; I can imagine invigorating pressure on my thyroid gland when I'm holding the Rabbit pose. The stronger I learn to make my mental images, the more effective the yoga routine. I took my good health for granted when I was younger, but not anymore. It's a prime ingredient for the life I want to live and I have become willing to make the effort necessary for it. I want to live in the glow of good health. I want to feel candescent.

A wise man said that all man's troubles come from his "not being able to sit still in a room." The purpose of all yoga poses, or asanas, with their widely varying degrees of difficulty, is to develop the capacity for stillness, the ability to sit without strain for long periods of time, and to meditate. All that stretching and sweating and balancing and strengthening was not originally intended by the ancient yogis to make your figure pretty so you could be on television. Astounding, isn't it? They figured out all that so we could "send our mind to the blue skies."

Our lives begin with breathing in and end with breathing out. When we breathe in, we are literally taking in life. Yoga, like life, begins with the breath and ends with the breath. The verb *inspire* means "to breathe in, to animate, to put life into," as well as "to infuse with feeling or thought." Yoga practice reminds us of this fact over and over and teaches us not to take our breath for granted.

Sam Keen, in his book *Hymns to an Unknown God*, says, "Follow the movement of your breathing, and it will take you to the prime mover." He gives us this beautiful conception: "I am a gossamer curtain hanging in a window separating time and eternity, blowing back and forth in the everlasting breeze."

When I begin my own yoga practice, I sit cross-legged in half-lotus position (one foot on one knee) and close my eyes. I try to feel my sit-bones making contact with the floor, and at the same time feel my spine extending up toward the sky. The head is forward of the spine, so that the crown of the head lifts straight up and is the tallest part of the body. My hands resting easily on my knees, I breathe slowly in and out, letting my stomach relax and move with the breath. I become aware of the air as it is drawn in through my nostrils, how it feels against the skin, cool as I breathe in and warmer as I exhale.

Now I let both arms float up as I inhale, stretching way out to the side, then meeting over my head, stretching way up, and holding the breath in for just a moment. As I exhale, I let my arms float slowly out to the side and then down gently to the floor. I repeat this movement very slowly five or six times, until I'm ready to begin stretching over to the side. Then I rest one hand on the floor and as I inhale, lift the other arm out and up and over, so that I'm stretching way over toward the side, neck relaxed, weight down on my forearm. Here I stay for several long deep breaths. Then I change and stretch to the other side.

Sounds so simple, looks so simple, but let me tell you, the results are breathtaking. It's the beginning of going from whatever cloud you may have been under to feeling *good*. By the time I've done just the little bit I've described, my body is waking up and wanting more, more oxygen riding in on the breath, and feeling so good.

I enjoy my little jest: Hey, everybody! Start breathing as if your life depended on it! It's really a matter of life and breath!

Once we have connected the mind with the breath and have become aware of the simple act of taking in and expelling it, we can learn to envision its passage through the body. As we are able to slow down our breathing rate more and more, which is possible with practice, we will become capable of breathing "into" areas of muscle tension or pain.

Most remarkable of all the benefits of yoga for me is the sense of serenity that comes over me. At the end of a session, unless time is an overriding concern, I go back to a seated position and remain in reverie for a little bit. I'm not of the "stay turned in on yourself all the time to find true happiness" school of thought; I find isolated spirituality selfish. However, a period of contemplation should hold the world at bay long enough for one to regain a balanced perspective, to let the spirit bubble up. The human spirit, if encouraged, will be pleased to keep on bubbling up.

What about dreams that don't materialize? Do we have to forget about them and concentrate on other things in order to stay positive? A letter came to me not long ago that included this quotation: "It's never too late to become what you wanted to be." Is that true? I think it depends on what you want to be. If your ambition can be defined by what you hope to become inside yourself, then the statement can be true.

I wanted to sing grand opera, and more I wanted to sing at the Metropolitan Opera. When I was a tiny little girl, I became intensely attracted to the Saturday afternoon radio broadcast from the Met; at four years of age I announced to my parents that I was going to sing at the Metropolitan Opera in New York City. I was used to looking into the radio as I listened, in an effort to see the little creatures inside it who made those thrilling sounds. I could never catch a glimpse of them; I guessed that they must be some very special variety of leprechauns, who hid behind the flickering tubes when they saw me coming, or that maybe they were invisible. Whatever they were, I knew it was my destiny to join them some day in the Metropolitan Opera in New York City, which I thought was in the radio, but I secretly dreaded the mysterious process by which they'd have to shrink me down to get me in there. When I confided to my Mother and Daddy my glorious plan for the future and expressed my concern as to how "they" would know when I was ready to sing at the Metropolitan, I remember a certain kind of smile that passed between them and how my father dignified my question with a pause for thought before he answered, "Those people at the Metropolitan Opera have ways of knowing these things, precious. Don't you worry."

That was my dream and my destiny, and I hoped for it unreasoningly. As it turned out, my dream did not become my destiny. I needn't have worried about getting shrunk down and put in the radio, because I did not have enough voice for grand opera or enough discipline, or maybe the tonsillectomy that left my throat a mess of scar tissue did me in. I'll never know for sure. I do know that it's been a twenty-five-year struggle to adjust to the disappointment, and I've been not entirely successful in the attempt. So, as to whether it's never too late to become what we wanted to be, I can't say that it's never too late for me to become an opera singer, 'cause it ain't goin' to happen. However, I can say that it's not too late to keep studying, to live with music, and to delight in my cabaret career. They say genius does what it must and talent does what it can. I'm afraid I fit in with the talent.

It can be too late for the literal manifestation of a dream but not too late to return to the source of the desire. It will never be too late for me to sing.

> *Thanks to the human heart by which we live,*
> *Thanks to its tenderness, its joys, and fears,*
> *To me the meanest flower that blows can give*
> *Thoughts that do often lie too deep for tears.*
>
> —WILLIAM WORDSWORTH

A KIND HEART

I guess I was a crybaby when I was little; I remember being called that by the same sensitive playmates who called me Horsetooth. I turned to tears easily for such a happy child as I was, experiencing extremes of joy and distress from infancy. It

followed that at a very early age I became uncommonly at-
tuned to the blessing of an act of kindness. My brother and
sister accommodated me at every turn and behaved in a pro-
tective way toward me even when we were all very young.

I was afraid of lots of things and I could not endure pain.
Midge wasn't that way at all; she was glad to go first into the
kitchen at night if the lights were out and we wanted a snack.
It didn't bother her one bit, but I saw things in the dark.
(Certain things I didn't have sense enough to be afraid of, like
jumping off the barn roof hoping an old umbrella would operate as a parachute, in which hope I was disappointed but relieved to get off with a sprained ankle.)

At a very early age I became afraid of losing my mother,
even before I could comprehend enough to be afraid that she
might die. Daddy seemed an invincible fortress of protection,
but Gina, even though she could work like a man and was
dynamic to the same extent that Daddy was, seemed perish-
able, threatened. I tried to hide that fear, from myself as well
as anybody else, lest the thought of it would bring it about. I
learned to hide most of my fears and not to cry every time I
wanted to. I became afraid of crying.

I was not afraid of performing until puberty. For eleven
years I jumped up and sang or made a speech or recited a
poem at the drop of a hat with no nervousness. When I was
almost fourteen years old I stood up in the choir loft one
Sunday morning to "sing a solo," as I had been doing almost
since I could walk, and started shaking horribly. I got through
the song somehow but not without causing grave concern in
the ladies who were sitting in the pew behind me, watching
me tremble. That was my first experience of stage fright, and
it was not my last. Ever since that day, performing has put
me somewhere between extreme nervousness and scared sick.
Usually the panic subsides once I begin to perform, and most
of the time I'm able to do a good job in spite of it, or maybe
because of it.

I'm afraid of other things: not being liked, failing my children, failing the promise I was born with, mice and rats, snakes

and lizards, strange dogs, heights and flying, my husband's displeasure, and on. Daddy has always said that anybody with good sense and a conscience is afraid of some things, that there's no disgrace in being afraid, so long as you go ahead and do what you see as right. It's always been a comforting thought to me, because I'm secretly ashamed of being a scaredy-cat. My demeanor doesn't often give me away; knowing what I sometimes cover up in myself allows me to suspect the superconfidence I run into so often in my business and to excuse it as I do my own pretenses.

If you're wondering why I would first bring up fear when I mean to talk about kindness, please bear with me. A fragile psyche has deep appreciation for a compassionate act. When you've spent your life with your heart fluttering in your chest *and* on your sleeve, starting at your own shadow, for Heaven's sake, the comfort offered by a tender heart seems much and begets profound gratitude for kindnesses that come your way, large or small. Well, let me back up.

There are no small kindnesses. Anytime a gentle thoughtful *word* comes my direction, I'm grateful, especially now that just about everyone I encounter has his or her head down over a computer screen while conducting business, rarely looking a person in the face to pass a pleasant time of day. How barren those impersonal transactions are, worse than having to talk on the telephone, which is bad enough.

Every time some unknown motorist, a total stranger in another car, allows me, feeling helpless and stupid, into a lane I've missed in traffic, in that moment my heart beats along with that person's. Car after car seems bent on preventing my getting where I need to go, and on the freeway it's purely dangerous. I sometimes wonder why so many people want to send my car all the way to Ventura or else run over me. When someone waves me in ahead of him and out of my trouble, I am suffused with gratitude, made glad again to be out in the world among others like me, trusting again in our common ground and the hope of "good will toward men," all from a stranger's simple gesture of graciousness. Wordsworth's beautiful phrase, "little, nameless, unremembered acts of kindness," he used to describe the "best portion of a good man's life."

I have an ambition to school my heart in kindness. I want very much to give what I have received. Tennessee Williams's "tenderness of the heart" applies to many of the dear hearts I've known and to none more than to my grandmother, Mama Carter. She was extremely shy, inordinately so, as I look back on it. Evelyn Bramley Pace told me once that she had been bowled over when "Miss Ethel" (Mama Carter) attended a bridal shower in her honor, because everyone in McLey knew that Miss Ethel didn't go anywhere but to church. Mama was smart and funny and very resolute when she needed to be, but she didn't promote that picture of herself. She loved to say that she was a simpleton and ought to just "go to the garden." I believe that "go to the garden" meant about what "get lost" would mean now. We would always raise up a merry alarm against such a thing, and the threat would subside in laughter.

Mama was the kindliest person I have ever known, except for Uncle Jack. The pretty English face she got from both her mother, Samantha Adeline Bailey, and from the Harveys, her father's side of the family. She looked to me like I thought angels probably looked. If she heard me say that now she'd probably add, "It would have to be a plump angel." She kept her house in perfect order, cooked three meals a day, and had time to read the Bible morning and evening, so that she read it through entirely each year.

Mama was a wonderful haven of comfort for the recently punished. I remember getting my soft little piece of torn sheet and heading across the driveway to Mama's house after a spanking one early evening. I wasn't more than three or four years old, and ordinarily Gina wouldn't have let me go over there so close to dark, but because she'd just spanked me, she felt sorry for me and allowed me to escape. I remember how sorry for myself I felt standing outside the kitchen door peeking through the glass and calling for Mama to come let me in, then when I saw her appear, launching a new freshet of tears and holding my sheet up over my face in the most heartrending and pitiable way possible. Mama opened the door and I made my grab for her. I remember how her apron felt against my hot face and how she kissed and petted me and gave me a biscuit with butter and sugar on it, which was one of the things I was hoping for. Then she took me up in her lap and rocked me, another thing I was hoping for. After a while Gina came in, kissed Mama, kissed me, and carried me home to bed.

Mama was naturally musical, as were all on that side of the family. She sang and played the piano for us and gave us our first piano lessons. I learned to play "Hard Times, Can't Make a Dime," "Three Blind Mice," and "Bringing in the Sheaves." She taught us our first scales, and when we started official piano lessons, she helped us to practice. In the fourteen years I knew Mama, although she must have had plenty of provocation, she never raised her voice to me except once, when I was eleven years old.

It was after Papa had died and she had begun spending the bad weather months living in our house with us. One Sunday morning I got up and came downstairs earlier than the rest of the family, consumed with my desire to see if I could replicate Becky Presson's spectacular performance at the talent contest in Huntingdon the night before. We hadn't started to school in Huntingdon yet, so I wasn't in the contest, but at least we did get to go see it. Becky, blessed with a startling set of pipes for a youngster, had wiped up the stage (and won the contest, a point that wasn't lost on yours truly) with "You Gotta See Mama Every Night." On this particular morning, as I was pouring the bowl of cold cereal we were allowed to have instead of a hot breakfast *only* on Sunday, I had forgotten about singing at the Metropolitan Opera. I wanted to scald the air. I tore into what had overnight become my dream number, "You Gotta See Mama Ev-ver-ry Night." Every note, word, gesture, jerk, and wiggle of Becky's was seared into my brain and I was reproducing it verbatim, working up steam as I went along. I was somewhere around "I don't like the kind of a man, who works on the installment plan" when Mama appeared, disbelief and revulsion writ large on her brow. She wasted no

time or words in notifying me with heat that she never wanted
to hear me singing a song like that on the Sabbath day again.
She must have regretted having to reprimand me; nonetheless
I had offended her sense of decency and she had no choice. It
was clean, clear, and final, an uncomplicated and complete
comeuppance. For all her gentleness it didn't do to make
Mama mad.

Those years Mama lived with us thunderstorms would often
cause power failures. It was best when the electricity went out
at night, because we would light candles and sit by the fire and
say nursery rhymes, even brother Hal, going around the room
one at a time until we ran out. The person who could keep
coming up with another rhyme longest won the game. Mama
would hold Midge on her lap and I would sit beside her so she
could help us if we got stuck. I can hear Mama saying this one
as if she were saying it now:

> Who has seen the wind?
> Neither you nor I,
> But when the trees bow down their heads
> The wind is passing by.
>
> Who has seen the wind?
> Neither I nor you,
> But when the leaves are dancing
> The wind is passing through.

And this one:

> The north wind doth blow
> And we shall have snow
> And what will poor robin do then,
> Poor thing?
> He'll sit in the barn
> To keep himself warm
> And hide his head under his wing,
> Poor thing!

which was so sad to us, as we chimed in together, "Poor fing." If it was wintertime, Mama and Gina would hold blankets in front of the fire until they got toasty, and then we'd all hurry up the stairs to our cold bedrooms with the warm blankets around us and jump into our beds piled high with quilts, "me and Midge" snuggled in together.

Wise people say that happiness isn't having what you want but wanting what you have. That standard and the beatitudes —every one of them, particularly "The meek shall inherit the earth"—would have assured Mama's state of grace: she reaped the "harvest of a quiet eye." As one who loved where she was and had no desire to leave it, she derived a lifetime of pleasure from what was at hand; she loved her family and doted on them, especially us children. She loved silly fun and she loved to laugh. She knew all the birds by their songs and all the constellations. She loved always being able to tell what the weather was going to be like and helping us to find the Big Dipper and the Little Dipper, and she genuinely enjoyed her daily ritual of rinsing out the cow's water tub and refilling it with cool clear water. I have heard many times how my brother, just barely walking, stood beside her, watching the cow stare placidly at the tub Mama had just filled, and commanded, "Cow! Gint it! [Drink it!] Gint dee wat-ter!" His grandmother's kindly efforts weren't to go unappreciated, even if he had to exert himself to come up with his first sentence, which I think that was. One day while she was petting and fussing over him, she asked him playfully, as one will ask a tot, "Hal, are you Mama's baby?" He had to tell her the truth. "No, ma'am, I'm Gina's baby." Mama enjoyed repeating that little story; that's how it was supposed to be.

I don't suppose Mama Carter in her humility would have guessed at the lasting influence of her benignity. I hope she knows how many times we talk about her, how we've missed her, and how we remember her with utter devotion. I hope she knows how grateful her progeny are for the translucent example of her life. I hope she knows how much we loved her.

The world stands out on either side
No wider than the heart is wide;

The soul can split the sky in two,
And let the face of God shine through.

—EDNA ST. VINCENT MILLAY

A GROWING SOUL

In the spring of 1981, shortly after we had started keeping company, Hal Holbrook took me over to Marina Del Rey to meet his New Zealander sailing mate Robert Rossiter. The year before Hal had sailed single-handed from San Francisco to Hawaii in the Transpac race. He had later taken his sloop, the *Yankee Tar*, on to Moorea in the Tahitian Islands. Now Hal and Rossiter were getting ready to go back to the South Sea Islands and sail to Pago Pago and the Tongas. I knew that Hal was thinking of inviting me to go sailing with them but that he wouldn't consider doing it unless Mr. Rossiter brought it up by himself. I didn't know what I would say if they asked me to join them. I am a poor swimmer and had never set foot on a sailboat. I had been fishing plenty in the Tennessee River, and Daddy had taken us out deep-sea fishing from Sarasota, but this was a horse of a different color.

Rossiter was working on a boat when we picked him up to go to lunch. What a sight he was—tall, broad, and tanned, snow white hair blowing around a leathery face, blue eyes glittering. "Hay-ee, Edmirel," he called out to Hal. I thought at once of Errol Flynn and Douglas Fairbanks, the swashbucklers. Hal said later he'd had the same reaction when he first met him. We went to lunch; they talked mostly about provisioning the boat, charts they needed, how ready *Yankee Tar* was for the voyage, how she was faring at anchor in Moorea, where she had just weathered a hurricane, what additional equipment they might need, and a little about Peggy Slater's boat business. (Peggy Slater was a raw-boned redheaded tyrant whom I was to meet later on and who never liked me because I got in the way of certain fantasies she had about her friendship with Hal. She sold sailboats for a living and had homes in L.A. and Hawaii. Peggy was held in high regard by even the saltiest sea dogs. She had skippered all-male crews in the Los Angeles–Hawaii Transpac and in the Hobart-Sydney Race. She had sailed single-handed since she was a girl and had survived more than one terrifying situation at sea, the most memorable the time when she was thrown overboard while sailing solo through the Hawaiian Islands. With one hand broken and twisted in the trailing jib sheet, she was dragged through the sea for hours, until finally, through ingenuity and herculean effort, she managed to save herself. She was pretty tough to handle even if she liked you, and since she patently thought I was about as worthwhile as a Crackerjack prize and treated me accordingly, I was scared of her. The funny part is that I saw why she couldn't stand me—a big sissy trying to horn in on her territory with the sailing fellows—and I didn't much blame her, and although I was never comfortable around her, I grudgingly liked her. Anybody who can do something as well as she could sail has got to be admired.)

I sat quietly through the meal, laughed when they were being funny, and once in a while asked a question. I knew I'd never get invited if I appeared to be a talker. Sailing expertise was not required to figure out that nobody would want to be confined in a small space with a big mouth. Sure enough, and as fate would have it, just as we were parting company, Mr. Rossiter smiled and said, "Whay-ee douwn't yew come too?"

My heart leapt up. "Why, thank you," I said, looking for Hal's reaction. "I'm not much of a swimmer."

"Douwn't worry about thet. if yew fawl awf the boat, yew *dree-own* enywaey."

Strange comfort, but strangely comforting. I called Midge that night, told her about the invitation, and asked her advice.

I knew better than to call my parents and ask theirs. (One of my axioms: Don't ask your parents' advice unless you intend to take it.) Midge was unequivocal. "At forty years of age, I don't think you can expect to receive too many more invitations to go sailing around in the South Seas, Didi. Go."

I made three sailing trips over the next thirteen months with Hal and the Mate, as we call him, from Pago Pago (pronounced *Pango Pango*) to the Tonga Islands (if they could put an *n* in *Tonga*, why couldn't they put one in *Pago?*), where we anchored at the Port of Refuge Hotel on Vava'u, then at Nuku Island and Kapa Island. Next we sailed from the Tongas to New Zealand, a 1,504-mile voyage, and last cruised around the Fijis, from Suva to the Great Astrolabe Reef. We hear the expression, "I wouldn't take anything for it." Well, *I would not take anything for it.*

After flying 4,500 miles in three legs, each leg in a smaller aircraft, I arrived in Pago Pago carrying, along with my duffel bag, a bottle of Taittinger Blanc de Blanc and a few ounces of caviar on dry ice, I was greeted warmly, allowed to sleep a couple of hours in the local hotel, and taken thence to the *Yankee Tar.* I was told *exactly* where to put everything I had with me and was told for the first of many times to get used to holding on to something with one hand all the time, even when we were anchored. Having received my initial instruction in boat behavior, I was left alone with a bucket of ammonia water and a sponge, *to wipe off every article and surface in the galley,* while they went out shopping for provisions. Hal explained before they left that this exercise would serve two purposes: at the same time everything was getting cleaned, I would learn by feel where each thing was—every knife, flashlight, etc.—very important to my safety if we encountered rough weather. They were gone all afternoon and I was pretty squeamish by the time they returned. You try spending two or three hours down under in a gently rocking boat with your face in a bucket of ammonia, and tell me if you don't feel a little squeamish, especially if you've gone off to the back side of nowhere to entrust your life to a couple of adventurers whose first act of protection is to leave you alone to get sick at your stomach.

When they got back, I was so glad to see them again, and they were so impressed with how hard I'd worked, that my dismal thoughts disappeared. We spent that evening rubbing Vaseline on the eggs, to seal the air out and keep them fresh, and wrapping them, and wrapping and stowing the other foodstuffs they'd brought aboard, ever careful for any cockroaches, the bane of the South Seas sailboat. That night we stayed on land again, and the next day we got the boat ready to go midafternoon, and then we were off, motoring out of the harbor and away from land. I can't remember being as nervous as Hal has told me I looked to them. He says with a fond smile, "You were very pale and very quiet." There was no wind, so we had no sail up. Hal said we were to take three-hour watches around the clock and galley duty every third day. The first night they let me have the nine o'clock watch to give me a break, so that I could sleep from midnight until six in the morning.

Sometime in the middle of that six hours I woke up. The motion of the boat and my tiredness had put me into such a deep sleep the moment I crawled into my berth that at first I didn't know what had waked me. Then I realized that I had waked because there was no sound. The motor had stopped. A soft rain was blowing down into the aft cabin where I lay. I heard the muffled voices of the two men on the deck and the soft clinking of steel against steel, and *then* I felt a sensation impossible to describe and impossible to forget. The boat began to move forward in a way different from before. I felt all at once lifted and cradled and moved and rocked, as if a great being had lightly taken me up like a little baby in his arms, and at this moment I entered a state of bliss that I cannot ever think of without a thrill of emotion.

The wind was in the sails.

We were sailing. I fought against the sweet sleep that kept trying to pull me down again, wanting to put it off and inten-

sify the exquisite pleasure of the cool wet air on my face and
the boat like a living creature moving under me, the only
sounds occasional murmurs between the men and gentle slaps
of the balmy sea against *Yankee Tar*'s hull, as she lifted and
slipped along, sliding us through the night.

Just as the spirit is not the same thing as consciousness, the
soul is not the same thing as the spirit. We shouldn't confuse
them with each other. The human spirit is that animating
essence the French call *l'élan vital*, the vital spirit. It is this
spirit that makes Aunt Helen someone no one forgets. It is
this spirit with which we engage the rest of the world, fight
our battles, revel in our successes, brave hard times, restore
our hopes, laugh and love and keep on trying. This is the juice,
the fuel for living. Although it is life in us that comes from
God, the spirit has a great deal to do with us in the world.

I believe that the soul doesn't have much to do with the
world or with other people, except as a dividend. The soul has
to do with just us, inside of ourselves, and God. The soul is
the part of us that is part of God. It's the only secret we have.
It's the only true privacy we know. Different people are born
with different souls, greater or smaller; you can see it in the
eyes. Those of us who feed our soul will be able to feel it
growing. If we do not nourish it, it will shrivel. If we nourish
it, it will grow.

I suppose I should have known that making the sailing trips
would be good for my soul. I didn't. I was thinking how exciting it would be, and how romantic. Looking back on it, I'd
have to admit having some idea that going all out to join Hal
in his passion for sailing would help to set the hook and reel
him in. That it did; that it did. Mission accomplished there.
What stuns me about it is not what happened to my darling
Hal but what happened to me.

I hadn't thought about getting stronger, much less hoped
for it. I don't think I knew it was happening until I got home
from the first trip and noticed that the Hollywood scene was

less intimidating than it had been. It wasn't a big deal; my mind was on the next sailing trip, not on me vis-à-vis show biz. The second trip was the long one, from the Tongas down to New Zealand. I had passed the test of the first one and was invited to come along again. The Mate had christened me the Bosun and had presented me with a bosun's whistle at the end of the first voyage. Now we all had names: Hal was the Admiral. (Rossiter had started calling Hal "Edmirel" a couple of years before, at the end of their first voyage together to Hawaii, when Hal, using only his sextant and celestial navigation, had brought them to a perfect landfall.) Rossiter was the Mate, and I was the Bosun. We could as well have been Robin Hood, Little John, and Maid Marian, for all of me; I had fallen out of time and into one of the adventure books I'd been glued to all my young years.

Hal was proud of me, especially proud of Rossiter's approval, and I was thrilled with everything about it—the storybook adventure, the magical beauty of the places we'd been, and my having measured up in the sailors' eyes, not to mention what had happened to me in my own eyes. Without malice aforethought I had been put, or had put myself, to what was for me a big test, and I had passed it. I was filled with glory. My avid and intemperate desire to make the next voyage, four times as long and probably fraught with gale force winds, defied common sense and judgment and resulted in a basically selfish decision to throw caution to the winds, as it were, and go, hoping and trusting that I wouldn't drown and leave my daughters without their mother.

In early October, after climbing the 135 stone steps from where we tied the dinghy to have our last breakfast at the Port of Refuge Hotel, where we watched the cook shinny up the palm tree outside to cut down the coconuts for our breakfast juice, convinced as ever that Sidney Greenstreet and Peter Lorre were both lurking just out of sight, we sailed out of Vava'u Harbor, just ahead of some rowdy weather. The wind was brisk, and we cleared the coral reefs of the Tonga Island chain with two reefs in the mainsail, after which Hal put us on a beam reach (a course at a 90-degree angle to the wind, the optimum sailing condition) and managed to keep us there. We stayed just ahead of the weather, made our landfall at Cape Brett, and docked in Auckland harbor in ten days to the hour, having averaged 150 miles a day. We were fairly flying a good part of the time, to make it in ten days even with having been becalmed for two days about five hundred miles out from New Zealand. Although we had the motor going and so were not absolutely standing still, those two days of calm were a little eerie; the atmosphere was strangely warm; we saw more than one albatross, which made me think of Coleridge's "Rhyme of the Ancient Mariner": "Water, water everywhere and not a drop to drink," and schools of dolphins and beautiful strange fish and whales. At night we often talked about sharks; the Mate had had a few run-ins with sharks, and I was endlessly curious to hear about them, repelled and attracted at the same time. With a queer mixture of feelings I can't find a name for I upped and slid myself into the dark silent sea one of those afternoons, just to see how it felt. That was some fast research; I found out how it felt swimming in the middle of the ocean, and then I found out how it felt to zip back up into the boat ever so hastily and be greeted by a couple of big old macho "I told you so's." We busied ourselves as best we could, washing clothes, washing our hair on deck with our jury-rigged shower, singing along with Waylon and Willie, practicing our shooting (cruising yachts usually carry guns in the unlikely but possible event of pirates), watching constantly for weather signs, and waiting for the wind, hoping it would get to us before the big storm we knew was a day or two behind us did.

I won't try to tell you about the whole trip, but I do want to talk about the night watches. Since there were three of us, the hours we were on watch, three hours each, changed every twelve hours. There was an easy case to be made for preferring the nine P.M. watch or the six A.M. or even the midnight watch —cold, cold, cold. But the fact is, the miserable three A.M. watch turned out to be my favorite.

The Mate was before me; when he'd pat my shoulder to

turn me out of my nice cozy berth, he'd have made a cup of tea, so at least there was that warmth. A sip of tea, into my foul weather gear, hook myself into the safety harness and the harness to the boat, hoist myself up into the helmsman's chair with a sea biscuit or two, check the compass heading, and get set for the next three hours' duty. Every five to ten minutes stand up on the side of the cockpit, clinging for dear life, literally, to the monkey bars (Hal's name for a crosspiece of steel he installed over the cockpit that attaches the dodger to the boom gallows), and check the horizon, all 360 degrees of it, for any shape against the sky. A big ship can run over you in less than twenty minutes from the time you see it on the horizon. At the end of each hour log the compass heading, distance run, speed, and significant weather changes, if there are any. Watch the sky for changing weather, particularly for squall lines. At all times and under all circumstances, hold on to the boat.

The simple act of holding on to the boat became increasingly interesting to me, especially during the dawn watch. Alone in the cockpit, no one else awake, holding steadfastly to the crossbar so I could stand up on the side of the boat to see over the dodger to the horizon as the boat rose and pitched along at seven knots, I would find a simile arranging itself in my mind, a simile that likened my willing my hands to hang on to a person willing himself to *live* in the broader and more abstract sense. The thought would recur there in the middle of the night: one instant of ambiguity about whether I wanted to be alive or not could send me into the dark fathoms below, to participate in this life no more. My mind had to keep instructing my hands to hold on. My hands had to do it full out, not halfway. I wondered if it wasn't a good thing to have that constant decision pushed in a person's face. I wondered if it would be possible to live that way all the time, grabbing on to life with both hands. I thought that I was very lucky to have been given new chances at life again and again, even though I had been apathetic, listless sometimes, not always holding on to it with all my might. I wanted to do better and be stronger.

The first days of the trip it was raining all the time, and the nights were too dark to see much of anything, even the horizon; Hal was having to navigate by sun-shots because we couldn't see the stars. We had been out maybe three days when the weather broke. I happened to have the three o'clock watch, and I saw the sun rise for the first time. I expected it to come up in the east, as usual. Nobody had told me about this. The dark sky gradually grew paler, the stars began to fade and then were suddenly gone, and next, unbelievably, a light pink color started up out of the western horizon, of all things, reflecting light from the sun, which hadn't shown up quite yet, heralding its arrival. Then that pink quickly changed to coral, then titian, then brilliant breathtaking rose. Color began chasing around the edge of the world in various hues of pinks, peaches, yellow, orange, fuchsia, and gold. In a few minutes the entire horizon was lit up, apparently the cue for old Mr. Sun to make his appearance. There he came, up from the east, in all his fiery glory; but his glory was not restricted to the east; it was all around and all above. All the heavens participated in his advent. I couldn't figure out where to look; the sunrise was happening everywhere and I didn't want to miss any of it. The eastern sky was dazzling; all the atmosphere around the sun was different shades of rose and scarlet, fanning out forever; but wait, get hold of your breath, the west was more dazzling than the east! The whole western dome had turned into a lavender dream, then the lavender was shot with gold, then in a few seconds, just as the sun edged up clear of the eastern horizon, all the way across the ocean the sky in the west burst into joyous purple applause. The sky over me and around me on every side was a rapidly changing kaleidoscope of rubies and amethysts dodging through gilt-edged clouds, a sight beyond dreams. I was awed, swept away, and utterly humbled. The sunrise at sea lasts longer than it does on land, or it seems to, but it doesn't last long enough to lock it into the mind's eye second by millisecond, as I would have wished to do. The colors won't hold still for an instant; one is constantly reflecting another, shooting out, fading, mutating, racing, and bouncing back and forth across the happy sky as if the great orb of heaven were no bigger than the inside of a china cup. When God takes out his paintbrush, He doesn't piddle around.

Hal and I talk sometimes about going ocean sailing again. If there were no practical aspects to consider, and if I had no other reason, I'd go out again just so I could see the sun rise.

> *Not in entire forgetfulness,*
> *And not in utter nakedness,*
> *But trailing clouds of glory do we come*
> *From God, who is our home.*

> —WILLIAM WORDSWORTH

My third trip with Hal and the Mate was the following spring, May 1982. In November of 1981 they had taken the boat out of the water and put her up "on the hard" in Auckland, where the Rossiter family lives, and had overseen major overhauling, scraping of barnacles, and repainting. Hal had gone back in January to sail in the Bay of Islands when the steering went out on them in a gale, causing them barely to miss going onto the rocks at Red Dog Island—very hairy business. They put the boat back up on the hard for more work after that and Hal returned to California and his by now desultory interest in his career. We all looked forward to joining up again in May. Early in May Hal flew back once again to New Zealand, and the fellows bade a fond farewell to Bob Rossiter's father, who had helped him work on the boat there, as well as to the rest of the family, and headed north. They beat hard against the wind for eleven days and brought dear *Yankee* into Suva in the Fiji Islands, where they anchored in the Hurricane Hole off the Tradewinds Hotel. In mid-May I flew to join them. There is one particular memory of this trip I must share with you.

As soon as I arrived in Fiji, the Mate began to educate us in native custom, as he did wherever we were. An important Fijian ceremony involved drinking a special brew made from a root, the root and the brew both called kava. He produced the kava root itself and boiled some up one night so we could try drinking it. I didn't take much; it tasted like mud and smelled bad too. It wasn't to his liking particularly either, he said, but if offered it, we should accept it and drink it as if it were good. He explained that it was imbibed from a coconut shell and that it had anesthetizing properties that made the drinker a little dopey. He told us that one was expected to get down the entire contents of the coconut shell at one go, then after finishing it, clap cupped hands twice together and say, "Boola boola."

I went through the motions with Hal, privately thought the Mate must surely be romanticizing the Fiji Islands to expect that we'd be likely to receive such a bizarre invitation, and forgot the whole thing. We went about our day sailing, gorgeous, beautiful, every day just one long smile, dinghying in to the hotel to shower and have dinner, or cooking dinner on the boat and eating under the stars, luxuriating in paradise. After a few days of this we went out for a week's cruising around the Great Astrolabe Reef and anchored at Mara Island, where I spent the afternoon of my birthday on the beach with Hal while Bob baked me a cake on the boat. It was darling, the way they plotted that out. Two days later we were sailing close to Ono Island and came across a little boat drifting along with three Fiji fishermen in it; their motor had played out and they needed a tow. As we were towing them back to their island, it was decided that we would have to go ashore if invited. I knew that these people used to be cannibals and I was scared. The Mate suggested that I put on my long cotton skirt and a long-sleeved shirt; apparently it was not nice manners for females to show much skin. As we drew closer to our destination, I decided to stay on the boat. When we got there and saw two long canoes full of young native men rowing out to meet us, I reversed field again; better to be eaten up on the island with the boys than to be eaten up alone on the boat, I figured as I buttoned that long-sleeved shirt up to my chin.

Some official personage of the village in a colorful sarong

waded out to meet the dinghy. He made signs that indicated how happy he was to receive the kind people who had hauled in their fishermen, then made more signs for us to follow him. The Mate could understand enough to know that we were being taken to meet the chief. We walked among several big thatched huts until our guide stopped at the door of the biggest one and motioned for us to enter. As soon as my eyes adjusted to the dark interior, I saw to my abject horror an enormous cauldron steaming in the middle of the space, by the center support pole. Two red-eyed young men were squatting beside it stirring the bubbling contents with big long wooden sticks. *Oh brother*, I thought, *there's the cooking pot*. All around the periphery of the hut were native men, older than the two acolytes, sitting cross-legged on the straw floor. There was not a woman in sight.

The head honcho, obviously the chief, stayed put and motioned with authority for us to come and sit by him. As we circled around the hut, each member of the unsmiling enclave rumbled, "Boola boola." The fellows answered back a couple of times. I answered each and every one with what I hoped would come across as a heartfelt wish for brotherly love and the end of cannibalism all over the world. Hal Holbrook has told that even at the time he couldn't get over the ferocious charm with which I was dealing out the boola boolas.

Hal was seated on the right side of the chief, I was on his left, and the Mate was on my left. The chief offered both men cigarettes, which they accepted. The apparel of choice seemed to be a single garment that looked like a diaper, and the occasional necklace. Apparently men got to show as much skin as they cared to. There was no window and no air and very few teeth. This group was a dentist's dream—or nightmare, depending. (Sadly, this observation was of no comfort just at that moment. Only after we were all the way back home did it dawn on me that the lack of teeth would make it difficult to eat you-know-what.) It was hard to see through the blue haze of cigarette smoke. Everybody was smoking cigarettes and drinking out of coconut shells. *Coconut shells!* Ye gads, maybe we had a chance to get out of here alive.

The chief called out something in his mumbo jumbo; the acolytes made two or three big whirls with their stirring sticks in the cauldron, which looked to be carved out of a giant tree trunk, and scooped up a dose into a coconut shell. As the kava brew was presented to Hal, I didn't dare look at the Mate and say, "Thank you for telling us about this," but I wanted to. Hal took it in both hands, downed it in one long gulp, handed it back, and clapped his hands twice. "Boola boola," he said, and a chorus of boolas answered him. More cigarettes were lit. The acolyte returned to the pot for another scoop and came to me. I was wishing pretty strongly that I had not been slipshod in my lesson. Now I didn't know if I could drink all that muddy stuff at once. On the other hand, I did know that the bigger question at this point was, Would the filthy broth from its filthy vessel kill me, even if I escaped getting tossed into the pot? Germs, worms, parasites, bacteria, or larvae notwithstanding, I was going to have to drink it down. So guzzle, guzzle, guzzle, I did. Amazing what you can do if you have no choice about it. It was down there, bugs and all. Everybody boola boola-ed and clapped along with me. Then, in his walking squat, the server presented Mr. Rossiter his portion, which of course the old Maeytee tossed off like nothing at all. Now we'd all done it, so there was a really big boola, a few more cigarettes were lit up, and the acolytes started refreshing the elders with the brew. By this time I realized that my entire mouth and part of my head had gotten numb and that a certain feeling of torpor (Dame Edith Evans, where were you when I needed you?) was stealing through me. Uh-oh, this was how they got you into the pot, I thought, drugged with the stuff they were going to cook you in.

It did seem as though it was time for something else to happen. We sat in silence for a long minute or two, as the elders muttered among themselves and the chief threw back a shellful of the old usual and lit up another Camel. Then the chief began to speak. "May I take this moment to welcome you to our village," he said. No mumbo jumbo. Measured and modulated tones. Prince Philip wouldn't have spoken in a more beautiful English accent. "I would like to thank you for your kind observance of our traditional ceremony of greeting. We see outsiders very rarely. Once in six months' time at most does a boat anchor here. When people do stop here, they are not usually respectful of us and our ways. Our customs are antiquated and primitive in the eyes of most strangers. You have dressed and behaved in accordance with our practices. You have treated us with respect. You are welcome here. Our village is open to you, and you are welcome to anything we have. You are welcome to remain at anchor in our harbor for as long as you wish."

Well, you could have knocked all three of us over with one feather. It turned out that the chief had been to school at Oxford and had lived for some years in England but had decided finally to come back to this place that was his home, this tiny isolated island, where he sat on the ground day after day in a dark and foul-smelling hut, quaffing a root potion that made the eyeballs turn yellow. What a mystery, this educated, elegantly spoken man sitting out his life here. It must have been civilized enough to suit him.

> My crown is in my heart, not on my head;
> Not deck'd with diamonds and Indian stones,
> Nor to be seen. My crown is call'd content.
> A crown it is that seldom kings enjoy.
>
> —WILLIAM SHAKESPEARE

We left the council hut with many words of goodwill back and forth, were greeted again by the village youths, who walked through the village with us as we smiled and said hello to the women and children, bought a few seashells they held out to us, and dinghied back to the boat. As it got dark, we quietly put out to sea.

That experience amounted to much more than an amusing

anecdote to remember together and recount to friends; the wiry little yellow-eyed chieftain had been, in retrospect, the essence of human dignity and graciousness. When one encounters a noble nature, one is apt to feel lifted and ennobled oneself. The question I have never asked my two traveling companions because it's never seriously come down out of the upstairs playroom of my mind, is this: What happened to the folks who came to that little island and didn't behave nicely? Just kidding, just kidding.

> *Take all away—*
> *The only thing worth larceny*
> *Is left—the Immortality—*
>
> —EMILY DICKINSON

With all the things I am afraid of, I'm no longer afraid of death. Of dying perhaps, and of pain, terrified, but not of death itself. When my mother died, I realized that this was a fact. I believe that a change had begun in me with the sailing trips. Thank you, my husband, for knowingly or not knowingly putting me into a great big schoolroom where Mother Nature was the teacher and the visual aids were provided by the Almighty.

> *How many loved your moments of glad grace*
> *And loved your beauty with love false or true*
> *But one man loved the pilgrim soul in you*
> *And loved the sorrows of your changing face.*

And thank you, Mr. Yeats, for writing about Hal and me. Gee whiz, and you didn't even know us.

As soon as Gigi began to walk, a thing would happen when she came into a room where I was. There was a heartbreaking way she had of coming through a door on her toddler tippy-toes with unguarded delight in presenting herself to whoever was there. Something would clutch at my heart every time I saw her and saw that look on her face. I knew that one day she would come through the door into a room where I was waiting and I wouldn't get to see that look because somebody would have disappointed her or hurt her feelings or in some way let her know that her arrival wasn't as stupendously grand as she had thought. Worse yet, perhaps I would be the person who displayed impatience or indifference, or whatever would be the cause of her eventually protecting herself by covering up the expectation in her face. I couldn't bear the thought of that beautiful view of her soul being closed off. I knew from experience that the heart will cover up whatever got rained on when it was left open to the elements.

Miraculously, even though there are days when something troublesome predominates, most of the time both my daughters still have the innocent belief that they are bringing a gift with their presence, and they do still have that childlike look of expectancy. And *most* of the time that's the way the world responds to them, as if their presence is a gift. My father has the same quality, in his fashion.

If only we could go back into ourselves and find the naïveté we cast aside for something safer; if we could see the possibilities in readopting our innocence. Cynicism is easy. Pascal said that evil is easy. Cynicism can be insidiously and secretly destructive, and then I think it can be evil. I believe that a person can choose to pursue innocence, expecting good instead of bad, and in so doing lighten the soul.

Within a month of my arrival in New York City, all atremble with ignorant hopefulness, I met the most sophisticated person I had yet encountered in my young life. Thirty-two years later, John Wallowitch, my brilliant, original, inspired, goofy, profound, funny friend, is still the most sophisticated person I know, and maybe the most guileless. During the first stage of our friendship he was the teacher (musical coach), and I was the pupil. My audition appointment began late and nervously. Confused by his Greenwich Village address at the corner of Eleventh Street and Fourth Street (a girl just up

from Tennessee doesn't expect those streets to cross one another), I was making the fastest time my black patent high
heels would allow along Eleventh Street when I spotted, even
before I got to the corner of Fourth, a trim young man on the
other side of the intersection, out in front of a brownstone
building. He was using a big old-timey watering can to water
his flowers, and as I got closer I saw that he wore round
eyeglasses and a yellow polka-dot bow tie. He wasn't pleased
that I was late, but he was pleased when I started to sing, and
told me so in a stirring way; for my part, I could have stayed
forever listening to him play the piano, which many a time
since I have done. That afternoon a chord was struck between
us, and what has been for me an exquisite and intimate pairing
of my soul with another soul had begun.

We have seen each other suffer. We have tried to help each
other keep up our pluck. We have laughed together and
played and sung through the night and watched the sun come
up to wake us, as it were, from our dream of life the way it
can be in song. Through the rare delight of our countless
hours and days together over the years, in good times and the
other kind, I have absorbed a great lesson from John. I have
learned that experience does not have to dull or cloud one's
picture of life, that it's possible to insist upon goodness
and live with it. John's wildly clever and urbane pieces are
companioned by a very different kind, like the meltingly sweet
"Come a Little Closer." ("It's late and we can't play this
piano too loud / 'Cause the neighbors upstairs are asleep and
dreaming . . .") Worldly wise and world weary don't have to
go together.

My friend has led a citified life, and yet his heart is as pure
as snow. His days are spent writing, coaching, and performing
music; he looks for beauty in his students and in his friends,
and he finds it. He is an innocent and a truster by choice,
not because life has handed out experiences to promote these
qualities. The kind of renown that his genius and his achievement deserve has not yet come to him. Any one of his gorgeous songs or compositions for the piano should have made

him rich by now, but that hasn't happened. He is not unac-
quainted with personal sorrow, nor with disappointment, yet
he lives with gladness. He chooses to see the beauty in his
existence and to nourish his soul. And every year his writing
becomes more moving. These are the lyrics of a recently published song.

> This autumn day is growing old,
> A hint of winter dark and cold.
> But in the deepest night I see
> The world that means the world to me.
> I see a child. I see my friends.
> I see your face
> And nothing ends.
>
> A day in May will soon be here,
> Another spring, another year,
> Then all at once the summer sky.
> The clock runs on, and by and by
> Into the night the roadway bends.
> I see a light
> And nothing ends.

Dearest John, how glad I am to know you.

Sam Keen titles his book *Hymns to an Unknown God* because
he doesn't believe in the God of his Presbyterian childhood
anymore. He writes, "In truth, we cannot know enough to be
either theists or atheists. We have no alternative except to
decide whether to trust or mistrust this encompassing mystery." His decision is to combine agnosticism with trust. He
writes, "Considering the inherent limits of the finite human
mind and our nearly inexhaustible capacity for self-deception,
we may actually be closest to the truth when we remain acutely
aware of our ignorance." And "Problems can be solved by
accumulating data, but genuine mysteries cannot be elimi-

nated by any conceivable increase in knowledge." And "Not even self-knowledge is the goal of the authentic spiritual life."

Mr. Keen's points are beautifully postulated and well taken. Yes, we are ignorant, and no, data doesn't eliminate mysteries, nor does self-examination. But knowledge doesn't have to mean the acquisition of information, does it? There is another kind of knowledge; that's the point for me. And why would we desire to "eliminate" the genuine mysteries?

> *We cannot kindle when we will*
> *The fire that in the soul resides*
> *The spirit bloweth and is still*
> *In mystery the soul resides.*

—MATTHEW ARNOLD

I agree with Mr. Keen that we find ourselves today in the middle of a "spiritual freak show" and that great words— *spirit, soul, faith, hope,* and *love*—are made small in having been put to use in easy and cheap ways. And *growth:* Sam Keen doesn't want us to use the word *growth* anymore with reference to inanimates, like the economy, that only can get bigger, which is different from growing. He says that only organic things can grow, like our gardens, our children, and our souls. He makes sense, doesn't he?

And it's a sacrilege how we use the word *love.* We use it way too much and insincerely. My mother used to remonstrate with me if I said, "I love that dress," that a person "should not use the word *love* for inanimate objects." When she was talking that way, she hadn't seen anything yet. I would much more appreciate a nightclub performer's saying goodnight to us in the audience by extending his goodwill, which *might* be possible to extend to the entire crowd, to his gushing us his love, which is definitely *impossible.* "I love you" has gotten to be a substitute for "good-bye" in personal exchanges also and is tossed off without any thought whatsoever. They haven't started throwing it around in Tennessee yet; I'm dreading the day that my cousin Sam Carter leaves the house after dropping by with

Daddy's mail and calls out, "Bye, Dixie, I love you." And the thing is, Sam *does* love me, and he loves Daddy, and so do his sisters Louise and Madeline, and we love them and him, and we all know it. We know it, for one thing, because he goes to the trouble to walk over to the post office and collect Daddy's mail for him in the grimmest weather, which would be a great favor even without Sam's extra burden of having had a bad leg since childhood and his being no spring chicken anymore himself. It would diminish his act of love if we were to cheapen it with a word that's so tired now that one hesitates to use it when it matters, almost hoping that another, fresher word will come to mind. No, *cherish* isn't quite the same.

I have purposely not tried to talk about love in these pages, because in my opinion it's been talked out. This soft and powerful word, the only one we have to express our deepest devotion, has become a show-bizzy catchall. The way it gets babbled about glibly and mindlessly, by everybody from therapists to politicians to New Age gurus, makes me tired. The Bible says, in 1 Corinthians 13, that love suffers long, is kind, envies not, vaunts not itself, is not puffed up, does not behave itself unseemly, is not easily provoked, thinks no evil, rejoices not in iniquity but rejoices in truth, bears all things, believes all things, hopes all things, endures all things, and never fails. That's a tall order. If love is all those things, and it is, I don't think it's so easy to come by, either to get or to give. (In the King James version of the Bible, the word is "charity" rather than "love," a point worth remembering.)

I appreciate Mr. Keen's beautiful and forthright book, and its many moving passages. Some of us are blessed with not having had to give up our religion to find our faith and save our soul. I haven't. Maybe I'm lucky to have taken only one theology course and run away from the subject, sensing the danger in dissecting the mystery of God. I haven't managed to be a very good example of a Christian, that's the trouble. I'm afraid I've received all and given nothing and called myself a Christian. One thing I do know that I am is grateful. It is my desire to cultivate a pervasive sense of gratitude in every moment of my day. Living every minute from a grateful heart would indeed be Heaven on earth, and some people do it.

Another thing I know about the divine mystery is that sooner or later we all need to figure out what we believe. Figure it out, stand by it, and live by it. Wordsworth said, "Though inland far we be, our souls have sight of that immortal sea which brought us hither." Yes, we do. Accepting the assumption of immortality seems to be scarier to some people than not accepting it, though why that would be the case I don't know. Maybe human nature sometimes finds hope and promise and possibility frightening. Being afraid to hope for good news is awfully sad in any circumstance, especially this one. Maybe some people don't believe they deserve to want to live in eternity with their loved ones and all God's angels and the Lord Himself. I know for sure I don't deserve it, but I know I'm going to get to do it. What could be a more profoundly joyful thought, I wonder. What higher good could a person strive for? Why would a person count himself out of Heaven of his own volition?

We hear it in church, how we're supposed to nourish and expand our soul all the time and not just work on it a couple of hours on Sunday. We know we're supposed to, and we want to, but how and when do we do it?

I have learned that we nourish the soul by attempting things that are hard for us, by looking for things to be grateful for and then being grateful for them, by trying to seek the good for persons other than ourselves, by practicing loyalty, by accepting truths that are not pleasant to face, by looking as squarely as we can at just what our own life is and setting about to make it beautiful with whatever tools are at hand, and by consciously remaining innocent, not matter who laughs.

Two years ago I started calling to find my mentor and friend, George Touliatos, who started me in the Front Street Theatre in Memphis, which he had founded and run with his wife, Barbara. Sometimes we don't see one another more than once a year, and I had a job tracking him down in Paris (France, not Tennessee, and there is a Paris, Tennesee), and unfortunately for him it was five in the morning there. I was sorry about waking him but kept him up long enough to extract a promise from him that he would direct me in *A Streetcar Named Desire.* I had had dinner with Sonny McCalman, and (just this once) we had gone on into the night and started "gettin' ideas," like Sonny's idea that television wasn't the best place to use my talents, such as they are, completely. He asked about why I had never done Blanche DuBois, and I told him I had wanted to several years before and a close friend had told me that she wouldn't advise it, that mid-forties was—you guessed it—too old. The big *o* word again. Well, that night Sonny had convinced me that I wasn't too old if I could play the part well, and I knew there was a good chance he was right, so I called George and begged him to say yes. He had not directed in years, said he was too rusty, growled around, then finally said yes so I'd let him go back to sleep.

President Lane Rawlins at the University of Memphis gave us the theatre and raised the money and we came back to work together, George and I, after thirty years. We had a wonderful cast and George worked us hard. He has his sights on big game, and if he thinks you've got it in you, he will get it out of you, and the process can be excruciating. And yet. And yet. This was, after a lifetime of performing, the first great role that I had ever done. Feeling this play under me was not unlike feeling the *Yankee Tar* under me out at sea. There was something awesome about it, a thrilling sense of the profound in this play that lifted all of us in grateful communion. When George, with his dark sad Greek eyes, would stop me to tell me I was missing it or forcing it or not getting the point, I was always cast down horribly; then he would explain as if giving me a precious jewel, which indeed he was, what he believed Tennessee Williams meant, and we would try again.

Many moments of awful, beautiful truth rose up before me every time we rehearsed and every time we performed. Never once did I get through Blanche's speech about her death

("And I shall be buried at sea, sewn up in a clean white sack and dropped overboard at noon in the blaze of summer") without tears of gratitude for the privilege of being the conduit through which all the dear people sitting out in front of me were to receive Mr. Williams's compassionate understanding of them. Of them, of me, of all of us. Indeed a true communion, an expanding of the soul.

Now you may say to me, Dear Reader, "But Dixie, not all of us can go sailing with Hal Holbrook or perform a Tennessee Williams play with George Touliatos. How are we to keep our souls growing if we live in a more restricted (perhaps) situation?" And I say back, "Don't give me that. The examples I've just talked about happen to have been things *impossible* for me to do. Clearly impossible. Too old, too scared, too weak, too busy—you name it. I keep quoting William Wordsworth, but I can't help it. In "The Prelude" he describes "that false secondary power by which in weakness we create distinctions, then believe our puny boundaries are things which we perceive, and not which we have made." In a way it makes me sad to realize how long it took me to catch on to how I've made my own "puny boundaries." In another way I feel a certain elation that at last I can see them for what they are.

And so I offer to you a little shyly, yet with conviction and most sincere goodwill, my hope that some of what I've said will resonate of shared humanity, dreams that can come true, progress that can be achieved in every pilgrim, and last I set down these lines by William Wordsworth:

> . . . to intertwine
> The passions that build up our human soul
> Not with the mean and vulgar works of man,
> But with high objects, with eternal things,
> With life and Nature, purifying thus
> The elements of feeling and of thought,
> And sanctifying by such discipline
> Both pain and fear, until we recognise
> A grandeur in the beatings of the heart.

Coda
PRAYERS FOR MY DAUGHTERS

True worth is in being, *not* seeming,
In doing, each day that goes by,
Some little good—not in dreaming
Of great things to do by and by.
For whatever men say in their blindness,
And in spite of the fancies of youth,
There's nothing so kingly as kindness,
And nothing so royal as truth.

—ALICE CARY

*J.*F WE COULD WISH FOR THE REST OF THE
world what we wish for our children, things would get pretty
peaceful, I'll bet.

My children were born one year, one month, and nineteen
days apart, Ginna (Rosalind Helen Virginia, for Arthur's
mother, Aunt Helen, and Gina) on May 17, 1969, and Mary
Dixie (for Aunt Mary and me) on July 6, 1970. Baby Ginna, as
she was called until Mary Dixie's baby talk transmuted
"Ginna" into "Gigi," arrived three weeks before her due date,
the morning after my mother underwent emergency surgery
in Memphis for an intestinal blockage and poisoning caused
by diverticulitis. When Daddy called to tell me they had to
perform an exploratory operation on Gina, I felt as if an iron
hand was squeezing the back of my waist, and I knew to start
packing my bag for the hospital. Daddy called back four hours
later with the news that my mother had made it, that a section

of the intestine had been removed, and that she would be all right. I was overwhelmed with relief, but of course it was too late to stop the baby.

I stayed up the rest of the night thinking and walking and waiting. I carefully cleaned my wedding ring with ammonia water and wondered who this little boy, for I was sure it would be a boy, was going to look like. I wondered if he'd be like Arthur or Daddy or anything like me. I had been waiting joyously for this little being all along and felt that I already knew him pretty well. I walked around the apartment, from room to room, and thought about things. I think in those hours I began to guess at how my whole life until that moment would soon roll itself up into "before the baby came."

At six o'clock I woke Arthur up and told him it was time to go. We met Dr. Jack Squire next door to his office, at Leroy Hospital on East Sixty-first Street. (I don't know when Leroy was torn down. I'm sorry it's gone, in a purely sentimental way; a great medical institution it wasn't exactly. It was noted mostly for Jackie Gleason's dropping in occasionally to dry out, and also for the jokes about it, like how patients at Leroy ordered food in from the Regency Hotel, how you'd be fine there so long as you didn't require medical attention, how

Leroy had to "send out for oxygen.") At 11:21 that morning my baby was born—a girl, a rosebud miniature of her father, which fact made me instantly fonder of him than ever.

If my daughters put any stock in my advice, they will have no audience when they give birth to their children. I am so relieved that only Dr. Squire and the nurse were with me. Nowadays it's fashionable to have father, mother, sister, brother, aunts, and uncles too, as the song says. When a baby comes into the world, it's a miracle, and it's sacred. In my opinion it's just between the baby and the mother and God. No witnesses for me, please. Arthur and I were in accord there —as we were in many areas, as a matter of fact—and you may be sure I'm very glad today that there's not a man out there running around, now living another life with another woman, who once happened to see me having a baby. Good grief.

This tiny and perfect little girl opened her blue eyes and looked at me with an understanding that hurts my chest to remember even now. Time stopped. Slowly and curiously she opened and closed her eyelids with their long lashes at the outside edges, for all the world like a little woods creature in a fairy tale. She seemed interested in me, in the way one is who meets someone she's heard a great deal about beforehand.

This wasn't at all how I'd imagined it. I'd expected my baby to be a *baby*, a helpless little thing I was supposed to care for and instruct, not this wise individual who seemed to have come here to teach me something instead. Not this shimmering soul hardly contained by the wee package she came in.

I started talking to her right away. Every time they brought her in to me, we renewed our conversation wherever we'd left off. I got a bit of teasing from my sister-in-law Ellen, who caught me talking to my infant as if she were talking back, but I didn't mind; to me she was talking back. My baby was the be-all and end-all to me. Being her mother was perfect rapture. I loved to see each day's events, new achievements, what tickled her, what displeased her. If she didn't want to eat a certain thing, she had a way of waving it off delicately with her little palm extended toward the offending dish. She could sit still in my lap endlessly attentive to adult conversation, turning her head to observe whoever was talking; or if John Wallowitch was visiting, she would listen and gurgle while we played and sang until she drowsed off in her infant seat on top of the piano.

By the time she was a year old, she missed nothing whatsoever. She clearly understood my explanation of the present I was going to bring her shortly, her very own baby sister. She was all attentive and excited about the preparations that were being made. She and Mary Dixie had the exact same baby beds in the same room, but they didn't get delivered for either child until after she was born—Ellen's superstition, which I took up with. Gigi came in the car with her great friend Clifford Pullins, who drove for us, to pick me up at the hospital. I got into the back seat, where she was waiting, and laid the all-time great gift across her lap. She patted the blanket and cooed, "bay-bee siss-tah."

Mary Dixie was born at Leroy Hospital at one o'clock in the afternoon. When my second daughter was handed into my arms, I received another shock. She was a rosebud like her big sister, but the eyes that looked into mine were announcing a little variation on the theme. Mary Dixie Carter knew about me, all right, and she had come to teach me plenty; it was just that she wasn't going to let me know everything about her so easily. Her cerulean eyes tipped up just a touch at the corners, giving an impression of exoticism, and there were those long dark eyelashes sweeping down over them, wink-a-blink. She was a mysterious little bundle with a definite opinion about lots of things—including me, I feared. (I thought she was slightly miffed about her name, or the lack of it. For the first month after she was born she was actually Baby Girl Carter on the birth certificate, as Arthur was resistant to my naming her after myself. We called her Baby Sister.) The first time I went anywhere after she was born, I saw this poem by Dorothea Fox on a plaque in a store window, and I have it still, hanging in my bedroom. It has always reminded me of Mary Dixie in her infancy.

Dear Lord, I am so newly come
I do not know my name.
I do not even know yet, Lord,
If I am glad I came.
Grant me the time to grow in love,
Rejoice that I am here.
Bless those who make me warm and dry.
Lord, keep my mother near.

We talked back and forth, and before very long I was able to determine that she was glad she had come.

Everybody who visited us at that time would be treated to Baby Ginna's toddling him or her proudly into the nursery to show off her "bay-bee siss-tah." Baby Sister lived up to every dream and expectation. She had a cherubic disposition. She absorbed everything that Gigi knew so effortlessly that by the time she was a little more than a year old, she had just about caught up. They played together with no fussing. They each thought the other ultimately amusing and entertaining.

When against my will I was convinced that they had to go to nursery school in order to be accepted at a good private school later, I entered them at Christ Church Methodist, where I was a member and where they went to Sunday school. After they had been in attendance for a few months, the teachers told me that my children said good-bye three times: first they kissed in the hallway between their two classrooms and separated to go hang up their coats; then they went back to the middle of the hall and hugged and kissed again; then as they got to their respective classroom doors, they turned one last time and waved good-bye. When it was time to go home, they embraced in the hallway as if they had not seen each other for ages, I was told. This apparently happened every day.

From the first they were very different from one another, completely individual yet mysteriously close, and ineffably sweet. And from the moment they first looked into my eyes, I have known, in deepest wonder, that they came to be with me.

Oh, my babies. Oh, my precious little girls. How I wish that I could hold you for just a moment as I could then, one in each arm, one sweet head on each shoulder. How I wish that I could remember every word, every look and bounce and giggle, every touch, and every sweet expression. How I wish that I could take away every tear, every disappointment or uncertainty of those tender years. How I regret my every instance of impatience and thoughtlessness. How I wish that I could have perfectly fulfilled your trust in me.

My daughters are grown up; training and instruction are past, as are the days when I might have been a better mother. All I can do now is to be where they can reach me, and pray. I pray for them, all the time, as every mother does for her babies, no matter how old they are, and whether she calls it praying or not.

"Most merciful Father, in Your compassion forgive us our sins, known and unknown, *things done and left undone;* and so uphold us by Your Spirit that we may live and serve You in newness of life, to the honor and glory of Your name." Never do I repeat this beautiful passage from the Book of Common Prayer without thinking of my children and the things I left undone.

After Gigi got out of college, she decided to live in Los Angeles and to move back into the house for a while before she got into her own apartment. That was three years ago. Mary Dixie came to the decision just a few months ago that she would try her fortunes as an actress on the West Coast, having spent her first two years after graduation studying in New York. Since I've been writing this book, Mary Dixie has moved "temporarily" back home, and we have returned to the full complement: Hal and I, Daddy, Gigi, Mary Dixie, Sweetie Pie, the little cocker poodle whom Daddy named and who has become his constant companion, and Paladin, our giant black poodle, rightly named after the knights-errant of old.

Paladin is younger and more well bred than Sweetie, so for

both reasons he defers to her. We've all decided that his course is a wise one. Sweetie Pie has a strong grip on the idea that she's right all the time, and one comes to understand sooner or later that it saves pain all around just to go along with the notion. Sweetie Pie is never apologetic or humble. The funny part is that no one enjoys seeing her proven wrong, when it happens. Her need to be literally top dog is so overriding that we'd all rather put up with her airs than see her brought low. Does that remind you of anybody you know?

I knew this arrangement was to be short-lived; I knew the girls would be moving out in a few months, yet I have been unable to retain the adjustment to separation from them that I achieved by the hardest while they were in college. When we drove Gigi onto the Harvard campus at the beginning of her first year there, my heart was in my throat with pride in her and her accomplishment and the golden opportunity that awaited her at this great school. Two days later, the glorious freshman ceremonies having been concluded, my happiness in her happiness got lost in a panic of sorrow at having to drive away and leave her there. We had had great fun a month before, picking out a pretty flowered comforter for her bed, as well as sheets and towels, a small mirror to prop on her dresser, boxes to store sweaters under her bed, and other articles to make her room a little homey. When I first saw her quarters, I was glad for everything we'd brought and wished I could have done more. Harvard does not put a priority on physical surroundings, or on cleaning. On Sunday afternoon I went into her bleak little room to get my coat from her bed. Everybody else was out in the common room beginning their good-byes. I couldn't keep myself from standing there looking at the few little things that made up her outfit and last at her comforter, picturing her sleeping in this strange room, in the bottom bunk of this strange bed, all by herself in this strange place. I stood there staring at the bed and saw the baby whose damp silky hair I had leaned over the railing of her crib to cut while she was sleeping, the baby in the shoe store who stood perfectly still and wept from the betrayal of having been laced into her first pair of shoes, the little girl who said, "I fell down in ballet practice today, Mama, but I pretended it was part of my dance," then the little girl who said to me once with tears lipping over her eyes, "Mama, you spoke *hardlish* to me." I wanted to take back the eighteen years and start with her all over again from the first moment I held her in my arms and pay closer attention to everything about her. For long moments I hung on to that hateful bunk bed and cried, my heart squeezing shut, unable to get hold of myself enough to face the roommates and their very nice parents, rejoin Mary Dixie and Hal, and leave. Leave my child, my firstborn, there among strangers, and fly across the country away from her.

She was scared too (on Sunday morning before church she had clutched me and said, "Mama, you can't leave here until I find one person I know from Marlborough!" and then we ran into Cynthia Kim on the church steps), but she has always been a brave little thing, and I knew she was going to be fine. It didn't matter what I knew; it didn't keep me from feeling that the most precious chapter in my life was coming to a conclusion. The start of a new chapter for my child ended mine with her. I wanted to feel only joy as she put on her new wings. I tried to grab on to the cheerful mood of the other parents. To no avail. I regretted having encouraged her to go to Harvard instead of Stanford, where she wouldn't be so far away. I regretted having encouraged her to do so well in school, to do anything, to go anywhere at all. There was nothing about it that I didn't regret. Edith Piaf I wasn't.

I was sad for myself, selfishly sorry for the blessing of a healthy passage of time and events. I cried off and on for weeks, mostly in the car or in the bathroom because I was ashamed of myself. My saving grace was Mary Dixie's lambent presence, still at home for her last year of high school. We missed Gigi together, and pretty soon we began to realize that we were having our year together as Gigi and I had been together the year before Mary Dixie was born, and there was much sweetness in it.

My mother died on March 1 the following spring. When

Hal and I headed out for Boston that fall with both girls, Gigi returning as a sophomore, Mary Dixie entering her freshman year, we were in trouble and we all knew it. They were stricken over the loss of their grandmother; along with their own grief they worried about their grandfather and me, cognizant of how their departure would add to the desolation of our home. Moreover, our home was to change while they were away. We had bought a house; finally years of living in rentals had come to an end, a happy prospect except for one problem: the girls dearly loved the rental home we were leaving, and the morning they left that house for the airplane to Boston, they were leaving it forever. At Christmas they would come "home" to another house. For the umpteenth time they were being moved, this time without even being there to participate.

Hurrying along a narrow Cambridge sidewalk beside me, going to look for coat hangers or something, Mary Dixie whispered, "Mama, I am scared sick. I feel like I'm dreaming all of this." I smiled reassuringly and did my best to allay her fears in a confident manner. I had hoped to find my own comfort in Gigi's being there with her sister, knowledgeable and secure, knowing both their ways around. I had hoped that Mary Dixie's room wouldn't seem hostile to me, that this time I could be bigger than those shriveling feelings of loss to me, me, me, and show the girls a good face. I had hoped not to dampen their spirits. I had hoped not to be an embarrassment to them.

But no. Every time Mary Dixie was turned away from me so that she couldn't see me looking at her, I watched her go back in time, saw her sitting in her diaper and squishing her plump little hand into her first birthday cake, saw the expression of intrigue on her bitsy countenance when she told me that she and Puppy had been hunting in Central Park, saw the expression of fear and determination on her two-year-old face just before she let go at the top of the slide, saw the same expression at eleven, as she stuck it out to win third place in a French "speak-off" she'd gotten herself into with a bunch of high school girls. I had to keep reminding myself that she was a champion; she would be fine. They would be great, the two of them together again, two little champions, and at Harvard, no less.

I watched the two of them together and remembered the day three years before when we had come there on a trip to "look at schools." I remembered dropping behind them, watching them walk together across Harvard Yard and thinking, "This is the place for them. They will score well on the SAT tests. They are both going to go to Harvard." Then I thought of how Mary Dixie had been pretty much set on Princeton, wanting to go to a school other than her sister's, until right up to the last minute, when Gigi was home for spring vacation and they had called out for me to come into their conference room, the bathroom between their bedrooms. Shyly smiling, Mary Dixie had said, "We think maybe one year is enough for us to be at different schools, and that has been this year. So I believe I will go to Harvard with Gigi after all." How the three of us had laughed and hugged and jumped up and down. I remembered how relieved, how jubilant I had felt, how happy that they would be together again. Two little champions together at Harvard College. Great, great, great. When the taxi with Hal and me in it pulled away from the dormitory where they stood in the rain waving good-bye, they were weeping as horribly as I was. Childhood was over. For all three of us.

At the time he and I married, I was not aware that Hal Holbrook was a saint. Well, it has turned out that he is. We made it through that year and the ones after that and I gradually became more or less adjusted to the incomprehensible idea that my children—the miracles of my life, closer than my skin, divine gifts of Heaven, many times such small but mighty bulwarks between me and despair—were going to be for the rest of this life parted and away from me. Me, me, me. Oh, me.

So now they've been here and we've all gotten used to it, and they're moving out again and we're going through much the same thing all over. Many a time when they drop by and leave again, memories come around to take their place. I remember how during their first year at the Buckley School I played the piano for them to try out for *The King and I*, all three of us feeling new and shy in the grip of unmanageable nerves. I was missing notes and they were frozen until midway through their song, when I saw Gigi nudge Mary Dixie with her elbow and beam her a radiant, if tremulous, smile, as if to say, "Buck up, stout," and amazingly we all did. Immediately following that ordeal, they went with me to Burbank, where I auditioned for *Filthy Rich*, my first show with Linda Bloodworth Thomason, while they waited in the outer office, doing their homework. On the way there I said, "Girls, that audition was enough for me. I'm drained and I'm still scared. I'll never get this job." And they said, "Oh yes, Mama, you will. We know you will." The next day we were elated to find out that they were going to be the Siamese twins in *The King and I*, and I got my part too.

I remember how after we had been apart, they always came running toward me with their arms outstretched, laughing and smiling, happy to be together again. What gets me is that they still do.

Naturally Daddy happened to be the first to start helping them furnish their new abode (rental "assistance" from their doting father), via the mail order catologues; boxes began arriving regularly as soon as he got the news that the dreaded exodus was imminent. Hal gave them beautiful glasses. I gave them our blue velvet tuxedo sofa, the same age as Gigi. One girl or the other pops in almost every day to spend a few minutes with their grandfather and once a week to have dinner, and then they're off again, eyes shining, hair flying, out into the world.

I lean against the front door and think of my mother when her children left home, how gallantly she sent us off, always happy for what made us happy, no matter how far away that took us, never wearing us down with any sighs or sad looks. I think about that now and know that it was much worse for her than for me, because Midge and I both moved away for good and much too far away for Sunday dinners; I think about it

and wonder how she did it. I think about her faith and fortitude and about her great patience. I pray that my girls will be
like their Grandmother Gina.

I pray that they are able to tell right from wrong, which I
know to be a hard thing to do. Their pure natures do not
necessarily make it easier. Maturation is almost entirely a
function of learning how to figure out the difference between
right and wrong on our own, and we can't be sure we know
until we've seen wrong all dressed up and looking good, and
recognized it, and walked away. Right and wrong we learn
from example or we do not learn it. There are no moral lessons except examples, in practical matter. On the other hand,
I don't think a parent should take the lazy way out and con-
done action that is not right, even if the child is determined to
do it, and even if the "child" is grown. I want to encourage
my daughters to do whatever they want with their lives, whatever will make them happy. I do have misgivings about their
going into my business. The part of the entertainment business that's left isn't very rich soil for tender young things to
grow and bloom in beauty, I'm afraid. But then, I suppose the
same statement would apply in all professions and callings, and
as I keep reminding myself, there are good people everywhere.

I pray that they will not seek power, which goal builds to
desperation and takes away joy.

William Butler Yeats's poem "A Prayer for My Daughter"
ends with these lines:

> For arrogance and hatred are the wares
> Peddled in the thoroughfares
> How but in custom and in ceremony
> Are innocence and beauty born?
> Ceremony's a name for the rich horn,
> And custom for the spreading laurel tree.

I pray with Mr. Yeats's words that my daughters will find
for themselves, in the raucous barrage of contemporary incite-
ments, a life held stable and secure in custom and ceremony,

not to be confused with conformity, that crippler. I pray that I was able to give them enough to get started.

I become ever more grateful for the countless happy forms that were created in our family, not just what we did together but how it was done, so that even as a youngster I felt safe in knowing what to expect and what my own part would be. Each duty, as it became accustomed and familiar, fitted another stanchion into the little ship of self that my parents were helping me ready for my life's voyage. My mother would often tell me, "Happiness is the flower that blooms by the wayside of duty." At seventeen years of age I didn't much like the sound of it; now I know that it is true.

When I say in my nightclub act, as I often do, that my childhood was idyllic, I sometimes get a laugh; someone expects that I must be setting up a joke because the word "idyllic" sounds over the top. It's not though, for me. Never since I left home have I felt the same sense of inviolable safety. Sanctity. The sanctity of a place walled and roofed with love. We did have sweet handmade clothes and fresh orange juice and fresh milk and butter and buttermilk and bedtime stories and warm laps to rock in, but the luxurious aspect of all these things was the fact that they were material evidences of love, and even before I could talk, I knew that. My mother forgot her pride when she sang us to sleep. She was a proud woman and not at all a singer, so when she lullabied us with "On the Good Ship Lollipop" or "See That Harvard Student," there was risk and enchantment and transcendent beauty, and I knew that. I knew that my father and mother worked for us and that they would protect us. I knew that my brother and sister and I were treasures beyond price and that we were safe. We had chores to do and lessons to learn and music to practice and mosquito bites and sprained ankles and spankings, but we were beloved and we were safe. It was idyllic.

My father describes the same kind of memories "as a little boy, lying in bed listening to the wind moan around the north side of the house by the pear tree and feeling snug and warm and safe." I was born in that house too, and I know just what he's talking about. The pear tree is gone now, but the wind still moans as I snuggle up in bed.

I grew up mortified at having the longest feet in my grade at school, and I have always used every means at my disposal to make them seem smaller. One of my father's unnumbered kindnesses was his way of taking my bare foot in his hand sometimes, as I would nestle in his lap to say goodnight, and remarking that my feet were beautiful, "slender and delicately boned," knowing of course that to me they were long and gawky. His gentle sincerity assuaged my discomfort to a measurable degree and reminded me at the same time that I was watched over and protected from hidden hurts as well as obvious ones and that I was beautiful to him no matter how long my feet got.

Those of us who felt safe for the first twenty years of our lives ought to be giving thanks every minute. My husband and his sisters June and Alberta didn't. And it grieves me that my own daughters didn't. Divorce is a devastation to children. I was not with them enough; that I know now, when it's too late to do anything about it. The time we don't have to spend with our children when they're little we will spend eventually, either trying to repair the damage or grieving over it, or both. I pray that my daughters will bend their careers so that they can be with their own children consistently when they're little. I pray that they will make their families their first consideration, that they will respect their children from infancy, that they will pay attention, both in successes and disappointments, and that they will teach their children obedience, discipline, and loyalty. I pray that they will honor their children's dignity, that they will teach them the beauty of simplicity and the ugliness of arrogance, teach them to think of other people, to be grateful, and to be kind.

I pray that my daughters will stay in the church. They were raised in the church, and I pray that they will raise their children in the church, for their souls and for the beauty of an upbringing within a beloved and ceremonial tradition. I pray for their happiness, and I appreciate, these years down the road, what brings happiness and what takes it away. "Eternal God, heavenly Father, send us now into the world in peace, and grant us strength to love and serve you with gladness and singleness of heart."

I grew up in the Methodist church. My family were, both sides, religious people. My mother's side were Baptists, but when she and my father married, she offered to join his church with him because that was the correct thing to do. She did not, however, change what she believed about doctrine. And she did as she saw fit; my brother was baptized as an infant because he was the first child and she knew it would please Daddy so much, but Baptists do not believe in infant baptism (they think you should know what you're doing first), so my mother stopped with Hal. My sister and I were not baptized until we joined the church as adolescents, and then we were sprinkled at the Methodist church on Sunday morning, and for good measure immersed at the Baptist church by the Baptist minister later that afternoon. It was pretty scary to me, going down into that chilly water with my Sunday dress on and having a handkerchief held over my mouth and being laid over backwards in the water for what seemed a good long time and stepping out cold and slick as an otter, dripping and embarrassed. It was one of those times that I was especially thankful for my little sister, with whom I shared everything in life, good and bad. I guess all things considered, I can't count that Baptist baptism one of our bad experiences because it gave my mother such obvious relief and joy; now in her eyes it had been done right, and we knew that she was grateful in a way beyond expressing to us, and so for Midge and me it was well worth the discomfort.

The funny thing is that my girls felt, as I always have, just a little deprived that they were not baptized when they were babies. I wasn't because my mother was a Baptist; they weren't because their father was, is, Jewish. I have to shake my head when I think of it—all the conversations I heard growing up about the differences among various Protestant churches, not to mention the terrifying gulf between Protestants and Roman

Catholics, and how important and marked these differences seemed, nobody dreaming, me least of all, that I'd go to New York City and immediately marry a Jewish man. Now *that* was a difference. And a Jewish man, what's more, who was not religious. I guess when I was growing up, no one had thought about reviewing Methodist-Jewish differences.

Over the hours and days and years that I have spent agonizing, longing, puzzling, going over, and second-guessing about failing in this union with the father of my children, whom I loved with all my heart, I have had to accept the possibility that the difference in our religious views doomed us from the start. Two people from very different backgrounds may have grown up with different understandings of the kinds of experiences, people, language, and behavior to which children should or should not be exposed, and believe you me, when children are involved, points of divergence become mattersome. For those of us who think raising our children is the biggest deal of all, anything that affects them is indeed worth taking a stand about. Parents need to be in tune about everything that has to do with their children's future, what they hope for them, and what the rules should be. If they don't agree, the children sense it and are made anxious.

When children come into the picture, different religions become religious differences. When I'm making a speech that includes my sincere enjoinder against marrying into a religious background essentially different from one's own, I feel tension in the audience. This area of discussion is a little chancy, I've discovered. My girls look concerned when I talk this way to them, and I understand that I seem to be revealing a narrowness they're not proud of in me, that from what they've gathered in their well-educated young lives, this point of view isn't very nice. I treasure every bit of good opinion I can get from my daughters, and I would love to be in perfect accord with them all the time, but what little I do finally know comes from experience, some of it not pleasant, and I have to offer them the benefit of that experience, no matter what they wind up doing with it. The irony of the fact that they are the ones hardest hit by what went wrong with me and their father is not lost on them.

Parents who bring up their children without a strong emphasis on their cultural and religious origins may not face the dilemma I'm talking about, but it appears clearer to me with the passage of time that the trade-off is a sad one. Whenever I have the chance, I urge young people to introduce religion to their children at an early age and keep it up until the children are grown. A grand part of one's birthright is the tradition of generations past that belongs to each of us and courses through our blood.

Sometimes I wonder if we who call ourselves religious have lost our energy to represent our religion in a way that fosters respect for it. Are we ashamed of ourselves? And if so, what for? I'm reading a terrific book about opening oneself to creativity; I'm sorry that the author has repeatedly to explain and apologize for using the word "God," recommending that we think of it as "useful shorthand." I notice in the paper that an actor who hosted a television special about the Bible has felt the need for a disclaimer, saying in an interview that if it had been a "religious" show, he "would not have had anything to do with it." What would be so bad about hosting a religious show? Why the assumptive attitude about "organized religion." I don't notice any religions other than mine doing any better; I'm just naturally more aware of what's going on with my crowd. Somehow we Christians have allowed Christianity to become associated with people of ill will and bad intention. Or simpletons. The "Religious Right" means something close to Nazism in many people's minds. An intelligent person said to me recently that he would rather his children marry atheists than "born-again" Christians. I was too stunned to reply. Where have we gotten off the track so badly that people fear us? We are the custodians of the beliefs and standards we have inherited from our forefathers. We are supposed to hand them down to future generations in some kind of clean and beautiful condition, so that what our children and their children receive from us will be a true support and guide.

I often hear perfectly bright people say that they don't want to force religion on their children, that they'll let them grow up and then decide. Decide based upon what? No one can decide what they feel about something with which they have no acquaintance. Lack of a religious grounding in the early years is to my mind a deprivation. Later is too late. After high school there are too many more interesting, exciting, trendy things to do, especially since at eighteen everyone is immortal. And when someone they love dies, or they get in trouble or have children of their own to stay half-scared about all the time, what is their recourse?

When I die, who will my children look to to watch over them? They will have no shortage of devoted people around them, but as it says in the old gospel hymn, "His eye is on the sparrow and I know He watches me." I take comfort in knowing that the Almighty will have his eye on the sparrow, on my sparrows, and that they will know He's watching.

"Faith, our outward sense befriending, makes our inward vision clear."

Why do I pray that my girls will stay in the church, as distinguished from pursuing what is now called a "spiritual life" or "following a spiritual quest"? I've read a lot of "spiritual" material, especially since I've become so interested in yoga and since "spiritual" has become fashionable. The spiritual quests that one organizes on one's own strike me as a bit flaccid. The quest is generally at one's convenience and leads to one's own truth the way one wants to read it. The "spiritual search" can mean whatever a person wants it to mean, and from my observation it often means just another form of therapy, just another exercise in self-examination, introspection— me, me, and more me. All that's helpful and fine up to a point, but in my opinion we reached that point a few years back. Self-examination doesn't necessarily have anything to do with knowing God or indeed with becoming a better person. It should, but it just doesn't always work out that way. I don't believe that we gain a great deal of inner fortitude from making up our own rules, as it were. I know extremely self-aware individuals who are perfectly miserable. I don't believe that generalized "spirituality" can lead a person to a state of grace.

Worship, which is what we go to church for, requires learning and practicing humility, bowing down to a greater power. The object is to bend our will to the will of God. Worship is the opposite of exalting the self, the me, me, me, me. When we learn to worship—and I don't know any place to learn how except in church or temple or wherever people gather together for this express purpose—we can then carry the practice out into the rest of our lives. When we present ourselves along with others in humble supplication, we discover exaltation, but not through me, me, me; it happens that when we give our egos over to God, we become celebrants. God lifts up our spirits. We become magnified, beatified.

I believe the humility that worship requires to be the only way to true dignity and to a state of grace.

> Dear Lord and Father of mankind,
>   forgive our foolish ways;
> Reclothe us in our rightful mind;
> In purer lives, Thy service find,
> In deeper reverence, praise.
>
> Drop Thy still dews of quietness, till all our strivings cease;
> Take from our souls the strain and stress,
> And let our ordered lives confess
> The beauty of Thy peace.

I pray that my daughters have received those things which I had given me as a child, the ideas I grew up with which have stood me in good stead thus far. I heard many an aphorism many a time and now am glad for it, but even gladder for the countless stories and the lived-out examples. My maternal grandmother Hillsman would very often say, after a little lesson of some kind, or admonition, "Line upon line, precept upon precept, here a little, there a little." This meant that we were not to send knowing glances to one another when she was quoting something for the umpteenth time. Now I treasure all Grandmother Hillsman's dicta, as well as her daily Bible readings to us at breakfast and her prayers following the readings. The prayers were hard to understand, because just about as soon as she started to pray, always beginning with what she was thankful for, she would become overwhelmed with gratitude for God's goodness and begin to weep as she prayed, so we got more of the general idea than actual words. The idea, however, was powerful enough to have impressed itself on me permanently, and it came, as these things do, I guess, from what Grandmother was and the fierceness with which she lived her beliefs.

She had married my grandfather when she was twenty-two years old. He was forty-nine. She called him "Mist Hillsman." She idolized him and so did the five children they had together. I couldn't guess how many times my mother has told us how Grandfather Hillsman, whom they called Papa, would tip his chair back a little at the table and light his corncob pipe. They knew this was the sign that he felt like staying at the table a little while and telling them stories. Although he was a tiny little boy at the time of the Civil War, his memories of it were vivid, and by all accounts he was an exceptional raconteur. He was also handsome, slightly built, fast moving, and white-headed from the time he was twenty-nine years old. He promised his little girls a dime for any black hair they could find on his head. It didn't matter that they never once collected; they loved the game. Aunt Helen remembers cutting the tags off a new suit he'd put on to go to church and watching him brush his hair and comb his mustache and saying to him, "Oh, Papa! You're so handsome!" He dropped dead out in the fields on July 5, 1927, when he was seventy-five years old, and Uncle Tom and Beecher Adkisson carried him up to the house packsaddle on their crossed arms, Uncle Tom crying and Beecher saying over and over, "Don't cry, Cap'n. Don't cry." (Beecher worked on the farm with Uncle Tom and had refused to change over from calling him Thomas as a

boy growing up to the "Mr. Hillsman" that Uncle Tom
thought was proper now that he was over twenty-one, so Beecher had compromised with "Captain.") The family was dev-
astated with grief. Daddy hadn't met Gina at that time, but
his family heard that Mr. Jim Hillsman over in Trezevant had
died and that it had just about killed his whole family too.

Grandmother was forty-eight years old, her children were
still young, and the Depression was getting under way. They
all worked. Four of the five went to college and made the
highest marks possible. The farm was lost. Aunt Helen, the
baby, started to work right out of high school. For the rest of
her life Grandmother lived mostly with Aunt Helen, spending
protracted periods with her other children when they could
and she could. She spent summers with us.

To say the least about the most, she was dramatic; she would
stand and call with great urgency, "Halbert Leroy Carter, Jr.!
Dixie Virginia Carter! Melba Helen Carter!" When we ran to
answer her summons, we would like as not be met with "Stop!
Look at the beautiful sunset!" She loved everything heavenly,
particularly astronomy. (Oh, how both my grandmothers
would love knowing about Hal's navigating the boat by the
stars and seeing the sun rise and set on the ocean. Well, they
probably do get to see it from where they are.) There was the
story Grandmother's children told on her about the time she
was stargazing after supper, as was her wont, fell asleep standing up, pitched off the back porch in the dark, and broke both
wrists. There were many such stories, none exaggerated. You
didn't have to exaggerate about Grandmother.

One wouldn't forget seeing her stand out on the porch in
the worst of summer thunderstorms, quoting aloud, "God
moves in a mysterious way, his wonders to perform; he plants
his footsteps on the sea, and rides upon the storm," as the
elements raged around her. My understanding of bravery is
carrying on in the face of fear. By that standard Grandmother's storm watches couldn't be counted brave, as she simply
was not afraid. I believe that she was out there in the tumult

so that she could feel God "ride upon the storm," absolutely secure in her faith that no harm would come to her so long as she trusted herself to his protection.

Grandmother was exceedingly intelligent and impossibly opinionated. She kept two large volumes open in her downstairs entrance hallway all the time—an English dictionary and the works of Shakespeare—I suspect so that she could easily refer to them to settle a debate. She enjoyed reading the dictionary and indeed read it through entirely more than once. When my brother Hal began his Latin class in high school, Grandmother loved to "help him study." I suppose my dear brother appreciated her help. There was no doubt about Grandmother's pleasure in giving it; she remembered every declension and conjugation she had learned at the Brownsville Academy for Young Women and couldn't resist the understandable temptation to show off.

I have many memories of my grandmother Esther Wingo Hillsman: her tearful prayers of thanks (which I understand now); her manner of getting about, which was full-bore at all times (even in her later years, when osteoporosis had bent her over and to the side, she traversed even the smallest spaces at a gliding trot); the way she listened to *Pepper Young's Family* and *Lorenzo Jones* ("Funiculi! Funicula!") on the radio with her chair pulled up very close, her head bent forward to catch every word; the ever expanding scrapbook she kept about General Douglas MacArthur, who reminded her a great deal of her late husband; her respectful fondness for my father and his family, derived from the way they all loved her daughter; her congenital inability to admit defeat in any area, in life or in discussion, which trait often prompted the conversation closer, "Listen to the beautiful birds"; her heroism in the face of whatever came. I remember how she took my baby sister Midge out of my mother's arms when Midge went into convulsions with something we all thought was going to kill her —diagnosed years later as poliomyelitis—and put a silver spoon in her mouth so she wouldn't bite her tongue and held her and walked with her while the ambulance took forever coming, and when Uncle Jack, who was there for the summer, said, "What can I do, Mama?" answered, "Get down on your knees and pray, Son Jack," and he did. Midge recovered; that's another story, and a dramatic one. I don't remember being born; however, I do know that Grandmother, not the doctor, brought me into the world and pressed my father off to find the doctor before my mother bled to death, and I have always been highly appreciative of both acts. And always the signs and ways that I was reminded that she was the mother of my mother, who was the goddess of all earth to me.

My mother. Apart from the crowd. Not given to overstatement or overfamiliarity. Not sentimental. Not social. Not impressed by the luxe, the glitz, not taken in by "palaverers," my mother, who knew who she was. My mother, the bluest of blue bloods, besotted with love for her husband, interested in him, their children, and their home. She must have been lonely sometimes, a beautiful and brilliant young woman, married at twenty-two and isolated in a hamlet of two hundred people, but if she was, it was her secret.

My mother, for whom her daughter-in-law, Margo, framed these lines by Stephen Vincent Benét:

> She was his wife, and her heart was bold
> As a broad, bright guinea of Border gold.
> Her wit was a tartan of colored weather.
> Her walk was gallant as Highland heather.
> And whatever she had, she held together.

My mother, who lost almost six inches in height the last years of her life, and never let it alter her perfectly erect carriage. I see her now as she must be in Heaven, tall and strong again, and shining.

I pray that my daughters will be like their Grandmother Gina.

(continued from page 4)

Song lyrics by Bob Dylan: Copyright © 1965 by Warner Bros. Inc., copyright renewed 1993 by Special Rider Music. All rights reserved. International copyright secured. Reprinted by permission.

Poems by Robert Graves:
For all editions published outside the United States: Copyright © 1955 by Robert Graves. Reprinted from *The Poems of Robert Graves* by permission of Carcanet Press Limited. Please note that the excerpt reprinted here is taken from two parts of the poem "Vanity," and that two lines have been omitted. For all editions published within the United States: Copyright © 1955 by Robert Graves. Reprinted by permission of Oxford University Press. Please note that the excerpt reprinted here is taken from two parts of the poem "Vanity," and that two lines have been omitted.

Song lyrics by John Wallowitch: © 1995 by Sky Witch Music, 411 East 51st Street, New York, NY 10022. Sole owner: John Wallowitch.

Poem by Dorothea Fox: Copyright © 1995 by Dorothea Fox.

"A Prayer For My Daughter" by William Butler Yeats:
For all editions published within the United States: Reprinted with permission of Scribner, a Division of Simon & Schuster Inc., from *The Poems of W. B. Yeats: A New Edition*, edited by Richard J. Finneran. Copyright 1924 by Macmillan Publishing Company, renewed 1952 by Bertha Georgia Yeats, Michael Butler Yeats, and Anne Yeats.
For all English language editions published outside the United States: Reprinted from "A Prayer For My Daughter" from *The Poems of W. B. Yeats: A New Edition*, edited by Richard J. Finneran. Reprinted by permission of A. P. Watt Ltd on behalf of Michael Yeats.

Poem by Stephen Vincent Benét: Copyright © 1927–1928 by Stephen Vincent Benét. Copyright renewed © 1955–1956 by Rosemary Carr Benét. Reprinted by permission of Brandt & Brandt Literary Agents, Inc.

PHOTO CREDITS: Page 75: Martha Swope. Page 95: Mitch Carter. Page 242: Beth Causey. Page 243: Sam Freed. All other photographs are courtesy of the author's personal collection.

The soul can split the sky in two
And let the face of God shine through.

—Edna St. Vincent Millay

If you would like to order Dixie's newsletter,
yoga videos, or recordings, please call:
901-986-3560